Jimmy Carter and the Horn of Africa

Jimmy Carter and the Horn of Africa

Cold War Policy in Ethiopia and Somalia

DONNA R. JACKSON

McFarland & Company, Inc., Publishers
Jefferson, North Carolina, and London

LIBRARY OF CONGRESS CATALOGUING-IN-PUBLICATION DATA

Jackson, Donna R.
   Jimmy Carter and the Horn of Africa : Cold War policy in Ethiopia
and Somalia / Donna R. Jackson.
       p.   cm.
   Includes bibliographical references and index.

   ISBN-13: 978-0-7864-2987-5
   (softcover : 50# alkaline paper) ∞

   United States — Foreign relations — Ethiopia.   2. United States —
Foreign relations — Somalia.   3. Carter, Jimmy, 1924–   — Political and
social views.   4. United States — Foreign relations —1977–1981.
5. Cold War.   6. Ethiopia — Foreign relations — United States.
7. Somalia — Foreign relations — United States.
I. Title
E183.8.E8J33   2007
327.7306309'047 — dc22   2006038824

British Library cataloguing data are available

On the cover: President Jimmy Carter (*Library of Congress*); Satellite
image of Africa (*Canadian Space Agency*).

Manufactured in the United States of America

McFarland & Company, Inc., Publishers
   Box 611, Jefferson, North Carolina 28640
      www.mcfarlandpub.com

For my parents

Acknowledgments

There are several people and organizations without whom this work would not have been possible, and whose help and support I would like to acknowledge. First and foremost, I would like to thank Dr. John Thompson for his support, patience and encouragement over the last few years. Words are inadequate to accurately portray my gratitude and appreciation for the counsel and wisdom that he has provided. I am also indebted to Professor Tony Badger, Professor Richard Crockatt, and especially Professor John Dumbrell, for their ongoing support and guidance.

This project necessitated much work in archives and research libraries, and I would like to thank all the staff at the Carter Presidential Library, in particular James Yancey; Christopher Beam at the Edmund S. Muskie Archives, Bates College, Maine; the archivists at Yale University Library; members of the staff at the Library of Congress; and the staff of the University Library, Cambridge. I am also extremely grateful to the people who gave so generously of their time to discuss with me their association with the Carter administration, and would like to take this opportunity to thank David Aaron, Dr. Zbigniew Brzezinski, Willard Hoing, General William Odom, Wardell Townsend, Admiral Stansfield Turner, and especially Paul Henze.

On a more personal note, I would like to express my deep gratitude to Congressman Brian Bilbray for introducing me to President Carter, and the members of his staff for their support, especially Justin Blackwell and Leah Hill. I would also like to thank my family and friends for their support, understanding and forbearance, especially when I have not been able to devote as much time to them as I should. I would also like to acknowledge the financial assistance provided by the Arts and Humanities Research Board.

Finally, and most important, I would like to thank my parents, Roy and Judith, for their constant love, encouragement and abiding belief in me. They have always done everything within their means to ensure my happiness, and any success that I have enjoyed in the past or may enjoy in the future is largely due to them.

One of the reasons that I am a historian of the modern era is the belief that we can learn important lessons from recent events that will enable us to make a better world for tomorrow. So, in conclusion, I would like to dedicate this work of history to the future: to Ashley, Louise, Georgia, Rebecca, Allen, Kenny, Austin, Aden, Sam and Brady.

Contents

Preface

Historians continue to be divided over the success, or otherwise, of Jimmy Carter's foreign policy. Some claim that Carter lacked vision or leadership, as evidenced by the reorientation of policy in 1980. Others are more positive, crediting Carter with success within unavoidable limits, and praising his introduction of human rights to the foreign policy agenda. Indeed, as Jerel Rosati argues, no orthodox position evaluating Jimmy Carter's performance as president has been established, nor is there a standard revisionist response.

Through an analysis of policy towards the Horn of Africa, this book, reflecting the more positive historiographical view, will argue that Carter adopted a consistent approach to foreign policy throughout the life of his administration. Although the actual policies changed, the motivation for those policies remained consistent and it was the changing context that provoked the changes in policy. If Carter should be faulted, it would be for his inability to "sell" his approach to the American people.

The book will argue that Jimmy Carter, ex-career naval officer, was as committed to the Cold War and the battle with the Soviet Union as any of his predecessors or successors in the White House. However, Carter was also the first president elected in the aftermath of both Vietnam and Watergate, and the first to have to fight the Cold War within the limits imposed by both. Without recourse to traditional Cold War weapons — including American military power and the support for the commitment of troops to overseas engagements — Carter adopted different weapons in his Cold War battle with the Soviet Union. Unable to compete on the military stage, he instead strove to put the Soviet Union on the defensive by attacking it on a moral level, by emphasizing, for example, regionalism and human rights. However, as the international context changed, allowing Carter more scope in his policy choices, so his foreign policy changed, and by 1980 his reorientation of foreign policy to a more traditional Cold War approach was complete.

An excellent case study for demonstrating this argument can be found in Carter's policy towards the Horn of Africa. In Ethiopia and Somalia, Carter was faced with violations of human rights, a strong Communist bloc presence, and a local conflict that had the potential to become yet another proxy war between two superpowers. For three years he resisted pressures both at home and abroad to confront the Soviet Union, and instead concentrated on efforts to improve the situation of the people living in the Horn. In 1980, however, the strategic location of the Horn, combined with the changed international circumstances, led Carter to reassess his policy priorities. He formed a military relationship with Somalia in direct opposition to the communist bloc presence in neighboring Ethiopia. By 1980 détente with the Soviet Union was dead, and Carter's policy towards the Horn of Africa, many (including Zbigniew Brzezinski) would claim, had played a major role.

This book will not only provide an in-depth study of American policy towards Ethiopia and Somalia during the years of the Carter administration, but it will also provide an analysis of the foreign policy decision-making process within the Carter administration. In addition, it will examine Brzezinski's claim that SALT (the Strategic Arms Limitation Talks) and détente were "buried in the sands of Ogaden," and explain how foreign policy towards the Horn of Africa fits into the history of the Cold War in general and détente in particular.

Introduction:
Does History Matter?

Does history matter? The answer in the Horn of Africa must be a resounding "yes."[1]

— Paul B. Henze

Jutting into the Arabian Sea, and reminiscent of the horn of the black rhinoceros that had once roamed through Ethiopia, the Horn of Africa is comprised of the East African countries of Ethiopia, Somalia, Eritrea and Djibouti. Paul B. Henze, in his study of the area, claimed that, to fully understand the region, a knowledge of its history was essential. While this is undoubtedly true, as any student of African history will attest, an appreciation of developments, events and actions in the Horn of Africa is equally important for those with wider academic interests.

The foreign policy of Jimmy Carter, president of the United States from 1977 to 1981, towards Ethiopia and Somalia demonstrates this. Zbigniew Brzezinski, national security adviser to the Carter administration, highlighted the importance of the Horn of Africa in the history of the Cold War when he claimed in his memoirs that détente was "buried in the sands of the Ogaden,"[2] a reference to the war between Ethiopia and Somalia that raged from 1977 to 1978. In addition, an analysis of Carter's policy decisions towards the Horn sheds light on both the style and substance of Carter's presidency, and provides further insight into the historiographical debates surrounding the 39th president, particularly the evaluations of Carter's reorientation of the bases of his foreign policy announced in the "Carter Doctrine" of 1980.

History certainly matters in the Horn of Africa, therefore, to any stu-

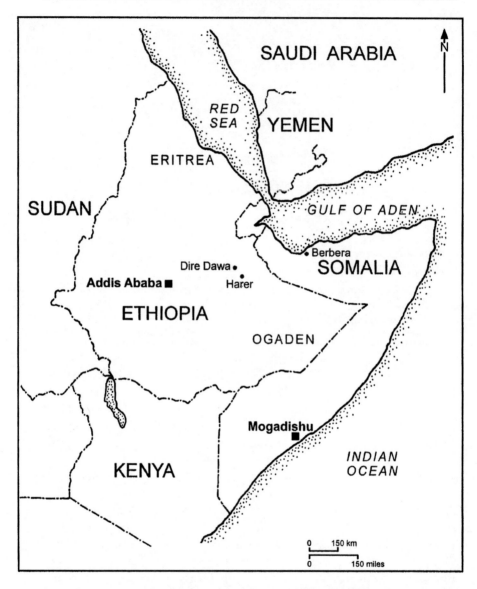

dent of the Carter administration and the Cold War. Although other events that occurred between 1977 and 1981 may have been given more prominence and received more attention, both during the years of the administration and since, the policy pursued towards Ethiopia and Somalia by the Carter administration provides a good case study for understanding what Carter attempted to do in his overall foreign policy design, why he was doing it, and the extent to which he ultimately succeeded in his aims. The events in the Horn between

1977 and 1981, and Carter's response to them, provided a test for the effectiveness and suitability of Jimmy Carter's approach. In the Horn of Africa, human rights abuses were evident, but Cold War concerns, exacerbated by the strong communist bloc presence, remained important, and both themes were complicated by violations of international law, and questions of self-determination.

Jimmy Carter was elected as the 39th president of the United States on November 2, 1976. When he assumed the office on January 20 the following year, he became the first president to serve in the aftermath of both the Vietnam war and the scandal surrounding the Watergate break-in and subsequent cover-up. Both events had wrought profound changes on American culture and society, and Carter knew that the context in which he had to operate was unlike anything that had been experienced before. The public and the media were much more critical and more suspicious of government activity; distrust and disillusionment abounded. The images of the evacuation of Saigon in 1975 had damaged American credibility both at home and abroad, and the "Vietnam Syndrome" led to an unwillingness to commit American military power to overseas engagements.

As president, Carter knew that he had a wealth of responsibilities, not least of which was to protect America's international image; Richard Nixon's attempt to achieve "peace with honor" in Vietnam had been motivated by a similar sense of duty. The Cold War still continued and evidence of persistent Soviet adventurism, for example in Angola, was plain to see. Yet Carter faced even more restraints than had Nixon. The experience and aftermath of the Vietnam War meant that the new president did not have access to the full range of tools of Cold War diplomacy, so Carter attempted to utilize different "weapons" in the battle with the Soviet Union. As a result of both his personal ideology and the wider attitudes within American society, Carter called for a new approach in foreign policy that seemed to de-emphasize traditional Cold War themes.

Carter's strategy in dealing with the constraints that he faced when formulating foreign policy was evident throughout his inaugural address. The United States had been so profoundly changed by recent events that Carter's inauguration as president marked, as he stated in the address, "a new beginning." Yet, even though he was leading the United States into its third century as a nation, Carter returned to America's initial principles and values in his attempt to restore pride and prestige both at home and abroad. He recommended that "our recent mistakes bring a resurgent commitment to the basic principles of our Nation" and added, "two centuries ago our Nation's birth was a milestone in the long quest for freedom, but the bold and brilliant dream which excited the founders of this Nation still awaits its consummation. I have no new dream to set forth today, but rather urge a fresh faith in the old dream." By basing policy on such principles, Carter believed that the United States could continue to demonstrate leadership and strength, even within the constraints imposed by Vietnam and Watergate. He contended that "we are a strong nation, and we will maintain strength so sufficient that it need not be proven in combat — a quiet strength based not merely on the size of an arsenal, but on the nobility of ideas."[3]

Translating this rhetoric into a course of action entailed a reorientation of the bases of foreign policy-making. Carter's new world order would be built upon community and cooperation, rather than conflict, not least because of the difficulties in utilizing traditional military weapons. By emphasizing a moral dimension to policy-making, through a focus on human rights, Carter aimed to demonstrate American power despite the fact that the Vietnam Syndrome limited his recourse to military means. To prevent "proxy" wars such as Vietnam, the relationship between the United States and Soviet Union would not be allowed to dominate foreign policy formulation. To encourage nations, especially those of the developing world, to ally themselves with the United States, there would be a greater emphasis on winning "hearts and minds" by formulating policy in a regionalist rather than a globalist context.

Some early goals of the administration's foreign policy reflecting this new approach were ratification of the Panama Canal treaties, peace in the Middle East through the Camp David Accords, the pursuit of détente and completion of negotiations on the SALT II treaty, as well as normalization of relations with nations such as the People's Republic of China and Vietnam. The new approach of the Carter administration, but particularly his emphasis upon regionalism, also resulted in a new attitude towards Africa. Although there had long been American interest in the Horn of Africa, particularly since the onset of the Cold War, Carter's reorientation of foreign policy led to a consideration of the region outside of an East-West framework.

Ethiopia was seen as the key to the Horn of Africa during the Carter administration and in the years previously, both because of the size of the country, and because Emperor Haile Selassie actively worked to assure Ethiopia's importance. Perhaps more important from an American perspective, however, was the strategic location of the Horn, and its proximity to the shipping routes of supplies, especially oil, from the Persian Gulf and Indian Ocean through the Red Sea to Europe. In 1953, Ethiopia and the United States signed agreements that gave the U.S. access to military bases in return for economic and military aid, instigating a special relationship that endured until the 1970s. Meanwhile, the USSR, determined to establish a presence to counter the Americans in an area that was strategically important in the Cold War, moved to consolidate its alliance with Ethiopia's neighbor Somalia, establishing relations as soon as Somalia was declared an independent republic in 1960 and providing economic and military aid. After Siad Barré seized power in a military coup in 1969, he publicly declared Somalia to be a pro-Soviet state and the relationship became even stronger. At the same time the Soviets actively supported Eritrean rebels who were demanding independence from Ethiopia, in the hope that the unrest would lead to a change of leadership in the major country of the Horn to one that might prove more receptive to Soviet overtures.

The Soviet hopes were boosted in 1974 when the Ethiopian Revolution resulted in the deposition of Haile Selassie and the country became ruled by a coalition known as the Derg. The United States continued to supply military aid until 1977, but no formal links with members of the Derg were established and increasingly Ethiopian military officers and leaders were sent to the USSR and Eastern Europe for instruction and training. In December 1976, one of the Derg leaders, Mengistu Haile Mariam, secretly visited Moscow and signed a military aid agreement further consolidating the new relationship between Ethiopia and the Soviet Union.

In Ethiopia, the initial response of the newly installed Carter administration was to invoke its focus on human rights and condemn the Derg-sponsored violence. Citing this, the United States cut off all military aid to Ethiopia in February 1977, the same month that Mengistu seized sole power by having his political rivals shot. Exerting his new authority, the Ethiopian premier used the administration's action to reduce ties with the United States and formally allied himself with Moscow. In rejoinder, the Carter administration, adhering to its regionalist approach, followed its plan to treat developing countries outside of a Cold War environment, and resolved to maintain ties with the Mengistu regime, albeit in a more limited fashion.

The Somali leader, Siad Barré, must have watched the growing relationship between Ethiopia and the Soviet Union with concern: although Soviet aid continued to flow into Somalia, Siad was aware that Ethiopia was the greater prize in Soviet eyes and feared abandonment. Playing the "Cold War game," Siad contacted the Carter administration and hinted that he could be wooed away from the Soviet bloc. Although, as part of the belief in global community and regionalism, Carter had indicated his desire to improve relations between the United States and Somalia, the priority of the administration remained its relationship with Ethiopia and talks with Siad proceeded cautiously. Rather than attempting to replace the USSR in Somalia, the administration, as it had with Ethiopia, adopted a long-term approach, ignored the Soviet presence in Somalia, and focused instead on ways in which the United States might aid human rights, especially through means of economic and humanitarian aid. Thus, by the summer of 1977, the Carter administration appeared generally pleased with policy towards Ethiopia and Somalia.

Concerns over human rights had been forcefully expressed; the Soviet presence was not allowed to dominate American policy; and a regionalist, long-term, humanitarian approach was underway in both Horn countries.

In July 1977, though, war erupted in the Ogaden between Ethiopia and Somalia. Supplied with Soviet arms and reinforced with over four thousand Soviet advisers, Siad was in such a strong military position that in the summer of 1977 he launched an all-out invasion of the Ogaden region of Ethiopia. The Ogaden was mostly inhabited by ethnic Somalis, although it had been formally incorporated into Ethiopia, and Siad Barré claimed the region should be part of the Somali Republic. The onset of war presented the Carter administration with possible involvement in a local conflict that potentially had global implications. With the Soviets increasingly involved on the Ethiopian side, and the Somali leader seeking accommodation with the Americans, the prospect loomed that the Cold War could be fought through proxies. Carter, however, refused to endorse the invasion of the Ogaden, arguing that it constituted a violation of international law and national integrity, and continued to apply a long-term, regionalist policy to the Horn, despite the immediate crisis. The president insisted that the Americans should remain neutral, stuck to the official administration doctrine that African problems should find African solutions, and called for the Organization of African Unity to sponsor negotiations.

American involvement in the Ogaden War remained at the diplomatic level. As well as promoting an arms embargo on both sides in the war, the administration concentrated its efforts on attempts to reduce or eliminate the Soviet and Cuban presence from the Horn, thereby facilitating an African-directed solution. However, despite efforts by the Organization of African Unity and the United Nations, it seemed unlikely that the conflict would be ended by peaceful resolution, mainly because of the lack of willingness on the parties involved to participate; neither the Ethiopians, Somalis, Soviets nor Cubans supported the idea of a mediated resolution to the conflict. Indeed, the Soviets appeared dedicated to a military solution to the war and undertook a massive airlift of Soviet supplies and Cuban troops into Ethiopia towards the end of 1977. The extent of Soviet support had the desired result from the point of view of Mengistu and his allies, and on March 9, 1978, Siad announced that all Somali forces had been withdrawn from Ethiopian territory.

The conclusion of the war eased the immediate crisis and the Carter administration continued to apply a long-term, regionalist policy to both Ethiopia and Somalia, hoping to improve human rights and decrease or do away with communist-bloc influence altogether through diplomatic pressure, economic and humanitarian aid. Perhaps the most interesting thing about this period is how apparent the conflicts between the State Department and the National Security Council, not just between Cyrus Vance and Zbigniew Brzezinski, became.

In Ethiopia, the long-term goal of the Carter administration was to restore American influence in this key nation of the Horn region. Despite his by now strong links with the Soviet Union, Mengistu had not completely broken ties with the United States, and appeared to respond to administration attempts to rebuild the relationship. Mengistu and senior administration officials conducted high-level meetings, during which the Ethiopian leader calmed American fears that the war would continue with assurances that there would be no counter-invasion of Somalia. Carter subsequently responded to Mengistu's request that relations be improved and increased the level of American representation in Addis Ababa with the appointment of a new ambassador. Problems remained in Ethiopia, however, especially in Eritrea where the level of secessionist guerrilla activity, and corresponding government military response, increased the potential for civil war and became the main area of concern for the Carter administration. As with the Ogaden conflict, the administration supported the doctrine of territorial integrity, sought a negotiated solution to the rebellion, and called for the removal of external, especially communist bloc, involvement. However, also in direct comparison to the Ogaden War, Ethiopian military might, reinforced by Soviet and Cuban supplies and advisers, was ultimately the main determinant in suppressing the rebels.

The Carter administration also continued in its efforts to improve relations with Somalia; Richard Moose of the State Department made an official visit and a new ambassador was selected. With the end of the Ogaden War, and the official withdrawal of Somali troops from Ethiopian territory, debates resumed within the administration over the question of military aid to Somalia. Siad was known to be desperate for external support, and some within the administration expressed concern that he might turn once again to the Soviets. Others suggested that American credibility would be at stake if the administration were perceived as going back on its word to aid Siad if he withdrew from Ethiopian territory, while others argued that Siad was not deserving of American military support, especially in the face of increasing evidence of ongoing Somali activity in the Ogaden and continued human rights violations. Eventually the latter group predominated, and the administration concentrated instead on its attempts to help the Somali people through economic and humanitarian aid projects.

The long debates over policy to Somalia and Ethiopia that had taken place within the administration from the end of the Ogaden War to November 1979 might well have continued indefinitely. However, two international events shook the Carter administration and caused a dramatic shift in policy orientation that was quickly dubbed the Carter Doctrine by the media. The seizure of the American Embassy in Tehran, followed shortly by the Soviet invasion of Afghanistan, radically changed the context in which Jimmy Carter was operating and led to the implementation of a more traditional Cold War approach. The emphasis on regionalism faded as the Soviet Union once again assumed the central role in policy formulation, with the international position of the United States safeguarded by military power, not simply moral certitude.

In order to fulfill Carter's pledge to use military force if necessary in the Indian Ocean and Persian Gulf, the administration sought the use of military facilities in the region from which to project American power. In addition to access to bases in Oman and Kenya, discussions were undertaken with Siad Barré for the use of the ex–Soviet base at Berbera in Somalia, despite the fact that the administration had evidence of persistent human rights violations as well as continued Somali activity in the Ogaden. Siad's record caused a great deal of concern in Congress, but the administration eventually overcame all objections. Having previously refused to form an alliance with Somalia because of Siad's violations of human rights and international law, the United States had, by August 1980, reached an agreement for use of Somali ports and airfields in return for which Somalia received $103.3 million in military aid over two years. At the same time, the administration accepted that its relationship with Ethiopia might need to be sacrificed as it consolidated ties with Somalia. The refusal of Mengistu to pay compensation for American industries that had been nationalized during the Ethiopian revolution led to the withdrawal of all U.S. aid, and in July 1980 the American ambassador in Addis Ababa was recalled.

By 1980, therefore, the Horn of Africa had become a microcosm of the Cold War, with the Soviets and Cubans in Ethiopia and the Americans supporting Somalia. The problems of the Horn of Africa were seen through the Cold War prism and globalism seemed to have triumphed over regionalism. Despite successes with many of the initial foreign policy goals, by the end of Carter's administration American foreign policy appeared to have largely reverted to a more traditional approach to the Cold War with policy based upon American military power, and relations with the Soviet Union once again the main priority. The administration's response to the Soviet invasion of Afghanistan in December 1979 — the Carter Doctrine — was arguably a classic piece of Cold War rhetoric.

The reasons why Carter found it difficult to implement his original approach, and thus undertook a second reorientation of foreign policy, remain a topic of debate for historians and form the basis of much of the evaluation that has taken place, with many different conclusions drawn. Indeed, as Jerel Rosati argues, no orthodox position evaluating Jimmy Carter's performance as president has been established, nor is there a standard revisionist response.[4] Some argue that his foreign policy was a failure, either because he had no clear vision of his own, or because the vision he did have was naïve and overly idealistic. His inability to establish a good working relationship with Congress or the media is also criticized, as well as his failure to win over the electorate. His style of government is condemned, including his attempts to micromanage, and his leadership abilities are called into question, particularly with regard to the way in which the discussions within his team of advisers appeared to present an image of discordance, chaos and internal disorder. These views tend to suggest that a better man or a better politician could have achieved different results with the same policies and in the same circumstances. However, other historians argue that Carter was unlucky and was overwhelmed by circumstances which neither he, nor any other leader, could have controlled. Still others praise Carter for his attempts to move away from traditional Cold War rhetoric and acknowledge his success in bringing human rights to prominence in the foreign policy agenda. Although it should be noted that assessments have generally become more favorable as time as passed, this is by no means universal.

Let us conclude this introduction, then, by examining some of the various appraisals of the Carter administration put forward by historians.[5] Perhaps the most important question to be addressed by these analyses is that of Carter's personal responsibility for the perceived failure of his administration. While most accept that Carter faced difficult situations while president, his leadership skills come under close scrutiny and the suggestion is made that someone with a different character, better qualified, more skilled as a politician or more experienced in the ways of Washington would have been better suited to handle the problems, and therefore to bring about more satisfactory conclusions. The severest criticism of Carter's leadership ability probably comes from Lawrence Shoup, who claims in *The Carter Presidency and Beyond: Power and Politics in the 1980s* (Palo Alto: Ramparts Press, 1980) that Carter lacked leadership skills and that the president did not determine policy but was dominated by others.[6] Shoup maintains that American politics are, at bottom, anti-democratic in nature, and argues that Carter's rise to the presidency and subsequent policies came as a result of the influence of the "ruling class," in particular the Trilateral Commission, which ultimately controls the United States.[7] By examining the sources of Carter's funding, his introduction to the Trilateral Commission, and that organization's ties with the mass media and Carter's staff, Shoup argues that Carter's campaign and policies were shaped by the unofficial elite; that "Carter's entire foreign policy, much of his election strategy, and at least some of his domestic policy has come directly from the Commission and its leading members."[8] For example, Shoup contends that Carter's move for peace in the Middle East was not motivated by humanitarian considerations or the search for global stability, but because "its oil is absolutely crucial to the stability of the U.S. and world economy."[9] However, while it is true that Carter had close ties with the Trilateral Commission, and relied on many of its members for advice, Shoup does not factor Carter's personal character and ideals into his analysis, nor examine the extent to which Carter's personal beliefs coincided with any advice he received. His conclusions regarding Carter's leadership abilities therefore leave many questions unresolved.

Among the other historians evaluating Carter's competence as a leader is Richard Thornton, who uses the Cold War as his basis for analysis in *The Carter Years: Toward a Global World Order* (Washington, D.C.: Washington Institute Press, 1991). He argues that Carter came into office determined to implement a new global order, but was deflected by the discovery during the first few weeks of the administration that the Soviet Union had made a major breakthrough in weapons technology. By perfecting the guidance system for SS-18 ICBMs, a "window of vulnerability" had been opened with regard to U.S. Minuteman missiles, thereby seriously threatening American second strike capability. Thornton claims that this discovery threw the administration into disarray, and forced a policy reappraisal that "produced a permanent split in the administration's ranks"[10] and created the image of incompetence. Thornton argues that it was concerns for Soviet achievements that drove all other aspects of the Carter administration's foreign policy. For example, normalization of relations with China was pursued only as a balance to the increased Soviet threat and human rights because it "allowed the United States to differentiate among communists and enabled a more positive ideological mobilization of public opinion."[11] As the Soviet Union was the main concern, Carter was wrong to attempt diplomacy and should instead have relied upon American power as the basis for his foreign policy. Thornton thus concludes that a "failure of leadership — indecision, a lack of imagination, and ... tentative adoption of half measures — characterized the Carter presidency" and the president was therefore ultimately to blame.[12] However, Thornton's approach, by basing his thesis on only one issue, neglects other significant events that may have contributed to the reorientation in the administration's foreign policy, and thereby over-emphasizes the importance of that issue within the overall policy program. His argument also relies on the theory that relations with the Soviet Union always dominated the foreign policy of the Carter administration, and fails to consider the substantial evidence that Carter spent a significant period of his four-year term in office deprioritizing the East-West conflict.

Evidence that Carter had poor leadership skills is provided for some historians through their evaluation of Carter's style of government, in particular the collegial approach adopted by the president. Carter not only allowed but also encouraged differing views and confrontational discussion among his advisers as part of his decision-making process, which exacerbated the image, these historians argue, that the administration was divided, discordant and incompetent. This viewpoint finds expression in the works of historians such as Burton Kaufman and Gaddis Smith, although it should be noted that their degree of disapproval of the Carter administration differs. The much more critical approach can be found in *The Presidency of James Earl Carter, Jr.* (Lawrence: University Press of Kansas, 1993) by Burton Kaufman, in which the author describes the administration as incompetent, leaderless and muddled, and attributes Carter's "mediocre, if not a failed, presidency" to the divisions within the White House staff.[13] These, Kaufman argues, presented an image of incoherence and lack of leadership, with the result that, by the final year of the administration, "the United States appeared to many observers as a hapless giant in an increasingly unfriendly world."[14] In *Morality, Reason and Power* (New York: Hill & Wang, 1986), Gaddis Smith shares Kaufman's view that Carter's style of collegial government deserves criticism, arguing that "the discordant voices of his advisers" led to the appearance of chaos — an image that could have been corrected by better leadership — and concludes that the president must assume the blame for the negative image of, and reaction to, his administration.[15] Similar deductions are found in the volume of essays edited by M. Glenn Abernathy, Dilys M. Hill and Phil Williams and entitled *The Carter Years: The President and Policy Making* (London: Francis Pinter Publishers, 1984). In the conclusion, Williams argues that Carter was to blame for all the faults of the administration for reasons including the president's style of government, his indecisive image, and the image of incompetence of the White House staff.[16] In the final assessment Williams contends that the administration "made more than its share of mistakes" and "in the final analysis the successes and failures of Jimmy Carter's foreign policies depended upon Jimmy Carter."[17]

Nonetheless, while accepting that a president inevitably must assume a degree of responsibility for the conduct and image of his administration, the negative evaluation of Carter's competence provided by historians such as Kaufman, Smith and Williams raises other issues within the historiographical debate. For example, those who place the blame for the perceived failure of the Carter administration on the president alone tend to overlook the inherent complexities of the American political system, while those who question Carter's leadership skills tend to overlook events such as the fight for the ratification of the Panama Canal treaties, or the Camp David Accords, where Carter exercised great leadership skills with positive results.

More positive analyses of Carter's leadership abilities are provided by historians such as Erwin Hargrove and John Dumbrell, who argue that the president was faced with a set of extremely difficult circumstances that would have challenged any leader, and that Carter, in fact, did as well as could be expected. One of the earliest, more complimentary analyses of the Carter administration was Erwin Hargrove's *Jimmy Carter as President: Leadership and the Politics of the Public Good* (Baton Rouge: Louisiana State University Press, 1988), although it should be noted that this is based on oral history given by the president and his staff, and it is therefore not surprising that it is not overly critical. Hargrove's focus is on Carter as a leader, his management of policy development and his style as a decision maker. Hargrove argues that Carter had "a clear and strong conception of the kind of leader he wished to be as president:" one who would act in the public interest and for the public good.[18] However, Carter's difficulties were exacerbated by the international and domestic circumstances with which his administration was faced, and Hargrove concludes that Carter's term should be considered one of "skill under unfavorable conditions."[19] Success within inevitable limits is also the approach taken by John Dumbrell, who provides a favorable analysis of the Carter administration in *The Carter Presidency: A Re-Evaluation* (Manchester: Manchester University Press, 1995). The self-proclaimed themes that run throughout the book are "compassion and competence," suggesting an analysis of both Carter's practical achievements and the way in which such achievements coincided with the president's ideals and morals. Dumbrell examines various aspects of Carter's foreign and domestic policy: the focus in domestic policies is on women's rights and black civil rights; in foreign policy relations with the Soviet Union, Northern Ireland, Nicaragua and Iran are studied in detail, as well as the foundations of Carter's foreign policy and the environment in which it was conceived. Returning to his theme of compassion and competence, Dumbrell contends that Carter merits a positive assessment; his final evaluation of the administration is that "within the ambit of the age of limits ... it can be concluded that Carter kept faith."[20]

Connected to the matter of Carter's leadership ability, a second historiographical theme surrounds the question of whether the president had a clear personal vision or foreign policy strategy. Williams discusses this issue, and argues that Carter failed to develop a clear strategy for foreign policy as is shown by the shifting emphasis on issues such as human rights and the East-West relationship.[21] In *The Uncertain Crusade: Jimmy Carter and the Dilemmas of Human Rights* (Lanham: Hamilton Press, 1986), Joshua Muravchik likewise criticizes Carter's lack of clear strategy with regard to his attempt to base foreign policy upon human rights. The president's lack of definitive vision, Muravchik argues, led to problems of consistency, definition and enforcement of the human rights policy, which Carter failed to resolve.[22] Although Muravchik acknowledges that Carter's emphasis on human rights in foreign policy has had a lasting impact, he criticizes the president's competence in carrying out the policies, arguing that Carter's efforts "left much to be desired."[23] He concludes that "the good that the Carter policy did for the idea of human rights by broadcasting it must be weighed against the harm it did by contributing to the miasma that surrounds the term."[24]

While it is true that Carter faced problems over definition and application of the human rights policy, other historians have argued that he does not deserve to be criticized for his seeming inability to completely redress these issues. In *Human Rights and American Foreign Policy: The Carter and Reagan Experiences* (New York: Greenwood Press, 1987), A. Glenn Mower compares the success of Carter and Reagan in incorporating human rights into each of their foreign policies. Mower argues that Carter was the pioneer president in including human rights among the basic factors for foreign policy decisions and, as such, he faced problems and obstructions with which the Reagan administration did not have to contend. Indeed, Mower asserts, Carter established precedents that made it easier for his successor to build human rights into his foreign policy to the extent that he chose to do.[25]

The idea that Carter's attempt to base foreign policy upon human rights was naïve, overly idealistic and unsuitable for the times or the international arena, has also been advanced by some historians and prompted scholarly debate. Donald Spencer, in *The Carter Implosion: Jimmy Carter and the Amateur Style of Diplomacy* (New York: Praeger, 1988), provides an example of those who criticize Carter in this area, contending that he "mistook strong words and constant attention for effective action."[26] Notwithstanding the good that Carter wished to do, Spencer argues that his plans were inappropriate and therefore Carter deserves a negative evaluation because "presidents must be judged by their achievements in protecting American interests at home and abroad — not by their dreams."[27] However, those who base their criticism of Carter on his naivety and idealism often do not incorporate into their analyses the fact that Carter was the first president elected in the aftermath of both Vietnam and Watergate, nor his need to factor the public's reaction to these two shattering events into policy formulation.

With regard to this area of historiographical debate, the middle ground is provided by historians such as Gaddis Smith, who recognizes the impact of Vietnam and Watergate on Carter's foreign policy plans but maintains that the image of incompetence that surrounded the administration and the president's inability to effectively project "what needed to be done ... [made] Carter's vision appear naive."[28] However, Smith also gives Carter credit, arguing that despite a general failure in application, the four years of the Carter administration were among the most significant in twentieth-century foreign policy because of the president's attempt "consciously and explicitly to discover and apply an effective combination of morality, reason and power in the conduct of American foreign policy."[29]

Dumbrell shares Smith's assessment that Carter deserves credit for his role in including human rights in foreign policy formulation but then provides a much more favorable evaluation of the Carter administration. Dumbrell analyzes the role of human rights in Carter's foreign policy, its hoped-for benefits of restoring consensus and providing a way to deal with both the communist world and the Third World, as well as the problems of definition, consistency of application and the lack of public support for specific policies. Rather than being naïve or inappropriate, Dumbrell concludes that Carter's emphasis on human rights was one of the strengths of his administration in that it helped to move the United States away from the "cripplingly hypocritical and counter-productive legacies of the Cold War."[30] Likewise, Mower praises the strength of Carter's commitment to human rights and commends the thirty-ninth president for ensuring that human rights became part of the policy agenda.

Those historians who claim that Carter either had a poor foreign policy vision, or that his vision was naïve and inappropriate, such as Williams, Kaufman and Muravchik, often cite the fact that the president reoriented foreign policy back towards a more traditional Cold War approach during 1979 and deprioritized human rights within the foreign policy agenda. They claim that such inconsistency is evidence for their position. However, these analyses often overlook other factors, particularly developments in the international arena, to which Carter felt bound to respond, such as Soviet adventurism and events in Iran. They also tend, as A. Glenn Mower points out, to overlook the fact that Carter intended his human rights policy as a "series of case by case decisions," and therefore the appearance of a degree of inconsistency would have been unavoidable.[31]

Jerel Rosati takes issue with those who condemn the Carter administration for the second reorientation of policy at the end of 1979 through his analysis of belief systems. Rosati argues that instead of reflecting confusion and disarray, the policy changes offer evidence of the consistency of the administration's approach. In *The Carter Administration's Quest for Global Community: Beliefs and their Impact on Behavior* (Columbia: University of South Carolina Press, 1987), Rosati attributes the administration with a collective "belief" or worldview formed from the interplay of Carter's, Vance's and Brzezinski's individual beliefs and ideologies. He then goes on to analyze the relationship between the evolution of this collective belief system and the foreign policy behavior of the administration, using this as a basis to evaluate the consistency and coherence of the administration's foreign policy. Rosati argues that throughout the four-year period there was a gradual move from an optimistic worldview that emphasized pluralism and sought global community, to a pessimistic view that emphasized security concerns and global stability. This change came about because of the Vance-Brzezinski split and the ultimate dominance of Brzezinski's influence on the administration's worldview. The two middle years of incoherence and indecision reflected Carter's wavering between the two worldviews. Rosati concludes that, throughout the four years, foreign policy behavior consistently reflected the collective worldview: the move from idealism to realism. Although Rosati does acknowledge some limitations of his analysis — for example, the question of the interaction between beliefs and behavior, and the fact that behavior can be affected by external circumstances and events — his assertion that beliefs are an important determinant of behavior merits consideration.

A further historiographical focus is that Carter deserves criticism because of his inability or refusal to recognize the reality of the framework in which he had to operate. Some historians deplore Carter's desire to micromanage and involve himself with all aspects of decision-making, arguing that such a detailed level of involvement was simply not possible for a man with all the responsibilities of chief executive. Donald Spencer contends that Carter failed because he lacked "any grasp of the limits of acceptable choice,"[32] while Gaddis Smith similarly criticizes the president for attempting to micromanage. He argues that Carter's efforts to be involved in too much made it impossible for the president "to see clearly what needed to be done," thus adding to the image of confusion that surrounded the administration.[33]

Carter's failure as a politician and inability to work within the Washington system is yet another issue that arises in the works of various historians. Phil Williams criticizes the president for his failure to develop good relations with Congress,[34] while Burton Kaufman contends that Carter neglected to establish the necessary base of public support and never came to terms with the realities of political life, and thus was doomed to failure.[35] Similarly, Spencer argues that Carter failed because he lacked "any appreciation of the tools that must be deployed to achieve even modest political objectives,"[36] such as the need to establish positive relations with Congress, with the Democratic party, and with other agencies, such as the American media; the latter is discussed in detail, with similar conclusions, by Mark J. Rozell in *The Press and the Carter Presidency* (Boulder & London: Westview, 1989). David Skidmore, in *Reversing Course: Carter's Foreign Policy, Domestic Politics and the Failure of Reform* (Nashville and London: Vanderbilt University Press, 1996), contends that Carter's failure lay in his inability to convince the public of the desirability of his policy objectives. His lack of success in gaining "domestic legitimacy" for his initial foreign policy approach was followed by a failure to "sell" the 1980 reorientation, ultimately leading to election defeat in November. Skidmore argues that Carter thus proved politically incompetent twice.[37]

The historians who criticize Carter for his inability to work within the Washington system often disregard the fact that, had Carter been more of a political insider, he would not have been elected in 1976. Nor do they adequately address the fact that events such as Vietnam and Watergate changed the way in which agencies such as the U.S. Congress, the Democratic party, the media, and even the American public viewed their own relationship with the executive branch of the government, and were much more adversarial than in previous years. These issues are, however, examined by Garland Haas, in *Jimmy Carter and the Politics of Frustration* (Jefferson, North Carolina: McFarland, 1992). Haas discusses how Jimmy Carter became president, how he dealt with that role and why he was unable to achieve re-election. While acknowledging the generally unfavorable opinion of the Carter administration, Haas argues that the president was overwhelmed by bad luck and "used any good luck he might have had in getting to the presidency."[38] He concludes that Carter was a man faced by impossible situations and that any president facing the same issues and "two Congresses as intractable as the 95th and 96th" would have been unlikely to achieve any more success than Carter.[39] The text concludes with a favorable analysis of Carter's post-presidential career, suggesting that as circumstances changed so Carter was able to succeed.

As previously mentioned, analyses of the Carter administration have tended to become more favorable as time has passed, and the reason for this is worth considering at this point. As well as the additional perspective provided by the passage of time, the change has been attributed to Carter's activities since 1981; even Carter's severest critics acknowledge him as one of the best ex-presidents that the United States has produced.[40] Douglas Brinkley, in an article for *Diplomatic History* entitled "The Rising Stock of Jimmy Carter: The 'Hands-On' Legacy of Our Thirty-Ninth President," and its expansion, *The Unfinished Presidency* (New York: Viking, 1998), comments on the fact that Carter's post-presidential career has influenced the way in which people have viewed him, thereby accounting for the more favorable analyses of his presidency. Brinkley argues that Carter's post-presidential successes mean that his four-year presidential term cannot be deemed a failure, maintaining that "what Kaufman — and others — failed to take into account is that Carter is the most successful American ex-president in the world *because* of his presidency."[41] For Brinkley, the four years of the presidential administration were but one element of Carter's career, which on the whole was successful; he concludes that Carter's life's work, and particularly the establishment of the Carter Center, has left a "permanent legacy that will extend well into the third millennium."[42] However, the question remains as to whether Carter's four years as president merits a more favorable consideration as a result of his post-presidential activities.

Carter's policy towards the Horn of Africa, and particularly the Ogaden War, features significantly in discussions among historians analyzing reasons for the failure of détente. As for the beginning of the Cold War in the 1940s, academic opinion is divided over the reasons for the hardening of relations in the late 1970s. Some historians argue that either of the superpowers was overly aggressive, thus betraying the spirit of détente. Fred Halliday, for example, claims that the American determination to rebuild its position of strength, damaged by the experience of Vietnam in particular, was ultimately responsible.[43] An alternative perspective, as put forward by Raymond Garthoff, Jussi Hanhimaki and Odd Arne Westad, assigns the responsibility to both superpowers. In general, this historiographical viewpoint argues that both the United States and the Soviet Union made the same mistake; they each had a different definition for détente, and this "fatal difference" ultimately proved critical.[44] For the Soviets, détente denoted the American acceptance of global parity, while the Americans saw détente as a way of maintaining global superiority in an era when American military and financial power was relatively limited. Each perceived the other's actions as a betrayal of its own definition of détente, thereby leading to the policy's failure.[45]

Regardless of their conclusions, a common point of discussion in all these works is the importance of events in the third world, particularly in the swath of countries that stretched from the Indian subcontinent, through the Middle East, to the Horn of Africa — a region collectively dubbed the Arc of Crisis.[46] Indeed an event involving two of these countries featured in perhaps the most famous comment on the failure of détente: in his memoirs, Zbigniew Brzezinski stated his belief that détente was "buried in the sands of the Ogaden."[47] His point was that Carter's new approach to the Cold War was put seriously to the test during the Ogaden War between Ethiopia and Somalia, and there its weaknesses proved. Such proof then encouraged Soviet adventurism, which further alienated the American public from Carter's attempt to fight the Cold War by de-emphasizing military power, leading to the withdrawal of the SALT II treaty and the collapse of détente. Brzezinski's quote is famous — perhaps, one might say, even infamous. As well as examining the responsibility, or otherwise, of the Carter administration in the demise of détente, this study will also consider the accuracy of Brzezinski's claim.

As the volumes discussed reveal, there are perhaps more questions surrounding Jimmy Carter's foreign policy than there are answers. There is no accepted view of the success, or otherwise, of the Carter administration; neither is there a basis of agreement about the reasons for the public's image of the Carter presidency. Carter's competence as Chief Executive is criticized — and praised. He is accused of being dominated by others in the formulation of policy — and dubbed a strong leader. He is maligned for mishandling the conduct of the Cold War — and commended for attempting to place world politics on a new footing. Additionally, between those who praise Carter's four-year term in office, and those who condemn it, the foundation for forming opinions frequently differs.

One of the reasons for the range of assessment, of course, is the fact that each reflects the personal viewpoints, ideologies or interests of the various authors. Thornton, for example, clearly thinks that the Cold War should form the basis for judging the conduct of foreign policy by presidential administrations between 1945 and 1991, while Jerel Rosati applies his interest in psychology to his analysis of the Carter administration. Those who provide more positive evaluations of Carter's attempt to base foreign policy upon issues such as human rights write from a liberal perspective while the strongest critics of Carter, for example Kaufman, reflect a more right-wing ideology in criticizing Carter for not effectively protecting America's national interest against threats posed by the Soviet Union. Indeed, the only sure thing about the Carter administration, with regard to both its internal workings and its place in the history of the Cold War, seems to be that the debates will continue and case studies of areas, such as the Horn of Africa, will provide useful contributions to the ongoing debates.

I

A New Hope

On July 4, 1976, the United States of America celebrated its bicentennial. It was a day of festivity, of congratulations and of pride. As the tall ships sailed into New York harbor, and the fireworks exploded over the Statue of Liberty, the nation cheered and patted itself on its proverbial back. But this image of the United States that flashed around the world was just that — an image. Beneath the façade was a troubled nation, not yet recovered from the traumas of Vietnam and Watergate. Still, the bicentennial seemed to symbolize a new beginning and, as America entered its third century, a more positive mood was apparent. The feeling was epitomized by the movie-going public; Americans lined up around the block to see the first film of George Lucas's *Star Wars* saga, subtitled "A New Hope."

A newcomer to Washington that year also embodied the new mood. In the 1976 presidential election the American people sought an antidote to recent chief executives who had embroiled the nation in political scandal and military defeat. They turned to Jimmy Carter who, with his status as a Washington "outsider" and his distinctive personal attitudes and beliefs, including his deep religious and moral convictions, was seen by many as the man who could and would restore the pride and prestige of the United States both at home and abroad. The *Time* report on Carter's inauguration noted that, with the election of the new president, the nation was "hoping again."[1]

However, much of the nation was also wondering about the little-known ex-governor of Georgia, who was now the leader of the Free World. *Time* saluted Carter as "Man of the Year" in 1977, and described his career to date — "Annapolis graduate, Navy Officer, nuclear engineer, successful farmer, businessman" — but also pointed out that "no president since Calvin Coolidge has

21

entered the White House with a briefer public record."[2] Indeed, outside of Georgia, Carter had never had a high profile; before the Iowa Caucuses and New Hampshire primary, his recognition rating was less than two percent. He therefore published his first autobiography during his presidential campaign to acquaint the American people with, he hoped, their future leader. Entitled *Why Not the Best? The First Fifty Years*, it outlined Carter's life, hopes and dreams, and most crucially described one of the defining moments in his life: when Admiral Hyman Rickover had asked Carter, then a lieutenant in the U.S. Navy, during an interview to join the nuclear submarine program, why he had not always done his best.[3] Although Carter got the job, he never forgot the question, or the fact that he had no satisfactory answer, and the theme, to do his best at any job, was to dominate his life. In his inaugural address as Governor of Georgia in January 1971, Carter declared, "I promise you my best,"[4] and during the presidential campaign five years later he vowed that he would "never be satisfied with less than the best."[5] He also admitted that he had not always wanted to be president of the United States, and while at Annapolis Naval Academy his goal had been to become Chief of Naval Operations.[6] The corollary was that once Carter entered politics, then he wanted the top job there too, and he wanted to do his best at it.

The "Best" Foreign Policy

Once in office, Carter wanted to provide the best foreign policy that he could. He had a comprehensive vision for the way in which the world should work, and also a clear idea of the role that the United States should play in the international system. However, although the most powerful man in the world, the president does not operate in a vacuum. The recent experience of the Vietnam War proved the importance of public opinion in formulating foreign policy, while the Constitutional system of government, with its principles of checks and balances, provides Congress with a key role in the policy process. Although both the 95th and 96th Congresses were overwhelmingly Democrat,[7] the post–Watergate effect meant that members, regardless of party affiliation, were inclined to demonstrate proven independence from the White House, and Carter knew that he could not afford to take Congressional support for granted.

The president is further constrained by the type of man that he is and the context in which he is operating. Carter's personality and personal experience were decisive to the way that he conducted foreign policy, and ultimately would prove crucial to the public's perception of his administration. Of most importance to his formulation of foreign policy was his military background. At Annapolis, and while on active duty, the young officer would have been inculcated with traditional Cold War doctrine and rhetoric, and while his intelligence may have allowed him to see through some of the more simplistic tenets, he agreed with the major theme. Thus President Carter, ex-career naval officer, was as committed to the Cold War and the battle with the Soviet Union as any of his predecessors or successors in the White House. He believed, at heart, in American Exceptionalism, and wanted the United States to maintain its position of superiority in the global battle with the Soviet Union. In a commencement address at Notre Dame in June 1977 Carter declared:

> We are confident that democracy's example will be compelling, and so we seek to bring that example closer to those from whom in the past few years we have been separated and who are not yet convinced about the advantages of our kind of life.[8]

But Carter was also a complex man and he recognized the complexities of the U.S. in 1977, particularly the impact of Vietnam and Watergate. Indeed, the context of the mid–1970s, which had proved so crucial in securing victory for Carter in the 1976 presidential election, was to prove equally important in the formation, implementation and ultimately, the success, of Carter's foreign policy. By the mid–1970s, the United States was in relative decline, exemplified by Vietnam, Watergate and the poor state of the economy. Richard Nixon, attempting to formulate a policy that would maintain American status without further draining American resources, instituted the era of détente — a period of rapprochement with the Soviet Union culminating in SALT, the Strategic Arms Limitation Treaty of 1972. However, Carter not only inherited the benefits of détente, he also inherited the problems, particularly with regard to the different ways with which both sides perceived the policy. For the Soviets, détente denoted the American acceptance of global parity, while the Americans saw détente as a way of maintaining global superiority in an era when their military and financial power was relatively limited. Thus, for the Soviet Union, détente sanctioned adventurism in the Third World; for the United States, such adventurism, particularly in the swathe of countries that stretched from the Indian subcontinent, through the Middle East, to the Horn of Africa — a region collectively dubbed the Arc of Crisis — betrayed its spirit.

Notwithstanding the legacy of détente, the beginning of a new presidential administration generally signals a reorientation of policy in some way, and Carter was to prove no exception to this trend. An intelligent man, Carter recognized the context of the mid–1970s and was determined that, under his leadership, the United States would regain its pride, beginning with its pride in government. Throughout the presidential campaign, Carter talked about the need for change in the United States, but added that "I don't want the people to change. I want the government to change."⁹ The main reason, of course, was the pervasive distrust in government felt by the American people, exacerbated, if not caused, by the crises of Vietnam and Watergate.

Carter, like his fellow Americans, had been deeply affected by the problems besetting those at the highest level of politics. In his autobiography Carter recalled that "our first movie in the White House was *All the President's Men*. I felt strange occupying the same living quarters and position of responsibility as Richard Nixon."¹⁰ He went on:

> As an American, I had been embarrassed by the Watergate scandal and the forced resignation of the president. I realized that my own election had been aided by a deep desire among the people for open government, based on a new and fresh commitment to changing some of the Washington habits which had made it possible for the American people to be misled.¹¹

During his campaign, Carter made it clear that he was going to be different; that he recognized the context and was determined to address it. He criticized the Ford, Nixon and Johnson administrations for "excessive secrecy in foreign affairs"¹² and more than once told the American people that "there are a lot of things I would not do to be elected. I wouldn't tell a lie. I wouldn't make a misleading statement. I wouldn't betray a trust. I wouldn't avoid a controversial issue. If I do any of those things, don't support me, because I wouldn't deserve to lead this country."¹³

The legacy of Vietnam in particular demanded a change in policy as well as a more open and honest government. The American experience in southeast Asia seemed to epitomize all the negative connotations of foreign policy. Carter acknowledged the problems when he pointed out, during the second campaign debate with President Ford, that "our country is not strong anymore; we're not respected anymore.... We've lost in our foreign policy the character of the American people."¹⁴ This he was determined to redress, telling the Chicago Council on Foreign Relations that "it must be the responsibility of the president to restore the moral authority of this country in its conduct of foreign policy."¹⁵ So, in order to increase respect abroad and restore pride in government at home, Carter, reflecting the context of the bicentennial presidential election, advocated a return to the values and principles upon which the United States had been founded 200 years earlier. In particular, Carter proposed that his foreign policy doctrines reflect the original ideals and values of the nation, with an emphasis on the importance of human rights or, as Jefferson and the Founding Fathers might have described them, natural rights. In his inaugural address, the new president proclaimed:

Over the years, our greatest source of strength has come from those basic, price-less values which are embodied in our Declaration of Independence, our Consti-tution and our Bill of Rights: our belief in freedom of religion — our belief in freedom of expression — our belief in human dignity.... These principles have made us great and, unless our foreign policy reflects them, we make a mockery of all those values.[16]

He went on to assure his audience that, for the Carter administration, the commitment to human rights would be "absolute," and added, in a speech to the American people on February 2, 1977, that his foreign policy would be based upon "respect for human rights ... [and] our own moral values [because] I want our nation's actions to make you proud."[17] Rhetoric became policy in the subsequent Presidential Directive that asserted that "it shall be a major objective of U.S. foreign policy to promote the observance of human rights throughout the world."[18] It should be noted that, as John Dumbrell points out in *The Carter Presidency: A Re-Evaluation*, in practice the commit-ment to human rights was not intended to be "absolute," and the subsequent legislation allowed for special circumstances and national security consider-ations.[19] Nonetheless, as A. Glenn Mower claimed, Carter's prioritization of human rights in American foreign policy represented a "quantum leap for-ward" in the movement to integrate human rights matters into the "machin-ery and substance" of foreign policy.[20]

As well as reminding the American people of the reasons why they should be proud of their country, Carter's emphasis on human rights was also a vital element in his new approach to the Cold War. While Carter's personality and military background may have made him a Cold Warrior at heart, the con-text of the mid–1970s required a foreign policy adapted to America's relative decline. Wanting to combat the Soviet Union but unable to use traditional "hard" power methods, including American military might, Carter, instead, emphasized policies utilizing "soft" power.

Thus, Carter's main weapon in fighting the Cold War was America's moral superiority, reflected in a foreign policy centered upon human rights. As well as attacking the Soviet Union and communism on a moral level, the president hoped that a program based upon human rights would increase the influence of the United States within developing countries, the support of whom had been sought by both the Soviet Union and the United States since the 1950s to increase or strengthen their respective spheres of influence, by winning the "hearts and minds" of the people. In his memoirs, Carter argued that "a human rights effort would also help strengthen our influence among some of the developing nations that were still in the process of forming their own governments and choosing their future friends and trading partners."[21]

However, it was not just the developing world that Carter hoped might be influenced or impressed by his prioritization of human rights. The aftermath of World War II had resulted in a global emphasis on the importance of the human condition. On December 10, 1948, the General Assembly of the United Nations had adopted and proclaimed the Universal Declaration of Human Rights. The preamble stated: "Whereas recognition of the inherent dignity and of the equal and inalienable rights of all members of the human family is the foundation of freedom, justice and peace in the world ... the General Assembly proclaims this Universal Declaration of Human Rights."[22] Patricia Derian, a State Department spokesperson for the Carter administration, explained in 1978 that international law and the Universal Declaration was "our guide to the definition of human rights."[23] More contemporary for the Carter administration were the Helsinki Accords, signed on August 1, 1975, by all the countries of Europe (except Albania), the United States and Canada, and which pledged the 35 signatories to respect human rights and fundamental freedoms and to cooperate in economic, scientific, humanitarian and other areas. The Accords declared:

> The participating States will respect human rights and fundamental freedoms, including the freedom of thought, conscience, religion or belief, for all without distinction as to race, sex, language or religion.... They will promote and encourage the effective exercise of civil, political, economic, social, cultural, and other rights and freedoms all of which derive from the inherent dignity of the human person and are essential for his free and full development.[24]

By publicly subscribing to such values, Carter perhaps saw an opportunity to enhance American integrity and credibility among other leading world nations.

As well as partaking in an international consensus on the importance of human rights in foreign policy, Carter hoped such an orientation would also help to restore the domestic foreign policy consensus that had been shattered by the Vietnam war. In a question-and-answer session with a group of editors and news directions in July 1977, Carter explained:

> We've been through some sordid and embarrassing years recently with Vietnam and Cambodia and Watergate and the CIA revelations, and I felt like it was time for our country to hold a beacon of light of something pure and decent and right and proper that would rally our citizens to a cause.[25]

Equally important was the need to restore an element of consensus between the White House and Capitol Hill. In response to recent presidential misadventures, both at home and abroad, Congress had moved to assert control over executive power, for example with the War Powers Act of 1973 which restrained the president's ability to commit U.S. troops overseas. However, at the same time Congress turned its attention to the role of human rights on the policy agenda. Following a recommendation in 1974 from the Fraser Subcommittee of the House Committee on International Relations, an office specializing in human rights was established within the State Department, and training in human rights was included in the preparation undertaken by foreign service and military officers. Congressional legislation also reflected the increasing importance of human rights on the political agenda. In 1974 Congress passed the Foreign Assistance Act which declared that aid should not be extended to countries with "consistent pattern[s] of gross violations" of "internationally recognized human rights" involving "torture or cruel, inhuman or degrading treatment or punishment; prolonged detention without charges; or other flagrant denials of the right to life, liberty and the security of the person."[26] Two years later legislation was passed declaring that it was "a principal goal of the foreign policy of the U.S. to promote the increased observance of internationally recognized human rights by all countries," and forbade assistance to any country engaging "in a consistent pattern of gross violations" of human rights.[27] One of the most active politicians was Senator Henry Jackson of Washington; in 1974 he had co-sponsored the Jackson-Vanik Amendment, which made the granting of "most-favored nation" trading status to the Soviet Union contingent upon Soviet reducing restrictions on Jewish emigration. The passage of the Jackson-Vanik amendment in 1974 was but one indicator of the importance of human rights in Congressional circles, and Carter's prioritization of it was a way of gaining support from an increasingly fragmented Congress for his foreign policy agenda.

Last, but not least, as Carter the Christian and moralist pointed out, emphasizing human rights "was the right thing to do."[28] Indeed, Carter's religious beliefs were as important as his military background or his experiences as Governor of Georgia during his presidency; the Bible provided the basis for Carter's research in preparation for the Camp David negotiations between Israel and Egypt.[29] "The presence of my belief in Christ is the most important thing in my life," Carter declared, and "I pray to ask God to let me do the right thing."[30] Carter was renowned as a "born-again" Christian, having undergone a "conversion experience" following his defeat in the 1966 Georgia gubernatorial race — he admitted that before then, "My Christian beliefs were superficial, based primarily on pride, and I'd never done much for other people. I was always thinking about myself."[31] However, following his spiritual rejuvenation, Carter made sure that his actions backed up his words. He became a lay missionary, spent some months "witnessing for Christ" in various parts of Georgia and also in Philadelphia, Boston and New York, and viewed his own political career as a form of ministry. When Billy Graham was asked whether Carter was "wearing his religion on his sleeve" during the 1976 presidential race, the noted evangelist remarked, "I don't believe it's on his sleeve; I believe it's in his heart."[32]

Carter's change of tactics in waging the Cold War involved several other elements, besides the emphasis on human rights. Up to this point, American Cold War foreign policy had concentrated on the containment of the Soviet and communist threat; the U.S.-Soviet relationship provided the central focus of foreign policy, with most other elements being, as Zbigniew Brzezinski pointed out, "derivatives of that relationship."[33] This globalist orientation led to the determination to "hold the line" in places such as Korea and Vietnam,[34] but Carter was well aware that the American people were unlikely to support him in a foreign policy that seemed too confrontational, nor one that involved the deployment of American troops to distant lands for abstract ideals.

To avoid future entanglements, such as Vietnam, the administration therefore sought to de-emphasize East-West conflict and competition, and implement a regionalist approach where Third World nations, in particular, would be considered outside of the framework of East-West relations. As early as October 1976, Paul Warnke, later to be appointed as Director of the Arms Control and Disarmament Agency and chief negotiator for SALT II, suggested that "in dealing with the smaller countries of Asia, Africa and Latin America, we should think primarily of their own interests, not of how they might fit into the complex global game we play with the Soviets."[35] While recognizing that the Soviet Union was, of necessity, an important factor in foreign policy, Cyrus Vance agreed in principle with Warnke, arguing that "U.S./Soviet issues will not be permitted to so dominate our foreign policy that we neglect other important relationships and problems."[36] Carter concurred. The recommendations made by Warnke and Vance became official administration policy and, in July 1977, Carter declared to the Annual Meeting of the Southern Legislative Conference:

> Our national security was often defined almost exclusively in terms of military competition with the Soviet Union. This competition is still critical, because it does involve issues that could lead to war. But however important this relationship of military balance, it cannot be our sole preoccupation to the exclusion of other world issues which also concern us both.[37]

De-emphasizing globalist concerns allowed the administration the scope to focus on some of these other issues, including the Panama Canal treaties and the Camp David Agreements for peace between Egypt and Israel in the Middle East. The new approach also involved a greater sensitivity to the variety of the Third World and to the particular cultures and problems of different countries included within it, including in Africa. In July 1977 Cyrus Vance addressed the Plenary session of the NAACP convention in St. Louis, and asserted:

> Africa matters very much to the United States. This is a fact more and more Americans are coming to understand.... We proceed from a basic proposition: that

our policies must recognize the unique identity of Africa. We can be neither right nor effective if we treat Africa simply as one part of the third world, or as a testing ground of East-West competition.[38]

Thus regionalism, like human rights, was a vital tool in fighting the Cold War in an era when previous methods were unavailable. It addressed the Vietnam syndrome; it sought to please developing countries by focusing upon their problems and needs, and thereby increase the respect with which developing countries viewed the United States; and it still projected an image of the United States as active and powerful in the world.

Jimmy Carter's foreign policy approach was also rooted in a belief in global interdependence and complexity; as Cyrus Vance declared, "global interdependence had become a reality."[39] For the new president, world order should be built upon community, not competition. Under Carter's direction, the administration worked towards cooperation with other nations with an emphasis, as Brzezinski summarized in a memo to the president, on "building new relationships with friends, with adversaries, with the developing world, even with the whole world — in the hope thereby of renovating the existing international system."[40] In October 1977, Carter told the UN General Assembly that the "power to solve the world's problems" no longer lay in "the hands of the few." It was "widely shared among many nations with different cultures and different histories and different aspirations."[41] As well as representing an idea that had taken center stage from time to time throughout American diplomatic history — for example, Woodrow Wilson's sponsorship of the League of Nations — the idea that a community of nations could share the load, if the need for outside military intervention arose, was also a response to the experience of Vietnam.

This approach led to the formation of ties with countries where the Americans had not had much, if any, of a presence. In the Horn of Africa, for example, this meant the development of a relationship with Somalia, and the maintenance of a relationship with Ethiopia, regardless of the presence of any of the communist bloc in that country. General William Odom, the military adviser to the National Security Council approved, pointing out that "as long as we have a foot in both camps, the amount of military required to maintain a stable regional power balance is small [*sic*]. When you lose your footing in one side the amount of military requirements goes up."[42] In the era of the Vietnam syndrome, no one in the administration wished to do anything that might require an increased American military presence.

Interestingly, Carter's emphasis on community not competition combined Wilsonian world-order liberalism with "realist" balance-of-power considerations, and reflected the cutting edge of academic thought on "complex interdependence" in the 1970s. Selling such diversity and complexity to the American public would be a challenge Carter would have to face throughout his administration, and one that would prove pivotal to his foreign policy approach in 1980, as we shall see.

The "Best" Team

As president, Carter wanted to do his best, as he had pledged after his interview many years before with Admiral Rickover. He vowed that his foreign policy should embody the best of America's traditions, and also that that it would be the best way to fight the Cold War in the constrained circumstances of the mid–1970s. To help him to achieve these ambitions he sought well-qualified advisers and assistants; at a news conference on November 15, 1976, the president-elect announced that his procedure for selecting his Cabinet and key personnel would be "careful and thorough and deliberate."[43] As well as those who had served with him in Georgia, Carter chose people who had, as he recalled in his memoirs, "demonstrated ability and knowledge of the issues we would be facing."[44] Into this category fell Zbigniew Brzezinski, Assistant to the President for National Security Affairs and Director of the National Security Council, noted for his expertise on the Soviet Union and Eastern Europe and who shared Carter's interests in China, the Middle East and Africa.[45] However, Brzezinski also shared Carter's complexity, and his apparent ambivalence over some issues — for example his tough anti–Soviet stance alongside his advocacy of interdependency — would not help the perception of confusion surrounding Carter's foreign policy.

As chief foreign policy adviser within the White House, Brzezinski was clearly going to be a key figure in the formulation of foreign policy, and he was delighted with the appointment, later remarking:

> I always wanted the job of Assistant for National Security Affairs in the White House, for a very simple reason. It was a more important job [than Secretary of State]. It was the key job. It involved the integration of the top inputs from State, Defense, and CIA. And, above all, it meant that you were close to a president whom I knew would be an activist. And, therefore, being close to him and working with him was centrally important.[46]

Brzezinski had been born in 1928 in Warsaw, but had moved to Canada in 1938 when his father was assigned to Montreal as consul general. Earning his PhD from Harvard in 1953, Brzezinski went on to become a professor of government and law at Columbia University by 1962. He took his first government job in 1966, although he had worked on Lyndon Johnson's re-election campaign in 1964, serving until 1968 in the State Department's Policy Planning Council. In the years between then and accepting the appointment from Carter, Brzezinski continued to teach, to publish, and to advise senior Democrats; during the 1976 campaign at least five other Democratic candidates, as well as Carter, sought Brzezinski's advice.[47]

Carter had first met Brzezinski through their mutual association with the Trilateral Commission, an organization established in 1973 by David Rockefeller, chairman of Chase Manhattan Bank, with the goal of influencing international affairs through fostering cooperation between, and the development of, the industrial democracies of Japan and the West. Rockefeller's idea for establishing the commission came after reading Brzezinski's *Between Two Ages*, published while he was a professor at Columbia University, which proposed an alliance between North America, Western Europe and Japan.[48] "Those Trilateral Commission meetings for me," Carter declared, "were like classes in foreign policy — reading papers produced on every conceivable subject, hearing experienced leaders debate international issues and problems, and meeting the big names like Cy Vance and Harold Brown and Zbig."[49] Indeed, these three men were to provide Carter with his three key foreign policy personnel.

Outside of the White House, foreign policy lay with the State Department, under the control of Secretary of State Cyrus Vance. Chosen because of his experience, knowledge and ability, Vance had also served as Carter's chief foreign policy adviser during the campaign and was another colleague from the Trilateral Commission. Carter later recalled that "in many ways Cy Vance mirrored the character of the organization he led. He was intelligent and experienced, thoroughly honorable, sound in his judgments, careful to explore all the facets of a question before answering, extremely loyal to his subordinates and protective of the State Department and its status and heritage."[50]

Vance was born in Clarksburg, West Virginia, in 1917,[51] received a law degree from Yale in 1942, and served in the U.S. Navy during World War II. He began his government career in 1957, as special counsel to the Preparedness Investigating Subcommittee of the Senate Armed Services Committee, chaired by Lyndon Johnson. Vance maintained his relationship with Johnson, and in 1961 was appointed general counsel of the Defense Department, where he worked closely with Robert McNamara. In June 1962, Vance was appointed as secretary of the army, and in 1964 became deputy secretary of defense. Although a back injury forced his resignation in 1967, Vance retained his close links with government service and continued to assist with special projects. Described by *Congressional Quarterly* as "a troubleshooter in times of crisis," Vance participated in missions to Panama, the Dominican Republic, Cyprus and South Korea. In the spring of 1968, Johnson included Vance in a meeting to discuss the future of American involvement in Vietnam, where Vance advocated increased negotiations, and subsequently was appointed as deputy to Ambassador-at-Large Averell Harriman at the peace talks with the North Vietnamese in Paris. Following this, Vance pursued another issue that had always been a major area of concern for him: the matter of the international arms trade. From 1969, he served as vice chairman of a United Nations association policy panel on conventional arms control, which released a study in 1976 deploring the continued growth in the world arms trade. Détente and arms limitation talks would remain Vance's priority throughout his tenure as secretary of state and, in the news conference on December 3, 1976, announcing his appointment, Vance stressed the importance of talks with the Soviet Union aimed at limiting the growth in nuclear weaponry.[52]

In a break with the traditional role of vice president, Carter was keen that Walter "Fritz" Mondale should play an active role in his administration. Primarily chosen because Carter was convinced, as he recalled in his memoirs, that he needed a member of Congress "in order to provide some balance of experience to our ticket,"[53] Carter wanted a longer-term contribution from the former senator from Minnesota. At a news conference two days after the election, Carter said of Mondale that "I expect him to play a larger role in the next administration than any previous vice president has ever played." On December 23, Carter elaborated on Mondale's role, describing it as "unprecedented in American history for a vice president. I look on [him] as my top staff person." Instead of the usual office in the Executive Office Building next to the White House, Mondale was given an office in the White House itself, and provided with the same briefings and information as the president.[54]

One of the main advocates of regionalism within the Carter administration was the man Carter appointed as Ambassador to the United Nations. Andrew Young first came to prominence during the civil rights movement, when he worked alongside Martin Luther King Jr., and served as vice president of the Southern Christian Leadership Conference. In 1972 Young was successful in his bid for a seat in the U.S. House of Representatives, where he became a leading spokesman for civil rights, an outspoken critic of the Vietnam War, and a passionate protector of funding for social programs. Rewarded for his early support for Carter's bid for the presidency, Young was determined to use his role as Ambassador to address Third World issues; in Africa, apartheid particularly concerned him.

Other executive branch officials would also have an input in the foreign policy decision making process, including Secretary of Defense Harold Brown (the third of Carter's foreign policy advisers chosen from his association with the Trilateral Commission), Director of the CIA Admiral Stansfield Turner, and General William Odom, who had previously served as defense attaché to Moscow, and was appointed as military adviser to the National Security Council. Although she played a less official role, the advice and counsel of his wife, Rosalynn, was important to Carter throughout his political career and indeed throughout his life,[55] as was the support and input of his whole family. In later years James "Chip" Carter, the president's second son, would recall how politics became the "family business," which would be reflected in every aspect of their lives — for example, during dinnertime conversation.[56]

Although he attempted to surround himself with the "best and the brightest," the new president took his responsibility as the *chief* executive seriously, proudly displaying the sign, borrowed from the Truman Presidential Library, bearing the words "the buck stops here," that had stood on Harry S Truman's desk when he occupied the Oval Office[57] — indeed, Carter acknowledged Truman as his favorite president.[58] Carter's plan was that, when possible and where appropriate, his advisers and subordinates should bring all options on an issue to him, and then he would make the ultimate decision. The chain of command in foreign policy decision-making was set out in a report by Brzezinski in the early days of the administration, and personally approved by the president.[59] Within foreign policy making, there would be both a formal system and an informal system, with both producing Presidential Directives (PDs) and Presidential Review Memoranda (PRMs) to implement presidential decisions. At the head of the formal system, the report stated, was the president who was "in overall charge" and would make decisions through "frequent and direct contact with the Secretary of State, the Secretary of Defense, and Assistant for National Security Affairs, and also through written reports staffed through the normal NSC system." Within the White House, beneath the president in the decision-making chain, was the National Security Council. This would hold "formal regular meetings" and coordinate the paper flow and decision process, which would be channeled to the president through Brzezinski. Instead of the previous seven committees, the NSC in the Carter administration would only have two cabinet-level committees, which would meet several times each week: the Policy Review Committee (PRC), usually chaired by Vance, and the Special Coordination Committee (SCC), chaired by Brzezinski.[60]

In his report, Brzezinski also acknowledged the informal systems through which information could be channeled to the president, and foreign policy decisions made. The president would have frequent personal contact with his chief aides, and would also preside over a Friday breakfast meeting, attended by Vance, Brzezinski, Brown, and also Mondale and Special Assistant to the President Hamilton Jordan, to ensure "interaction with domestic politics." Issues that could be resolved at the "sub-presidential level" were to be dis-

cussed at the weekly Vance-Brown-Brzezinski lunch, and White House senior staff would meet informally as necessary.[61] Jody Powell, the White House
press secretary, issued a statement on January 22, 1977, announcing that the
new structure was "devised and ordered by the president himself. It reflects
his desire for a more simplified and responsive organization through government."[62] The informal structure also reflected Carter's belief that, notwithstanding his acceptance of ultimate responsibility, his subordinates had their
own equally important roles and levels of responsibility. In remarks at the
swearing-in ceremony for cabinet members, Carter stated that "I believe in a
Cabinet administration of our Government. And although the major decisions will be made ultimately by me as president, which is my constitutional
prerogative and responsibility, the Secretaries will run their Departments.
And this is the way it ought to be."[63]

Why Not the Best?

Jimmy Carter was elected president in a year that, contextually, reflected
both the best and the worst that the United States could be. The shadows of
Vietnam and Watergate still touched the souls of the American people, the
bicentenary celebrated the ideals and values that lay at the heart of American
Exceptionalism, and the beginning of its third century as a nation brought a
new hope that the United States had a future of which Americans could be
proud.

Carter certainly believed that the United States could, and should, once
again be proud of itself. The new president was driven by a moment in his
life when he had had to admit to himself that he had not always done his
best, but he was determined to rectify this shortcoming. The United States
had clearly not done its best either in recent years, as epitomized by Vietnam
and Watergate, but there was no reason why this could not also be rectified.

So in presenting his foreign policy, Carter applied new tactics to the
Cold War as part of his hope to restore American faith and pride in the aftermath of recent disasters and tragedies. Constrained by the contemporary context, and unable to wield the might of American military force, Carter chose,
instead, to use moral certitude as the basis for American power and influence.
Gathering around him a foreign policy team that he felt would enable him
to do his best, Carter called for a move away from a preoccupation with the
Soviet Union, with an emphasis on regionalist rather than globalist concerns,
centered upon human rights.

Carter's new approach in foreign policy was to have a profound impact
on relations with the developing world. His ultimate strategy may well have

been to ally these countries with the United States in the global battle with the Soviet Union. Notwithstanding, Carter gave consideration to the needs of the individual countries, and particularly to the demands of the people, rather than leaders who had become adept at maintaining corrupt regimes through judicious playing of the Cold War game. In Africa, the initial idea was to address the racial injustice in the South, but developments in the Horn of Africa, specifically in Ethiopia and Somalia, soon widened the focus on that continent and led to the administration's "first foreign policy crisis."[64]

II

Shifting Alliances: The United States, Ethiopia and Somalia

The Importance of the Horn

While never the priority of the Carter administration, in the same way that perhaps the Camp David Accords were, or Iran would become, the Horn of Africa was nonetheless important — and an interesting prism through which to view the foreign policy process. However, in January 1977 there was little hint of the dramatic developments to come that would test the personal preferences of the members of the administration, as well as the fundamental policies of Carter's new approach to the Cold War.

American interest in the Horn of Africa began in earnest with the Cold War. Then, the geographical location of the Horn, with its proximity to Middle East oil fields, the sea oil routes and the Red Sea passage to the Mediterranean, as well as its role as a link in the technological chain of Western communications and defense systems, made it strategically important. William Odom, the military adviser to the National Security Council during the Carter administration, argued that the Horn of Africa should not be viewed within the African context, but as part of "the larger regional grouping of the Middle East-Southwest Asia states. Its ties to the Arabian peninsula and Egypt rival, and in some ways exceed, those to Africa."[1] Paul Henze, National Security Staffer responsible for the Horn of Africa, concurred, noting that the location of the Horn made it a crucial "link in the chain of

Western defenses against Soviet expansionism and radical Arab disruptive activities."[2]

Many, including Henze, argued that Ethiopia was the key country of the region. Covering an area of 455,000 square miles, it was one of the largest countries in Sub-Saharan Africa, and also one of the most important, mainly because of the effort put in by Emperor Haile Selassie. Following his restoration to the Ethiopian throne after the expulsion of the occupying Italians in 1941, Selassie determined to make Addis Ababa "the capital of Africa."[3] The Ethiopian capital became home not only to the headquarters of the United Nations Economic Commission for Africa, but also the Organization of African Unity, and many regarded Haile Selassie as the "father-figure" of African nationalism.[4] Indeed, for a major part of the twentieth century, Ethiopia was the only independent African nation, apart from Liberia. However, Ethiopia was not without its problems; the nearly thirty million people were ethnically and religiously diverse — twenty-five percent were of Amharic ethnic origin, forty percent were Galla, twelve percent of Tigre origin, while the remaining twenty-three percent included ethnic Somalis; with regard to religion, forty percent were Ethiopian Orthodox Christians, forty-five percent were Muslim, and fifteen percent animist — and secessionist movements plagued the Ethiopian leadership.[5]

Notwithstanding these problems, the dominant nation of the Horn region was also the one that it was most desirable to have as part of one's sphere of influence, and therefore the United States government was receptive when Haile Selassie decided that the future for his country lay with the West, and not the Soviet Union. In 1953, Ethiopia and the United States signed agreements that gave the United States access to military bases in return for economic and military aid, beginning a special relationship that would endure for over twenty years. One of the most significant gains for the United States was access to a communications facility at Asmara, in the province of Eritrea, on the Ethiopian coast. The facility was named Kagnew Station, in honor of the Ethiopian legion that had fought as part of the UN force in the Korean War,[6] and was to prove especially important to the American intelligence community until the 1970s, when technological advances in the era of satellites and improved communications reduced the number of relay stations necessary for the passage of information.[7]

The Americans were not alone in recognizing the strategic importance of both the Horn of Africa in general and Ethiopia in particular. The Soviet Union strove to gain a foothold in the area and courted the Ethiopian Emperor. In 1959 Haile Selassie accepted $100 million in Soviet aid, but did not change his overall alignment with the West. Unable to dislodge the Americans from Ethiopia, Soviet leaders, in line with Cold War mentality, sought to gain preponderant influence in another country of this African region that was thought to be of strategic importance. Hence, once Somalia was declared an independent republic in 1960, Khrushchev established relations, offered economic aid, and undertook a major port expansion in Berbera, beginning in 1962.[8] It should be noted, however, that during the period from 1954 to 1970 the United States also enjoyed cordial relations with Somalia and extended almost $60 million in aid.[9]

In 1969, though, the situation changed. In that year Mohammed Siad Barré seized power in a military coup, overthrowing, according to the American perspective, "an elected Somali government."[10] Siad had risen through the ranks, first of the police force and then of the military, to hold the rank of Major General and lead the Somali army at the time of the coup. Perhaps realizing that there was little chance of Western support for his regime because of the West's close ties with Ethiopia, Siad publicly declared Somalia to be a pro–Soviet state, creating, according to the Presidential Review Memorandum produced by the Carter administration on April 1, 1977, a "Leninist-style party apparatus" in Somalia, establishing formal links with the Soviet communist party, concluding a Soviet-Somali Friendship treaty, and going "out of his way to praise the USSR and to parrot Soviet policy lines."[11] In return, the Soviets increased their military aid to Somalia, making it one of the most heavily armed nations in Africa, and constructing various military facilities, including a naval base at Berbera. However, there were always questions surrounding the depth of the Soviet commitment to the Somali nation; Henze, for example, claimed that "the Soviets moved into Somalia bag and baggage because they couldn't get Ethiopia."[12]

The presence of the Soviet Union and United States in the neighboring countries of Ethiopia and Somalia, within a Cold War framework, provided the context in which one of the key, and arguably most dangerous, aspects of Horn politics might be exacerbated: the long-standing rivalry between Ethiopia and Somalia. As far back as the sixteenth century, Christian-ruled Ethiopia, backed by the Portuguese empire, fought Muslim Somalia, supported by the Ottoman empire.[13] In the twentieth century, the friction between the two nations was not prompted by religious differences, although these existed, but focused upon a border dispute concerning the Ogaden, a mostly barren desert that was officially part of Ethiopia but largely inhabited by ethnic Somalis. The fact that both the United States and the Soviet Union were supplying military aid to the parties involved provided the means with which territorial claims might be realized and increased the possibility of conflict, potentially at a superpower level.[14]

Indeed, Siad's motivations in consolidating the relationship with the Soviet Union in 1969 were more nationalistic and irredentist than the result of any strong ties to communist ideology. In Siad's view, the European "scramble for Africa" had destroyed Somalia in the late nineteenth century, dividing the country into five parts: British Somaliland; Italian Somalia; the French-controlled territory of the Afars and the Issas (which in 1977 became the independent state of Djibouti); a fourth part, the Ogaden, became part of Ethiopia; the fifth was merged with Kenya.[15] The end of colonial rule in Africa had led to the creation of the Somali Democratic Republic in 1960, formed from British Somaliland and Italian Somalia, covering an area of 246,155 square miles and with a population of some 3.2 million by the late 1970s. However, as opposed to the ethnic and religious diversity of Ethiopia, homogeneity characterized Somalia: the country was 98.8 percent ethnic Somali, and 99 percent Muslim,[16] and arguably this homogeneity contributed to the Somali people's support for Siad's determination to reunite all ethnic Somalis in one nation. Nor could any Somali easily overlook, or forget, the dream; the five-pointed star on the national flag of Somalia served to remind the people of the five parts into which the Europeans had divided the nation. Tom Farer, a professor at Rutgers University and specialist on the Horn region, remarked in testimony to the House Subcommittee on Africa that the creation of the Somali Republic in 1960 was "the first step toward the consummation of national unity," and warned that "it would not be the last."[17]

The problem of reunification, with regard to peace and stability in the region, lay in the Cairo Resolution, passed by the Organization of African Unity (OAU) in 1964, which stated that existing borders of African nations would be honored and maintained, and made the notion of territorial integrity almost a sacred principle.[18] Thus, it appeared to Siad that he would only be able to achieve his dreams through military conquest, and for this he would need arms and external support. Realizing that he was unlikely to find this among African nations, because of the Cairo Resolution, Siad accepted Soviet offers of help, and consolidated the relationship between the two states.

Nevertheless, despite the friction between Ethiopia and Somalia, and their own long-term relationship with Somalia, the Soviets seemed unwilling to give up completely on an alliance with Ethiopia. At the same time that they were actively involved in Somalia, the Soviets also supported Eritrean rebels who were demanding independence from Ethiopia, in the hope that the unrest would lead to a change of leadership in the major country of the Horn to one that might prove more receptive to Soviet overtures. The Soviet hopes were boosted in 1974 when social problems and discontent within the military over pay and conditions led to the overthrow of Emperor Haile Selassie. In his place, Ethiopia was ruled by the Provisional Military Government (PMG), led by the Provisional Military Administrative Council (PMAC) known as the Derg, the Amharic word for committee.[19]

The United States, absorbed by the aftermath of the Watergate scandal —
Richard Nixon resigned only one month before Haile Selassie was deposed —
and perhaps still stunned by the Vietnam experience, made no moves to
counter the Ethiopian revolution, but although the United States continued
to provide military aid, no formal links with the Derg were established. This
appeared to suit the Derg members, who were increasingly sending Ethiopian
military officers and leaders to the USSR and Eastern Europe for instruction
and training. However, the initial response of the Soviet Union to the
Ethiopian Revolution was to increase the supply of arms to Somalia: between
1974 and 1977 more than $300 million was supplied to Siad Barré, which was
more than the United States had provided to Ethiopia in the entire period
since the 1953 military aid agreement.[20] Nonetheless, the Soviets were aware
that the opportunity existed to gain the biggest prize in the Horn and increased
their attempts to form an alliance with Ethiopia. One of the Derg leaders,
Colonel Mengistu Haile Mariam, secretly visited Moscow and signed a military aid agreement on December 14, 1976, a clause of which demanded that
Ethiopia sever its ties with the United States.[21]

In *Ethiopia, the United States, and the Soviet Union*, David Korn described
Mengistu as "consistently extreme, consistently ruthless, consistently anti–
American and consistently pro–Soviet."[22] Mengistu's antipathy towards the
United States is believed to have developed from his experience of military
training in the United States, when his dark skin led to him being a victim
of racial discrimination while stationed in Alabama and at Fort Meade, Maryland.[23] Also, Mengistu's vision of himself as a revolutionary led to his ideological identification with the Soviet Union. The elevation of such a man as
Mengistu to a position of power in Ethiopia should perhaps have sounded a
warning note to the Carter administration when it came to power in January 1977. Nevertheless, Jimmy Carter had little reason to believe that within
a few months, relations between the United States and the Horn country
would change radically. Indeed, the State Department received a telegram
from Mengistu, one of several key figures in the Derg at the time, extending
"sincere felicitations" to the new president and wishing him every success.[24]
Likewise, the Carter administration continued to reflect the long-standing
American view that the Horn of Africa was strategically important, and that
Ethiopia was the most important country with which to maintain relations.

Indeed, Paul Henze had been appointed to the National Security Council in part because of his knowledge and expertise on the Horn region. Henze
had first visited the Horn of Africa in 1962, and was appointed as first secretary and political counselor at the American Embassy in Addis Ababa in 1969.
Although transferred to the Embassy in Ankara in 1974, Henze remained
abreast of developments in the Horn, publishing *Ethiopian Journeys: 1969–72*

in 1977, at which point Brzezinski, whom Henze had known since 1953 through their mutual acquaintance with Professor Carl Friedrich of Harvard, invited him to join the NSC.[25] Henze's expertise on the Horn region was widely acknowledged within the administration, but his pro–Ethiopian and anti–Somali stance was also commented upon. General Odom later remarked that "Paul Henze on the NSC staff knew a lot about Somalia, and he had very strong views. He felt we ought to stay out of Somalia. He wrote great tracts against anybody on the staff who as much as suggested that we ought to take advantage of Soviet difficulties in Somalia."[26] Brzezinski apparently shared Henze's bias in the NSC. Henze recalled that "Brzezinski had no sympathy for Somalia. He had a lot of sympathy for Ethiopia. He recalled how as a child he had played soldier during the period of the Italian invasion of Ethiopia and all his Ethiopian soldiers always won. Brzezinski had ... the natural sympathy the Poles have for invaded people who they regard as underdogs."[27]

Human Rights and Ethiopia

Clearly, then, the Horn of Africa was an important region geopolitically, and would be affected by Carter's new approach to the Cold War, beginning with the president's determination to link foreign policy with the human rights record of a country. It should be noted, though, that the prioritization of human rights was designed to apply to all of Africa, not just the Horn. As Cyrus Vance told the NAACP:

> Our deep belief in human rights — political, economic, and social — leads us to policies that support their promotion throughout Africa. This means concern for individuals whose rights are threatened — anywhere on the continent.... We will be firm in our support of individual human rights. Our concern is not limited to any one region of the continent. We must understand the diversity of African social and value systems. Gross violations of individual human dignity are no more acceptable in African terms than in ours.[28]

Although addressing the racial injustice in the south of the continent was a priority, particularly for Andrew Young, it was clear that Carter always considered other regions just as important. In December 1977, the president reminded the Black Leaders' Forum that "human rights standards are significant not only in relations with South Africa, but also with black African states, as illustrated by strong administration concern and action in response to deplorable human rights violations in Uganda and Ethiopia."[29]

Indeed, in Ethiopia, with whom the United States had enjoyed a "special relationship" lasting nearly twenty-five years,[30] the Carter administration was overwhelmed with evidence of human rights violations, including that perhaps most dear to the hearts of Americans: the right to free and democratic government. The internecine strife that had plagued the Derg for two years was resolved on February 3, 1977, when Mengistu seized ultimate power and set up a one-man dictatorship by eliminating all his rivals in a violent shootout that was described in the *New York Times* as one of the "bloodiest days of the Revolution" thus far.[31] The former Ethiopian ambassador to Egypt, Getachew Mekasha, depicted the coup through which Mengistu seized power as "a trap," explaining that when "Tefferi [Mengistu's chief opponent within the Derg] and the others arrived at the palace they were arrested one by one and shot. Mengistu believed his power was being threatened, so he simply had his rivals shot."[32] Furthermore, human rights abuses by the government pervaded every level of Ethiopian society. The Policy Review Committee of April 11, 1977, reported that "current intelligence ... indicates that the military regime in Ethiopia is becoming more brutal and more beleaguered."[33] In memos to Brzezinski in March, Henze described the internal violence in Ethiopia as an "orgy of killings"[34] with increasing numbers of "random shootings, as well as killings of students and regime opponents."[35]

As well as intelligence from agents in Ethiopia, the Carter administration was offered first-hand accounts of human rights violations from Ethiopians seeking to defect. Ambassador Mekasha, who sought political asylum in the United States, told the *Los Angeles Times* that his decision was motivated by the severe and brutal conditions that existed in Ethiopia, saying:

> Ethiopia is gripped by fear. The people are afraid of the Derg and the Derg's members are afraid of each other. At the slightest excuse, soldiers will arrest and kill anybody considered an opponent. Those of us who welcomed the military revolution are now embarrassed. At least under Selassie there were laws, a constitution. There was law and order. Under the Derg there is no law and no constitution. The only law and order is that imposed by the men with guns.[36]

Ethiopia's ambassador to Saudi Arabia, Abdullah Abdurahman Nour, fled to Britain and told the *New York Times* that "I was one of the strongest supporters of the revolution in Ethiopia but now under Mengistu there are mass killings and chaos. The army is told to kill anyone suspected of working against the revolution and everything is done to consolidate the power of Mengistu."[37]

Members of international organizations also provided evidence of the conditions within Ethiopia. Stefan de Vylder, who had worked in Addis Ababa for the Swedish International Development Authority, described the manner of execution for prisoners in graphic terms: "In mid–March some 120 students were collected in a field outside Addis Ababa and dynamited. Most of the 655 youths officially admitted to having been executed in May were found with their throats cut. This is now a common method of execution." He also reported that the authorities in Addis Ababa were charging families of the executed the equivalent of $51 to give the bodies a burial, then using the money to replenish ammunition supplies.[38]

Dr. Meyer-Lie, an official of Amnesty International, provided further evidence of the horrors when testifying before the House Subcommittee on Africa in March 1977. He stated that since the Derg seized power in 1974, Amnesty International regarded the human rights violations in Ethiopia "as a matter for urgent international concern." He went on to describe the conditions he encountered during his recent visit to the women political prisoners in Akiki prison in Addis Ababa:

> There were no beds and mattresses were laid directly on the floor.... The lavatory was a hole in the floor with barrels of water.... There were no chairs, tables or heating arrangements in either room despite the chilly weather.... The women were not permitted to communicate with their families. They appeared to be thin, hollow-eyed and mentally depressed.

He added:

> The atmosphere in Addis Ababa was one of total fear. People disappeared daily and almost every family has had some member shot or imprisoned. During the house-to-house search by the army, police and workers' defense squads, innocent people were shot or taken away to prison. This amounts to a manhunt, especially enforced after curfew.

He concluded:

> The violation of human rights in Ethiopia has escalated to a grotesque level. Detention without trial, the frequent use of the death penalty, the widespread practice of extrajudiciary executions and trial of civilians by military tribunals leads one to the conclusion that there is clearly a consistent pattern of gross violations of human rights under the rule of the Derg.[39]

The fact that the House Subcommittee on Africa had solicited such testimony boded well for Carter's attempt to reorient foreign policy. The American political system, with its practice of checks and balances, meant that no chief executive could casually ignore the feelings of Congress on matters of policy, particularly when embarking on a reorientation of foreign policy as was Carter. Fortunately for the president, Congress appeared as keen to address human rights violations as he was, a fact reflected by the appearance of Dr. Meyer-Lie. Indeed, even before Jimmy Carter took office, the 94th Congress had held hearings into the human rights situation in Ethiopia and were told by witnesses then, including William Schaufele, Assistant Secretary of State for African Affairs in the Ford administration, of the "widespread violations of human rights ... [including] tortures, killings, imprisonments on political grounds."[40] Members of the 95th Congress continued to show concern, including Representative Edward Derwinski (R-Il), who addressed the House on June 6, 1977, expressing his worries about the repression of freedom of speech in Ethiopia:

> Hardly a day goes by without some new report of the ruling military junta's political oppression that now appears to have reached pervasive proportions. The recent seizure by Government forces of the Radio Voice of the Gospel, Africa's most powerful broadcasting station, illustrates just how sweeping the crackdown has become.... It is now quite clear that the expropriation of the Radio Voice of the Gospel was part of the Ethiopian Government's policy of placing all forms of media under its control to further the social, economic and political objectives of the Ethiopian revolution.[41]

In addition to Congressional interest, a further reason for the Carter administration to respond to human rights violations in Ethiopia, and also a consequence of the American political system, was the extent of public awareness of conditions in the Horn. With the influence that public opinion could have on elected officials, and the publicity surrounding the administration's stand on human rights, the Carter administration could ill afford inaction when the American public was being inundated with press reports citing the brutality of life in Ethiopia. The *New York Times* of February 1, 1977, for example, described Ethiopia as "racked by political assassinations and unrest, military suppression and a war against secessionists in Eritrea, the northernmost province."[42] Indeed, according to the press, violence had permeated every level of society since the Derg had seized power in the 1974 revolution. For a regime dedicated to "scientific socialism," *Time* declared, the only thing scientific appeared to be the "methodical ruthlessness of their rule. The Derg seized power in Addis Ababa and other centers in the African nation of twenty-eight million people, confiscating weapons and executing anyone who opposed it."[43]

For journalists, it appeared clear that the violence with which Mengistu seized power in February was also the way in which he ruled the country, as he pledged to crush all rivals, creating "terror in their camps as they did in ours."[44] According to *U.S. News and World Report*, Addis Ababa was "a city cowering in fear and chaos. Each evening, machine-gun fire resounds in the streets."[45] *Time* reported that the government-controlled television station regularly broadcast:

> A prime-time horror show intended — quite literally — to terrify the nation's twenty-eight million inhabitants. Shots of racked bodies of political prisoners tortured to death, corpses of dissidents shot down by mobs of armed vigilantes — they all flicker across the screen as evidence of the ruthless determination of what may be one of the most brutal and arbitrary regimes in power today.[46]

The *New York Times*, on May 20, declared:

> It is impossible to tell how many people have died in Addis Ababa since February when Colonel Mengistu took over, but those familiar with the situation here have put their guesses in the thousands.... It is hard for residents of Addis Ababa not to notice a grisly comment on their situation: vultures have taken to roosting at a central location in the city, Revolution Square.[47]

An earlier report from the *New York Times* informed the American public that "dozens of parents [who] gathered at the gates of the National Palace, the headquarters of the military council, seeking information about their missing children [were] told to go home.[48] Meanwhile, *Time* reported in February that "fifty militants, mostly students who had been suspected of anti-council activity, were shoved against the wall of a suburban Addis Ababa shooting range and slain. Many more killings have taken place secretly. One woman was presented with her husband's bullet-ridden body along with an explanation of his death from natural causes."[49]

In addition to dealing violently with those who appeared happy to be Ethiopians, Mengistu's treatment of, and attitude towards, various secessionist movements in the country also raised questions about violations of human rights. In March, Professor Tom Farer, a specialist on the Horn region at Rutgers University, told the House Subcommittee on Africa that, in attempting to subdue the secessionist movement in the northern province of Eritrea, "the Ethiopian armed forces perpetrate My Lais and Guernicas in a random and obscene procession." He claimed that human rights violations included the "use of starvation, a 'weapon' that at one point in the conflict seemed to threaten virtual genocide, the bombardment of undefended villages, shooting of hostages, and all of the kinds of humanitarian delinquencies we associate with full-scale insurgency warfare."[50]

However, perhaps the most immediate area of concern for the Carter administration with regard to the violence and terror in Ethiopia was the risk to American personnel. There was a constant fear that reprisals would be taken against American citizens either visiting or working in Ethiopia, and to counter this threat Henze informed Brzezinski that "American tourists are being advised to avoid Ethiopia and there are discussions of possible evacuation of American official dependants."[51] Much of the discussion within the administration centered on Kagnew Station, the American communications base at Asmara in the province of Eritrea. The lease was due to expire in 1978 and, because advances in areas such as satellite technology had made the need for a communications facility in that location obsolete,[52] the decision had been made in 1976 to not renew the lease.[53] However, the internal situation within Ethiopia, and the threat to American personnel, prompted the Carter administration to bring forward the closure. In a memo to Brzezinski in

March, Secretary of Defense Harold Brown pointed out that "the situation in Asmara has become unpredictable and, therefore, that the security of our military and contract personnel there can no longer be assured."[54] Similarly, Henze warned Brzezinski that "our remaining personnel there are potential hostages,"[55] and the national security adviser concurred that "the risk to the safety of U.S. personnel created by the situation in Ethiopia" necessitated the early closure of the base.[56] The president agreed, and Mengistu was informed of the decision on April 22.[57]

Given the extensive evidence of human rights violations in Ethiopia, and the highly publicized rhetoric of the Carter administration, the question was more how the administration would respond to the situation in Ethiopia than whether it would. Candidate Carter had articulated the likely response in 1976 when he told a news conference that "I think the allocation of foreign aid and the normal friendship of our country would be determined or affected certainly by the attitude of those countries toward human rights."[58] Following approval from the president, Vance informed Congress that the administration had decided to reduce foreign aid to Ethiopia because of "arbitrary and wanton deprivation of human rights, including torture and execution of real and potential political opponents."[59] Talcott Seelye of the State Department explained to the Ethiopian government during a visit to Addis Ababa "that an important reason for the termination of our MAP [military aid] grant program was this gross violation of human rights."[60] Nonetheless, we should not forget that the realities of the Cold War also featured in the decision to reconsider aid provisions to Ethiopia; of particular concern was the growing closeness between Ethiopia and the communist bloc. The participants in the Policy Review Committee meeting of April 11, 1977, demonstrated their awareness of the many strands of Carter's foreign policy approach by concluding that the administration "cannot justify further significant support to the present government in view of its moves toward the Soviets, its ineffectiveness in governing its own country and its brutalization of its people."[61]

Any decisions reached by the administration, regardless of the reasoning behind them, could not, of course, be implemented without the support of the legislative branch of the American government. However, as previously discussed, Congress was also keen to prevent human rights violations, and both Houses supported the administration's action; on March 3 Representative Don Pease (D-Oh) introduced into the House a concurrent resolution expressing Congressional support for the administration's stand on human rights.[62] The House Subcommittee on Africa recommended in April "that for the reasons of gross and systematic violations of human rights ... all military assistance to the Mengistu government should be terminated."[63] On the north-

ern side of the Hill, the Senate Committee on Foreign Relations likewise recommended that the International Security Assistance and Arms Export Control Act of 1977 prohibit "military assistance, training and FMS [Foreign
Military Sales] credits for Ethiopia, and ... FMS cash sales and deliveries of
military equipment financed by military assistance, credits or guarantees."[64]
Again, it should be noted that although human rights factors were clearly as
important to the legislative branch of the Federal government as to the executive branch, the political orientation of Mengistu should not be ignored as
a possible factor in Congressional backing for the administration's stance.

Although economic aid was not affected by this decision — by way of an
attempt to live up to its commitment to human rights and related humanitarian concerns, the administration pledged to continue its "economic aid
program there to demonstrate our sense of commitment to the Ethiopian
people"[65] — all military aid to Ethiopia, totaling some $100 million was
stopped as of April 19, 1977.[66] The media took note of the administration's
action and, although arguing that it was "symbolic," the *Washington Post*
nonetheless acknowledged that it still took "the new administration's overseas human rights policy beyond verbal protest, to tangible action, for the
first time." [67]

A Regionalist Approach from the Carter Administration

When appearing before the Democratic Platform Committee in June
1976, Jimmy Carter had made it clear that he wanted a new approach in foreign policy with regards to the developing countries of the world when he
declared that "our policies toward the developing countries need revision. For
years, we have either ignored them or treated them as pawns in the big power
chess game. Both approaches were deeply offensive to their people."[68] In contrast, the president resolved that his administration would treat developing
nations as important in their own right, and increase their priority within the
foreign policy agenda, by applying a regionalist rather than a globalist
approach. This meant, of course, that most of the African nations became
more important in the formulation of American foreign policy. Cyrus Vance
told a meeting of the NAACP:

> Africa matters very much to the United States. This is a fact more and more Amer-
> icans are coming to understand.... We proceed from a basic proposition: that our
> policies must recognize the unique identity of Africa. We can be neither right nor
> effective if we treat Africa simply as one part of the third world, or as a testing
> ground of East-West competition.[69]

Rather than allowing local conflicts in Africa to become proxy fights in the Cold War, the policy of the Carter administration was instead based upon the belief that African problems should have African solutions, with outside involvement limited as much as possible. In a statement on April 4, Philip Habib, a close adviser to Henry Kissinger and colleague of Vance during the early stages of the Paris negotiations on Vietnam,[70] and appointed by Carter as the new undersecretary for political affairs in the State Department, declared that "we believe firmly that the people of Africa hold the key to the solution of African problems.... It is not for us, or for any other external power, to attempt to impose its own ideas and solutions." Such a strategy should improve the standing of the United States in the eyes of the African people and perhaps help to win "hearts and minds," not least because it might reduce the scale of some conflicts by, as Habib pointed out, avoiding "situations which make Africa an arena for great power rivalry, as happened in Angola."[71]

The Carter administration therefore resolved that developing nations should be removed from the arena of East-West competition. Developed nations had long been involved in the internal affairs of the newly independent African countries, but the Carter administration was vocal in its opposition to external interference, as opposed to involvement, especially with regards to conflicts, and particularly from the communist bloc. On January 31, when asked in a news conference about the Cuban presence in Angola, Vance asserted that "the presence of any outside forces is not helpful to a peaceful solution. I think that this is a matter that should be settled by the Africans themselves."[72] At a further news conference in March, he reiterated "with respect to the presence of Cubans in Africa ... it is appropriate for African problems to be resolved by the Africans rather than by outside forces."[73]

The Carter administration certainly did not advocate that the United States should remain distant from Africa, but argued instead that American interest should be long-term and productive, rather than short-term and reactive. Accordingly, as Vance informed the NAACP during a speech in July, the administration would adopt "affirmative" policies towards African nations and not be "reactive to what other powers do, nor to crises as they arise. Daily headlines should not set our agenda for progress ... [because] a negative, reactive American policy that seeks only to oppose Soviet or Cuban involvement in Africa would be both dangerous and futile." In the same speech, Vance also pointed out that the "long-term success of our African policy will depend more on our actual assistance to African development and our ability to help Africans resolve their disputes than on maneuvers for short-term diplomatic advantage."[74] Indeed, the long-term approach that would be attempted by the Carter administration had been agreed during the campaign, following

Vance's suggestion that "in its conduct of its foreign policy, the new administration will proceed with gravity, not flurry; will not try to do everything at once or solve all the world's problems; and will keep its mind focused on long-term general objectives, not just the crises of the moment."[75]

During the first few months of 1977 the "crisis of the moment" was arguably under way in the Horn of Africa, as the Ethiopian regime continued to improve relations with countries of the communist bloc. Perhaps the most serious development had occurred before the Carter administration formally took office, in December 1976, when Ethiopia signed a military aid agreement with the Soviet Union, worth some $100 million.[76] Subsequently the Carter administration received intelligence reports from various sources on the growing signs of friendship between Ethiopia and the Soviet Union. The Soviet president, Nikolai Podgorny, included Ethiopia on his itinerary when he toured Africa, and the Ethiopian leader later reciprocated the visit. Mengistu left Addis Ababa on May 3, 1977, for a visit to the Soviet Union that according to Western sources produced extremely positive results for the Ethiopian leader. The two days of talks resulted in a formal alliance between Ethiopia and the Soviet Union, and ended with a ceremony in which the leaders of both nations signed a declaration that proclaimed their friendship and pledged continued Soviet military aid as well as economic and technical cooperation.[77] In an interview conducted in the 1990s, Henze recalled that, to the Carter administration, "it was all very obvious ... large numbers of Ethiopians were taken off to the Soviet Union for training, including military people. The Ethiopian press and media became completely communist oriented, repeating all of the standard themes."[78]

The administration also watched as Cuba moved to strengthen its ties with the East African nation. Fidel Castro, who had been one of the first world leaders to congratulate Mengistu after his seizure of overall power on February 3, 1977,[79] visited Ethiopia in March. According to a memo sent by Henze to Brzezinski, the press in Addis Ababa went into "an orgy of delight over Castro's just-ended visit and envisions all sorts of benefits from the new relationship with 'Freedom Island' (i.e. Cuba)."[80] Recently declassified documents reveal that Castro was impressed with the Ethiopian leader, finding him to be "a quiet, honest and convinced leader who is aware of the power of the masses [and has] an intellectual personality."[81]

It therefore should have been of little surprise to the Carter administration to find that by the middle of April, the Cubans were supporting Mengistu with more than words. A spokesman for the State Department confirmed that it had received reports that about fifty Cuban military advisers had arrived in Ethiopia as well as "unverified reports that several hundred Cuban troops were being sent."[82] The *Washington Post* stated that the Cuban mission was to "train Ethiopian troops in guerrilla war tactics and countertactics,"[83] and although Castro declared that he had "the right to send military instructors if the Ethiopian government asked," he insisted that only Cuban "diplomats and doctors were in Ethiopia."[84] This assertion appeared to be met with some skepticism within the United States however. The *Washington Post* commented that "the beginning of Cuban military assistance to the Ethiopian military government appears to indicate that Fidel Castro is prepared to involve his country in yet another major internal African conflict in direct conjunction with Soviet aims and designs on the continent. This time the scene is in north-eastern Africa, along the vital Red Sea waterway."[85]

The Carter administration, however, seemed less concerned than the media and, in line with its policy of de-emphasizing East-West factors in policy formulation, tolerated the immediate presence of communist bloc countries in the Horn of Africa. Although a memo from Henze to Brzezinski in March warned that the "Soviets are currently calculating that they can be influential in both Ethiopia and Somalia,"[86] in the Presidential Review Memorandum (PRM) on the Horn of Africa at the beginning of April the administration noted its willingness to accept that "present leftward trends in Ethiopia cannot be arrested," and, at least in the short term, acknowledged that there would be "a decreased U.S. influence in that country."[87] After all, once Mengistu had moved into accommodation with the Soviets, for whatever reason, reduced relations with the United States was to be expected; as a State Department official remarked, "they couldn't be taking Soviet money and keep walking around in our GI fatigues."[88] In addition, the closeness between the United States and the previous government of Ethiopia suggested that the Carter administration was unlikely to be too popular with the Derg, as the PRM on the Horn acknowledged: "our quarter-century of close friendship and of generous support for Haile Selassie make it difficult for the PMAC to believe that the U.S. can sincerely desire a co-operative relationship with those who overthrew the Emperor."[89]

Nonetheless it should be noted that the Carter administration's response to the communist bloc presence in Ethiopia was arguably so restrained because of a belief that the relationship between Moscow and Mengistu would not endure, even if the Americans took no action. Some members of the administration shared the view expressed by Andrew Young, the United States ambassador to the United Nations, who remarked, when on a visit to the Ivory Coast, that the Ethiopian alignment with the Soviet Union had given the Kremlin "more trouble that it can handle."[90] Also, the administration was aware of the difficulty the Soviets faced in attempting to pursue relations with both Somalia and Ethiopia. One State Department official commented that the Soviets were "in the position of the fellow who is pinned to two girls on the same campus. Let's see if they can pull it off."[91] There was also a belief within U.S. government circles that the role of religion in African society would hinder Soviet attempts to establish a permanent presence in the Horn. A Congressional delegation that visited the Middle East and Africa reported back to the House Committee on Armed Services, noting:

> There is a widely held feeling that the Soviet influence in Africa will not be of permanent duration and that countries would take Soviet help, but once they got independence, would throw off the Soviet yoke. Two reasons given for the African aversion to communism were that many Africans were religious and believed communism was opposed to their religion, and that Africans had strong belief [*sic*] in the private ownership of property and believed communism threatened their property rights.[92]

Indeed, a Soviet official, commenting on the Somali "annoying insistence that its road to Socialism could include Islam too," confessed that the "religious problem was our worst enemy."[93]

As it emerged then, the initial policy of the Carter administration was to accept the immediate presence of communist bloc nations in the Horn of Africa and to seek to maintain, as Talcott Seelye of the State Department explained to the House Subcommittee on Africa, "a long-run relationship with Ethiopia that would not be affected by regime changes."[94] However, hope persisted within the administration that Mengistu would not survive as the Ethiopian leader, and would be replaced by someone more attuned to the United States instead of the communist bloc. The Presidential Review Memorandum of April 1, 1977, noted:

> The instability of the present Ethiopian regime raises the presently remote possibility of its replacement over the medium or longer term by a leadership more amenable to co-operative relations with the U.S. This prospect, plus the fact that Ethiopia is the second-most-populous country in Africa, gives us an interest in so tailoring our policies that we are in a position insofar as possible to capitalize on possible future developments favoring a resumption of closer Ethio-U.S. ties.[95]

The members of the Policy Review Committee, who met on April 11, 1977, agreed that "we should not pull out of Ethiopia entirely, because we wish to be in a position to reassert ourselves there if a friendlier and more humane government comes to power."[96]

However, although intelligence reports from Ethiopia acknowledged that "an assassination or coup is always possible,"[97] there was a general recognition within the administration that any such hopes in that vein were likely to remain unfulfilled, at least in the immediate future. The intelligence service estimated that "the military regime can maintain itself in Addis Ababa for an indefinite period of time," and also cautioned that there was a great deal of uncertainty "as to what kind of a government would follow the overthrow of the present military regime."[98] There were, perhaps inevitably, discussions within the administration as to the role the United States might play in aiding or encouraging dissension against Mengistu's rule. However, Carter's desire for a more open government contributed to the decision that no covert action should be taken. Instead, the priority would be to maintain a presence in Ethiopia, despite the relationship between the Mengistu regime and the Soviet Union.

However, it soon became apparent that the Ethiopian leader had other ideas. In April 1977 the tension between the United States and Ethiopia exploded into a decision by Mengistu that would vastly reduce the American presence and influence in Ethiopia. The break between Ethiopia and the United States came from the Africans at the end of April 1977 when, on the day after the United States officially informed Addis Ababa of the closure of Kagnew Station, the Ethiopians retaliated by ordering the closure of that and other American facilities in the country, including a naval medical research unit, and the United States Information Service. From over four thousand, American personnel in Ethiopia were reduced to seventy-six staff and five Marine guards at the U.S. Embassy and the Agency for International Development in Addis Ababa. In addition, Mengistu expelled the three remaining Western journalists from the country.[99]

Mengistu's decision was greeted by the administration with "an official sigh of American regret ... [and] the hope that the strains will not worsen." Hodding Carter III, the State Department spokesman, added in this statement to the press that "it is no secret that our relations with Ethiopia have deteriorated over the past two years, despite our efforts to maintain our former close ties ... we hope this trend can be arrested."[100] Indeed, the sentiments expressed by Hodding Carter appear to accurately reflect the administration's position; there is no evidence that suggests that the administration hoped that Mengistu would take the initiative in breaking relations, nor any indication of relief that he had done so — a conclusion borne out by subsequent reactions to Mengistu's announcement.

The Carter administration, adhering to its belief in a long-term approach, made no immediate response to Mengistu's action, apart from an official protest through diplomatic channels.[101] There were both practical and moral considerations behind the administration's restraint. The emphasis on human rights, for example, required a continued relationship for the sake of the Ethiopian people — Henze later recalled that the United States "was in Ethiopia because of support for the Ethiopian people, not for support for any particular Ethiopian regime"[102] — while the importance of Ethiopia within the African community of nations also made the maintenance of ties desirable. This reasoning predominated in the discussion as to whether the United

States should formally break relations with Ethiopia following Mengistu's action. The administration followed Henze's recommendation to maintain an Embassy in Addis Ababa because, as he argued:

> Satisfying as it would be to [break relations], I think it would be a mistake for we still have a good many unofficial Americans and many American interests in Ethiopia to which we should give some protection. Beyond that we have thousands and thousands of friends there — American-educated and trained Ethiopians, including large numbers of officers and noncoms in the armed forces — who will be encouraged if we keep some presence. A further reason for maintaining our Embassy in Addis Ababa is the fact that it is accredited to the various international bodies that are located there: the OAU, UN/ECA, the ILO office, etc., with which we have extensive business. The military regime wants to keep Addis Ababa the "capital of Africa" and is unlikely to take initiative to break relations with us for this reason.[103]

Mengistu's decision to greatly reduce the American presence in Ethiopia was variously attributed to different factors. *Time* argued that "President Carter's emphasis on human rights clearly played a role in the Americans' expulsion." The article also praised the Carter administration's determination that foreign policy should not be dominated solely by East-West factors, pointing out that although "Mengistu's move may advance Soviet aims in Africa, it also relieves the U.S. of the moral burden of backing yet another bloodthirsty dictatorship."[104] However, as much as the administration might have liked for its human rights policy to take the credit, there was an awareness that more practical reasons most likely prompted the Ethiopian leader's action. Anthony Lake, who had served in the National Security Council as a special assistant to Kissinger in the Nixon administration until 1970 when he resigned over the administration's decision to expand the war to Cambodia, then served as head of the State Department transition team, before accepting the position of State Department analyst for the Carter administration, contended that Mengistu's decision to scale down involvement with the United States "probably stemmed more from the new regime's desire to seek a more ideologically compatible political and military relationship with Moscow than with unhappiness with our human rights advocacy."[105] In *The Horn of Africa: From War to Peace*, which was part memoir, part history, Paul Henze later claimed that Mengistu "feigned rage" and "seized upon the human rights report as the pretext to terminate the American military relationship."[106]

It seems likely that the desire to establish a military relationship with a superpower was Mengistu's primary motivation, and if the United States was unwilling to continue to supply Ethiopia with military aid because of the human rights situation then the Ethiopian leader was going to look elsewhere. Mengistu's need to guarantee a source of military supplies was driven by conditions both within Ethiopia — for instance, in Eritrea — and by external threats, particularly from Ethiopia's long-time enemy, Somalia. Indeed, the Carter administration received intelligence reports from Ethiopia in May stating that "Mengistu said he accepted Soviet aid for pragmatic reasons and that he is primarily interested in getting Moscow to restrain Somalia in its claims to Ethiopian territory."[107]

As we have seen, the Somali leader, Siad Barré, was strongly motivated by his personal desire to reunite all ethnic Somalis within the borders of a Greater Somalia, but the terms of the Cairo Resolution of 1964 asserted that there should be no territorial restructuring in Africa. This meant that Siad's desire to incorporate the Ethiopian-controlled but Somali-inhabited Ogaden into Somalia had to be carefully phrased in his official declarations and diplomatic dealings, lest his hoped-for allies perceived his dream as a violation of both the Resolution and international law. The Somali leader therefore deemed the fight of the guerrillas in the Ogaden to be a matter of self-determination and publicly supported the notion of autonomy for the region, no doubt with the hope that, after independence had been declared, the Ogadeni people would then choose to legally incorporate their nation into the Somali Democratic Republic. Siad insisted that Mengistu "must give the nations living in the Ogaden, including both the Eritreans and the Somalis, the right to self-determination,"[108] and claimed that the Ethiopians were "suppressing colonized people struggling for their freedom."[109] However, Siad appeared willing to support the Ogaden freedom fighters with more than words and in February newspapers reported that an "undeclared desert war in East Africa has heated up with a raid by 1500 Somali troops into south-eastern Ethiopia's Ogaden region."[110]

Meanwhile, in the northern part of Ethiopia, secessionists in the province of Eritrea were also fighting for their independence. Since 1962, when Eritrea formally became part of Ethiopia as opposed to a separate province merely administered by Ethiopia,[111] rebels had fought "simply to liberate our land," according to Tesfai Woldemichael, the secretary general of the Eritrean Liberation Front. In the first few months of 1977, the Eritrean rebels held the upper hand in the secessionist struggle; a *New York Times* correspondent, invited to join the guerrillas of the Eritrean Liberation Front for two weeks, described the rebels as "a full-fledged army ... heavily armed and highly trained."[112] In conjunction with the other main rebel group, the Eritrean People's Liberation Front, the secessionists controlled about eighty-five percent of the 50,000-square-mile province of Eritrea and all but about 300,000 of its 3.5 million people.[113] However, the overall situation was not as desperate for Mengistu as perhaps it might seem. A glimmer of hope existed in the differences that beset the different secessionist groups. A spokesman for one of them commented that despite the Eritrean Liberation Front's recent successes, there would be no all-out offensive in the near future; "we must resolve our political differences first," he said in an interview.[114]

The Implications of Global Complexity

The aspirations of the Carter administration to apply a regionalist policy to the Horn of Africa and de-emphasize East-West relations was linked to a further tenet of the new foreign policy approach: the belief that the world constituted a complex international system and that this must be factored into foreign policy formulation.[115] The administration's credo was that the United States must be considerate of other nations in the making of foreign policy and, indeed, encourage their input. On assuming office, Jimmy Carter declared that the "United States alone cannot guarantee the basic right of every human being to be free of poverty and hunger and disease and political repression. We can and will cooperate with others in combating these enemies of mankind."[116] Reflecting this view, Cyrus Vance told a news conference on May 23 that "we have kept in close touch with others in the area, including the other countries in the Horn of Africa, and with others who are interested in the situation which is developing in the Horn of Africa."[117] Indeed, as part of the process of détente, Carter expressed his hope that the United States and the Soviet Union would work together on the problems of Africa. In his news conference of March 24 Carter announced that "we are going to express our concern about the future of Africa and ask the Soviet Union to join with us in removing from that troubled continent outside interference which might contribute to warfare in the countries involved."[118]

Nonetheless, the role of communist bloc nations in the Horn remained a cause for concern, rather than one of hope, for many nations with interests in the region. The Presidential Review Memorandum of April 1977 conceded that "Moscow's efforts to displace the U.S. as the dominant foreign influence in Ethiopia are causing concern among moderate states in the region, notably Sudan and Saudi Arabia."[119] Also, at a time when a priority of the Carter administration was to normalize relations with the People's Republic of China, the impact of that nation in the Horn of Africa was a matter that needed to be investigated and considered. Although the Soviet Union supplied the largest amount of military equipment to the Horn countries, the PRM noted that China was "the largest single communist donor of economic aid to Ethiopia" and also provided "light weapons, ammunition and training assistance to the peasant militia forces" together with some economic assistance to both Somalia and the Sudan.[120] However, the PRM went on to argue that there was unlikely to be much Sino-American co-operation in the Horn because "the longer-term thrust of PRC [People's Republic of China] policy lies in demonstrating commonality with the Africans on major North-South issues and in defining Third World interests as basically opposed to those of both the U.S. and the USSR."[121]

The Israeli interest in the Horn of Africa was perhaps the best indication of the accuracy of Carter's belief in a complex international system. Israel, which, although its relationship with the United States changed during the years from 1948 to 1977, was generally seen as pro–Western, aligned itself alongside the Soviet Union in supporting Ethiopia but only because it opposed the nations of the Arab League, who were aligned against Ethiopia. The Israeli position came not from support for the Soviet Union or for communist ideology, but because of fears of Arab, and Muslim, domination of the region; the PRM on the Horn of Africa noted that the "primary interest [of Israel] is to prevent an alignment of Arab strength in this area that could further isolate Israel and place it at a geopolitical disadvantage."[122] Thus the administration was faced with Israeli pressure to focus more on strategic concerns and less on abstract ideals such as human rights. Henze warned Brzezinski in May 1977 that "the Israelis persist in trying to persuade us that Mengistu is just a simple, benign nationalist whom we really ought to support, no matter what he does to his own people or to his country's basic interests."[123]

Strategic concerns also dominated the thoughts of nations of the Arab League, who were mainly concerned that the increasing Soviet influence in the Horn of Africa might pose a threat to the conservative Arab regimes in the region. Intelligence provided to the Carter administration warned that "Sudan, Yemen Arab Republic, Egypt and Saudi Arabia are all alarmed at the potential threat to their security and to the security of the Red Sea posed by Soviet advances in the Horn of Africa."[124] Anwar al-Sadat, whose views were shortly to become very important to Carter as he worked on peace proposals for the Middle East, declared that the Soviets were engaged in "somber maneuvers from one end of the continent to the other," particularly in Zaire and Ethiopia.[125] The administration was also aware of Arab hopes that the growing closeness between the Soviet Union and Ethiopia could be exploited to loosen the ties between Somalia, a member of the Arab League, and the USSR, and Soviet influence consequently lessened. The Presidential Review Memorandum of April 1977 reported that the Arab League nations were:

> Undertaking initiatives designed to facilitate self-determination — preferably independence — in an Eritrea which would be induced to hew to an anti-communist path by Saudi money. They are also attempting to use Somalia's disenchantment with Soviet military supplies to Ethiopia, plus the carrot of substantial Saudi financial aid, to woo Somalia away from the Soviets.[126]

Indeed, James Akins, former American Ambassador to Saudi Arabia, had informed the Senate Foreign Relations Committee back in May 1976 that the Saudis had agreed to furnish economic aid to Somalia, plus finance military aid, if Siad Barré agreed to reduce or remove Soviet influence from Somalia.[127]

The efforts of the Arab nations to tempt Somalia from the Soviet bloc were well publicized in the United States. As early as February 1977 the *Washington Post* reported that "anti–Soviet Arab states led by oil-rich Saudi Arabia are already promising Somalia massive financial and military assistance, reportedly running into the hundreds of millions of dollars, if it expels the Soviet Union as Egypt did three years ago."[128] *Newsweek* was more specific, stating that "Saudi Arabia has offered Siad Barré $400 million to $500 million worth of arms, and Iran is also helping out with equipment."[129] In May, *Newsweek* added that the Saudis, who "fear Soviet influence in the Red Sea and the Horn of Africa, have reportedly urged Siad to preserve Muslim solidarity in the area."[130] At the same time, *Time* noted that the "spread of Soviet influence on the Horn so distresses Arab leaders that four of them [Sudan, Somalia and North and South Yemen] recently convened an extraordinary summit at Ta'iz, in the Yemen Arab Republic.... They set aside differing political views long enough to agree on a pan–Arab, pro–Moslem program against Ethiopia."[131]

In the same way that Israel hoped that the United States could be persuaded to support their cause and Mengistu, the Arab nations hoped that the Carter administration would join their mission to woo Somalia from the Soviet bloc. Reportedly, the Shah of Iran had shipped small arms to Somalia, and urged the U.S. to do likewise.[132] Similarly, Saudi Arabia attempted to elicit military aid for Somalia from the Carter administration, in the hope of supplanting Soviet influence with Siad by that of the West.[133] However, the administration refused to be pressured into a deeper involvement, despite the pleas from its Arab allies. In June it was reported that "Saudi Arabia's Prince Fahd brought away one disappointment from his talks with President Carter: he failed to win help in wooing Somalia — just across the Aden Gulf from Saudi Arabia — out of the Soviet camp."[134] Notwithstanding, American-Somali relations were to feature in Carter's new approach to foreign policy.

Global Community: A New World Order for the Carter Administration

In accordance with his belief that international politics had become more complex, Jimmy Carter asserted that world order could no longer be based on the simplicity of an East-West balance of power; administration policy instead contended that the international system be founded upon the ideal of global community.[135] In an exclusive interview with *U.S. News & World Report* on May 30, Zbigniew Brzezinski declared:

> It is our view that we are now at a stage in world history in which the United States again has to undertake a creative process of building a new world system. This must take into account the cumulative effect of all the changes that have occurred in the past fifteen to twenty years: the appearance of a massive number of new states, the extraordinary [sic] rapid decolonization, the surfacing of new social and political aspirations, the doubling of the world's population.... What is important is to try to create a framework of cooperation which inhibits competition and which prevents aggression.[136]

One way that this rhetoric would be transformed into policy was through discussion and cooperation, particularly with those nations with whom the United States had not always enjoyed good, if any, relations. Cyrus Vance told *U.S. News and World Report* that "it's very important that we have a dialogue with as many countries as possible" and the administration would therefore try "to normalize relations in a measured and reciprocal fashion between ourselves and countries with whom we have had no communications because we had cut off relations for one reason or another."[137]

In the Horn of Africa the nation to which this policy applied was Somalia. In March, Brzezinski made Vice President Mondale aware of a potential opening for the United States, pointing out that "Somalia is upset about Soviet support for the Ethiopian military regime, feels it may be left in the lurch and is looking for ways to lessen its dependence on the Soviets."[138] Following Carter's instructions to "move in every possible way to get Somalia to be our friend,"[139] the administration sent messages through diplomatic channels on at least two occasions, stating its interest in better relations.[140] The next step was taken on April 11, 1977, when the Policy Review Committee issued instructions to the American Ambassador in Mogadishu to arrange a meeting with Siad in order to discuss the possibility of closer ties between Somalia and the United States, and discover the Somali leader's expectations if such a relationship should go ahead.[141] At the same time, the administration decided to send an exploratory aid mission to Somalia to examine options for economic and humanitarian aid.[142] However, because of concerns over guerrilla activity in the Ogaden, the Carter administration resolved to withhold military aid, although it recognized Siad's need for support. Thus the Policy Review Committee suggested that Saudi Arabia should "take the lead in offering money for military aid."[143]

It should be noted, though, that the aims of the administration with regards to improved relations with Somalia differed somewhat from those of

Saudi Arabia; whereas the Arabs wished the Americans to replace the Soviet Union in Somalia regardless of the cost, the goal of the Carter administration was to forge a relationship with Siad Barré within a regionalist framework. This is not to say, however, that geopolitical factors did not figure in the thoughts of policy-makers. In the era of the Vietnam syndrome, the administration was well aware that the American public would be reluctant to support the deployment of troops abroad, and the way in which to maintain stability and minimize the risk of an American military commitment in confrontation states, such as Ethiopia and Somalia, was to form a relationship with both sides. Nor were members of the administration unaware of the potential benefits should improved American-Somali relations result in the displacement of the Soviet Union. Henze recalled:

> The idea of detaching Somalia from its Soviet embrace appealed to some of the more liberal elements in the Carter team, including Vice President Mondale, although they had no firsthand knowledge of Somalia. By taking over a Soviet client such as Somalia, they calculated, they could placate conservative Senate opposition to a new SALT agreement with Moscow, the highest strategic priority of some members of the Carter team.[144]

Regardless of American aims, the Somalis seemed to share the administration's desire for improved relations. The Somali ambassador to the United States, Abdullahi Ahmed Addou, requested an audience with Jimmy Carter to discuss the possibility of closer relations between Somalia and the United States,[145] a request that the president was encouraged to approve by both the National Security Council and the State Department. Brzezinski argued that "this is a good opportunity to pass word directly to Siad that we are interested in closer relations. The symbolism of this meeting is at least as important as the substance."[146] Meanwhile, Peter Tarnoff, a career Foreign Service officer before joining the State Department at Carter's request,[147] pointed out that a meeting at the presidential level "would clearly demonstrate our interest in improving relations and should strengthen the hands of the officials in the Somali government who are arguing for a reorientation of Somali's [*sic*] policies. The president's reception of Addou would also be welcomed by Egypt, the Sudan and especially Saudi Arabia."[148] Subsequently Carter met with the Somali ambassador and expressed his desire for a closer relationship between the two nations. The American president admitted to Addou that he had been "concerned about the closeness between Somalia and the USSR which had been a reason for doubt on our part that our friendship could be strong," but added that he believed this might be changing.[149] Carter also expressed the hope that Somalia would be "non-aligned and not dominated by anyone ... [because] we want the Somalis to recognize their own destiny."[150]

As previously discussed, the Carter administration was seeking to apply a long-term policy to the Horn, and wished to avoid immediate reactions to current circumstances. Therefore, as in Ethiopia, it was willing to tolerate, at least in the short-term, the Soviet presence in Somalia. Indeed, despite the increasingly close ties between the USSR and Ethiopia, and the traditional enmity between the two Horn nations, the Carter administration had no reason to believe that the Soviet presence in Somalia was under threat. In testimony to the House Subcommittee on Africa, Tom Farer acknowledged that "the Russians would be extremely reluctant to risk loss of their Somali redoubt. In the first place, particularly coming after their just preceding exile from Egyptian bases, expulsion from Somali facilities [at Berbera] would be intensely humiliating."[151] Also, members of the Carter administration were aware of practical considerations that led them to believe, as the Presidential Review Memorandum on the Horn of Africa pointed out, that even though "the prospect of a major Soviet military supply relationship with their Ethiopian foe has caused the Somalis to consider whether it might be in their national interest to readjust their relations with the USSR and with the U.S.," this could not be accomplished without risks to Somali national security, because "Somalia depends on the Soviets for virtually all its military supplies and equipment. It also relies on the USSR for some economic aid. Given the unrest and tensions in the Horn, Somalia is loath to take any step which might weaken it militarily."[152]

Throughout much of 1977 Siad was insistent that he would not break ties with the Soviet Union. In the first interview granted to an American journalist in three years, the Somali leader spoke with *Newsweek* correspondent, Arnaud De Borchgrave, in June 1977 and maintained that there would be no change in alignment as far as the Somalis were concerned. He admitted that he and the Soviets "don't see eye to eye on Ethiopia" but went on to declare that, "I can assure you there will be no conflict between Somalia and the Soviets.... We are not thinking in terms of divorce and remarriage."[153] Opinion in the United States seemed to believe Siad's declarations at this time. *Newsweek* stated that "despite frictions, it seems unlikely that Siad Barré will break completely with Moscow."[154] The *New York Times* reported that "Somalia has been subdued in its response to the reports of a Cuban presence in Ethiopia.... Although Somalia is distressed by the shipment of Soviet arms to Ethiopia, most observers do not foresee a sudden break with the Soviet Union, its long time ally."[155]

One way that Moscow hoped to retain good relations with both Ethiopia and Somalia was through the formation of one vast federated area under the influence of the Soviet Union, that would include Ethiopia, Somalia, Aden and Djibouti. However, as Somali Ambassador Addou told Mondale, and the House Subcommittee on Africa reported, the Somalis refused to join the plan.[156] The main problem for the Soviet Union lay in the enmity that had long existed between Ethiopia and Somalia. The *Washington Post* on July 16, 1977, quoted an African source on the situation who explained that the "Russians and Cubans never understood that, for the Somalis, socialism came after nationalism. Just because the Somalis and the Ethiopians claim to have the same ideology, that doesn't mean they could ever agree on anything."[157] An American official remarked that the "Somalis see everything in terms of their quarrels with Ethiopia.... Whoever is Ethiopia's friend is our enemy — that's their byword."[158] The Somali president certainly did not hide his personal feelings about his Ethiopian counterpart; in an exclusive interview with *Newsweek* in June 1977, Siad declared that "Mengistu is a sick mind conducting bloodthirsty genocide. Ethiopia is neither Marxist nor Leninist, neither socialist nor democratic. They only know how to kill."[159]

Bearing this in mind, therefore, it was not surprising that Siad Barré responded favorably to the overtures of the Carter administration with regards to improving relations. In his interview with de Borchgrave, Siad spoke in terms that appeared designed to impress the Carter administration. Practically parroting Carter's goals and policies, Siad stated that:

> What we believe is that the oil lanes must be kept open, free and peaceful. And the people around these seas must take the responsibility to ensure that there is no interference by either superpower. Our interest is to guarantee a two-way flow of oil and trade with the Western world.... [The Soviets] never interfere in the exercise of our sovereignty.... We would rather have good relations with all powers as this would reinforce our non-alignment policy.[160]

The fact that Siad was now declaring Somalia to be "non-aligned" is worthy of note. Until the consolidation of the relationship between Ethiopia and the Soviet Union, and the expulsion of the United States from Ethiopia, Siad had allowed his country to be seen as pro–Soviet. It appears that he believed a policy of "non-alignment" might prevent a breach with the USSR, while also gaining Western aid and support.

A similar approach was apparent from Somali Ambassador Ahmed Addou, during his meeting with the president. Addou told Carter that he "wished to convey greetings from President Siad and his admiration for the president's stand on human rights," and went on to suggest that the Somali government shared Carter's belief in the protection of human rights, at least in the political sphere, insisting that "Somalia's people are deeply democratic by nature" and there was "no political oppression in Somalia." In contrast was the Ethiopian regime, which was violating the human rights of "two million Somalis in Ethiopia" who wished to express the right of self-determination and wanted "to be free of Ethiopian rule."[161] Talcott Seelye, in his Memorandum for the Record of his meeting with Addou, noted also that the

Somali Ambassador had attempted to play upon Carter's well-known devout nature, stressing the deep religious feelings of the Somali people, and taking "his prayer beads out of his pocket to emphasize that he himself prayed five times each day."[162]

One of the first signs that relations between the United States and Somalia were improving came when Siad Barré agreed to accept economic and humanitarian aid from the Americans. Although the United States had provided aid to the tune of some $80 million to Somalia from 1954 to 1970, American aid was then suspended because of continued Somali-flag trade with North Vietnam.[163] The decision by Siad to accept the Carter administration's offer of aid represented "a significant shift on the part of the Somalia government," according to Peter Bourne, Special Assistant to the President on health issues. Bourne's comment came in a memo reporting that the Somalis were allowing Americans into the country to provide medical assistance, in this case with an outbreak of smallpox.[164] In addition, the team sent by the Carter administration to assess the economic needs of the Somali people was, according to the *Washington Post*, "given high-level attention in the Somali capital of Mogadishu and accorded red-carpet treatment, in notable contrast to the severe restrictions usually placed on the activities of the U.S. ambassador and other American officials there."[165]

However, Siad Barré's greatest desire was military aid, although Ambassador Addou, acting as Siad's emissary, insisted that the Somalis had no aggressive intentions but wanted only to be able to defend themselves to ensure peaceful coexistence with their neighbors.[166] Nonetheless, Peter Tarnoff reported that Siad had sent Addou to Washington with "an extensive military supply request,"[167] including "armored personnel carriers and mortars," which Addou asked for during a meeting with Walter Mondale.[168] Mondale also noted that Addou "indicated receptivity to arms being purchased for Somalia in Europe, but he repeatedly emphasized the need for the symbolism of U.S. military support, even though on a limited basis"[169] and insisted that "only the U.S. can help Somalia in dealing with the Soviet Union."[170]

Despite the desire of the Carter administration to improve relations with Somalia, caution nonetheless remained as to how far to go. The Presidential Review Memorandum of April 1977 acknowledged the danger of "rushing into too close a relationship with the Somalis too soon,"[171] especially with regard to military aid. In May Brzezinski informed the president that:

> I am very skeptical about our getting involved in providing even token direct military assistance to the Somalis, much as we want to encourage them to disengage further from the Soviets. Somalia is already one of the most heavily armed countries in Africa and makes no secret of its territorial claims against its neighbors. We cannot really gain by getting involved in this problem.[172]

One of the main reasons for caution was the fear that a close relationship with Somalia might hinder future ties with Ethiopia, which was still seen as the key nation in the Horn region. The PRM advised that "any improvement in our relations with Somalia and Sudan should stop short of activities perceived as hostile to Ethiopia as a nation."[173] In May, Henze warned Brzezinski that although the administration wanted to:

> Continue encouraging the Somalis to loosen their Soviet ties ... we must not take too short-term a view of this objective. If the present Ethiopian regime were replaced by a better one, we would not want to find ourselves so linked to Somalia that we couldn't shift back into friendlier relations with Ethiopia, the most important country in the Horn ... we need to keep our own future options open.[174]

Brzezinski agreed, telling Mondale that "even if we find the Somalis warming up to us rapidly, we will have to exercise some caution, for the situation in Ethiopia is very fluid, and we haven't reached the point where we feel we should give up Ethiopia in exchange for Somalia."[175]

Another reason for the administration's reticence with regards to military aid was a skepticism regarding the Somali need for such supplies. In his meeting with Addou in June 1977, Carter told the Somali Ambassador that, although the administration wished to "work with the Saudis and our European allies to see that Somalia has adequate defense capabilities without relying on the Soviet Union," there were doubts over the extent of military aid required by Somalia.[176] Indeed, in May, Henze sent a memo to Brzezinski warning that "Somalia has no desperate military needs. Nobody is going to attack it. The likelihood is much greater that it might be tempted to move into parts of Ethiopia."[177] The fear pervaded the administration that, should the border tensions between Somalia and Ethiopia erupt into war, a military supply relationship with Somalia could lead to greater American involvement in the conflict, potentially with Soviet involvement on the Ethiopian side. Nor was the American fear unfounded. In July, Peter Tarnoff of the State Department informed Brzezinski that the military aid requested by Ambassador Addou was "composed almost entirely of items readily susceptible of use in the growing Somali guerrilla campaign in eastern Ethiopia."[178]

In addition, the Carter administration was aware that, even if it desired a military relationship with Somalia, there was unlikely to be much support for such a position in the United States. In March 1977, Brzezinski in a memo to Walter Mondale stated his opinion that "while we could probably justify some economic aid ourselves and get Congress to go along, I am skeptical about justifying military aid."[179] Subsequently, Vance assured the NAACP that while the administration would "consider sympathetically appeals for assistance from states which are threatened by a build-up of foreign military equipment and advisers on their borders, in the Horn and elsewhere in

Africa.... Arms transfers to Africa will be an exceptional tool of our policy and will be used only after the most careful consideration."[180]

A third reason why the Carter administration was cautious about consolidating a relationship with Siad Barré was the reports of human rights violations from Somalia. Despite Somali protestations of their adherence to the principles of human rights, the administration had little evidence that action matched rhetoric. Henze noted to Brzezinski that "internally, Siad's regime in Somalia has been pretty much of a police state. When a group of religious leaders opposed him a couple of years ago, he had them all shot."[181] Brzezinski also raised the subject of Somalia's human rights record in the meeting with Addou in June 1977, asking about any public declarations Siad might have made on human rights. Addou pointed out that "Siad had condemned the killings that were taking place in Ethiopia and had taken Idi Amin to task for his cruelty," but, when asked whether Siad had made any comments on the situation in Somalia, Addou admitted that he had not.[182]

The Importance of Public Opinion

Like any American politician, Jimmy Carter was aware that public opinion mattered. Without public support for his policies and political decisions, the Carter administration would have only one term in office, and that one term was likely to be most unproductive because Congressional support was to a large extent dependent on public support. Political success depended on a politician's ability to do one of two things: either convince Americans that a chosen policy was the best way, or follow public opinion in policy formulation. Jimmy Carter was determined to lead and not follow in the matter of public opinion, and aides talked about "his stiff-backed reaction to suggestions that this course or that would be politically advantageous." An administration official told the *Washington Post* that the best way to get on the wrong side of the president was "to tell him that what you want is a good political thing to do."[183]

The determination of the Carter administration to reorient foreign policy from an excessive focus on the East-West relationship meant that the new president was faced with a test of his leadership abilities and strength of purpose in this matter, because concern remained in both Congress and among the general public regarding the perceived communist advances in the Horn. Indeed, there were rumblings on Capitol Hill that a stronger administration response to the communist bloc presence in the Horn was required. In March 1977 Representative Joseph Waggonner (D-La) warned the House that "while we are floundering, changing direction and wondering what our policies ought to be, the Russians and their communist allies are vigorously pressing for their goal of domination of all Africa."[184] Philip Crane (R-Ill) agreed in his speech to the House on April 25:

> Africa is fertile, manipulable soil for Soviet intervention. A persistent and highly visible Soviet presence in Africa is assumed to be stabilizing and legitimate, according to our UN Ambassador. The truth of the matter is that passive acceptance of the Soviet threat to isolate the West and the United States from the Third World, its resources, and its markets, encourages the Soviets to create further instability in Africa. We must not and cannot continue to ignore the Soviet presence in Africa in the hopes that they, too, will become isolationists.[185]

On June 2, Representative Larry McDonald (D-Ga) declared that "the drivel the president uttered at Notre Dame notwithstanding, we do not live in any 'new world,' but the same world of the postwar struggle between East and West. That is what Angola and Ethiopia are all about."[186] Six days later he spoke up again, stating that the "American presence is diminishing there [in Africa] daily, seemingly replaced by arriving Cubans.... Ethiopia is another piece of the mosaic known as the twentieth century — a century whose earmark is the betrayal of Western civilization by the leaders of the West.[187] Edward Derwinski (R-Ill) agreed. On June 6 he described the situation in Ethiopia as:

> Lamentable and, when coupled with all the other bad news we have been receiving lately from Africa, cause for real concern. Moreover, it points up dramatically the tough questions confronting the current administration as it shapes its African foreign policy. Tough questions require tough calls and I hope this administration can summon the courage to make them.[188]

Six weeks later he again criticized the Carter administration for its lack of response to the communist advances in the Horn, declaring that "President Carter's foreign policy initiatives with the Soviets are not supported by sufficiently strong military or diplomatic bases to be effective or credible. The Soviets by now should be able to sense that the Carter administration is strong on rhetoric and short on everything else."[189]

The concerns that were expressed in Congress were echoed in the American press and broadcast to the nation. As early as February the *Washington Post* argued that "the priority being given by the Carter administration to the human rights issue ... is playing nicely into the Soviet strategy" in the Horn.[190] The more right-wing *U.S. News and World Report* ran an article on April 4, 1977, entitled "Turmoil in Africa — How Moscow Capitalizes on Strife." It declared:

> Exactly four years after the last American combat troops were pulled out of Vietnam, the U.S. is under massive Soviet pressure to abandon yet another part of the

world — black Africa. The extensive travel in central and southern Africa of two communist leaders — Cuba's Fidel Castro and Russia's president Nikolai Podgorny — underlines an increasingly serious situation on a volatile continent. Their efforts are concentrated on gaining influence in the region as a long step toward helping Marxist governments to get into power.

The article claimed that Soviet goals were to "gain secure naval bases on both sides of Africa that could be used to choke off the sea lanes over which Middle East oil is transported [and] deny Western nations access to the rich resources in strategic materials possessed by many African nations," and warned that "the growing threat of trouble all around Africa — sanctioned if not instigated by Russia and Cuba — is a development that the U.S. as leader of the free world would ignore at its peril."[191]

Although the Carter administration did not overtly change its policy to reflect the concerns of Congress and the press, it is important to note at this stage that despite the efforts of Jimmy Carter to apply new tactics to the conduct of the Cold War by de-emphasizing East-West competition and creating a world order based on global community and moral values, the administration accepted that some things had not changed, and some traditional aspects of Cold War foreign policy must be integrated into, although not allowed to dominate, the new approach. In October 1976, when preparing an outline of the proposed foreign policy to be pursued by the Carter administration, Cyrus Vance had suggested that East-West issues should "not be permitted to so dominate our foreign policy that we neglect other important relationships and problems," but asserted that the relationship between the United States and the Soviet Union remained "of *central importance.*"[192] Meanwhile, in the second debate before the election, Carter declared that "militarily we are as strong as any nation on earth. I think we've got to stay that way and to continue to increase our capabilities to meet any potential threat."[193] After the election he told the American people that "as Commander in Chief of the Armed Forces, I am determined to have a strong, lean, efficient fighting force."[194] The Presidential Directive of August 1977 declared:

> It is clear that in the foreseeable future, U.S.-Soviet relations will continue to be characterized by both competition and co-operation, with the attendant risk of conflict as well as the opportunity for stabilizing U.S.-Soviet relations.... To fulfill this national strategy, the United States will maintain an overall balance of military power between the United States and its allies on the one hand and the Soviet Union and its allies on the other at least as favorable as that that now exists.[195]

Such rhetoric reinforces the argument of Carter as a Cold Warrior within contextual constraints.

The interplay between the Cold War and the complications and constraints of Carter's situation in the 1970s is particularly apparent in policy discussions regarding Ethiopia and Somalia. The Presidential Review Memorandum of April 1977 on the Horn of Africa acknowledged the Cold War context in its preamble, yet also highlighted the contextual complexities, noting that the "competition between the U.S. and the USSR for influence in Africa has been superimposed on the welter of ethnic, religious, ideological, and territorial incompatibilities existing between, among and within the African states of the Horn of Africa."[196]

The Summer of 1977

If events in the Horn of Africa had taken place ten or fifteen years previously, it seems unlikely that the American response to the usurpation of their influence by the Soviet Union would have been so calm. Citing the needs of national security, it is probable that American action would have been swift and vigorous. Indeed, the Carter administration did respond — but in a way that reflected its new approach to the Cold War, and the commitment to regionalism, the ideal of global community and human rights. The "improvement of relations with Sudan and Somalia" was cited by Henze as one of the accomplishments of the administration during its first six months in office, and he also suggested that the administration should congratulate itself for "disengagement from support of the Ethiopian military regime" because of its human rights record.[197]

By the summer of 1977, therefore, although events in the Horn of Africa had arguably tested many of Jimmy Carter's foreign policy aspirations, the administration appeared to be successfully pursuing a regionalist policy in the Horn of Africa, where the Soviet presence was not allowed to dominate American policy formulation, which instead was largely shaped by the perceived needs of the Africans and the principles of human rights. In an address to the NAACP on July 1, Vance declared that "our objective must be to foster a prosperous and strong Africa that is at peace with itself and at peace with the world."[198] However, events from the end of July caused the situation in the Horn to deteriorate and threaten this objective.

III

War in the Ogaden

The Start of the War: An American Role?

By August 1977 the border skirmishes between Ethiopia and Somalia had grown into full-scale war. Although by no means the only conflict in the world, the Ogaden war was widely argued to be the most worrying; the *New York Times* correspondent, James Buxton, contended that the "two most serious wars being fought in the world today are going on in Ethiopia,"[1] while a *Washington Post* editorial suggested that the war in the Ogaden "is probably the world's largest military conflict at the moment," where as many as "30,000 troops may be fighting on each side."[2] As we have seen, Somali irredentism led to the conflict, although the question arises as to why Siad Barré chose to begin his campaign for reunification by attacking Ethiopia as opposed to Kenya or Djibouti. The answer perhaps lies in the family history of the Somali leader: his mother belonged to a Ogadeni clan, and Siad had been born in Ethiopia, although he had hidden this for many years to enable him to be eligible to join the Somali police force and military. Indeed, there appeared to be no other reason why Siad Barré should be interested in an area of mostly desert, described by David Lamb, special correspondent of the *Los Angeles Times* in Nairobi, as a "hot, barren and inhospitable ... desperately poor region ... [with] little economic or strategic value."[3]

In the first few weeks of the conflict, it appeared that Siad Barré might achieve his aim of merging the Ogaden with Somalia. On August 3, a substantiated report from Radio Mogadishu claimed that "guerrillas had captured eighty-five percent of Ogaden,"[4] and Somali combatants told a *Time* correspondent that the entire region would be "liberated" from Ethiopian rule by the end of the month.[5] The gravity of the situation in the Ogaden was underlined to outside observers when Ethiopia and Somalia officially broke diplomatic relations with each other in September, and a government announcement from Addis Ababa warned that Ethiopia had "launched all-out war against the invading enemy" in the Ogaden.[6] Initially, however, the Ethiopians met with little success. By October, the Somali insurgents remained in control of all of the Ogaden, except for the strategic towns of Harar and Diredawa; Abdullahi Abdi, a Somali military commander, declared, "the Ethiopians know they do not belong here. That is why they do not fight well. We are driving them away forever."[7]

Despite the seriousness of the conflict, the importance of the Horn of Africa in the overall foreign policy strategy of the Carter administration should not be exaggerated; indeed in his memoirs Carter recalled that "Rosalynn, Cy, Zbig, and I discussed my first year in office and decided that, as far as foreign policy was concerned, 1977 had been the year of the Middle East."[8] Nonetheless, the war in the Ogaden could not be ignored by the administration, not least because military confrontation was a direct challenge to Carter's belief in a world order based upon global community, with peaceful resolution to international disputes. However, Carter perhaps also had a personal emotional commitment to bringing about conflict resolution without the need for one side to endure bitter defeat. In *The Other Side of the Story*, Jody Powell, Carter's press secretary, described a trip that the president took with Anwar al-Sadat, President of Egypt, and Menachem Begin, Prime Minister of Israel, to Gettysburg in September 1978, during the Camp David talks on the Middle East. Powell alluded to the impact that war had had on southerners, arguing that the "Civil War (or War Between the States, if your family was on the right side) provides for southerners a perspective that differs from that of most Americans. Tales of glory and valor are forever entwined with bitter memories of defeat, humiliation, and terrible loss."[9] Powell suggested that, as a Georgian, Carter was perhaps particularly sensitive to the impact of defeat, and during the trip to Gettysburg was "reminded of what he understood about war and the consequences of failure."[10] Obviously there were other reasons for the president's desire to mediate in world conflicts, but Powell's claim that the visit strengthened Carter's resolve that the Camp David talks should succeed may well have relevance to Carter's determination for peaceful resolution to all conflicts.

However, before the Carter administration could consider its role in ending the war in the Ogaden, it had first to answer its critics that it had been the cause, or the inspiration, of the Somali action. There were several reasons why Siad might have decided to increase Somali activity in the Ogaden at this time, such as the fact that the break between Ethiopia and the United

States suggested that Ethiopia would not be able to respond immediately because it had yet to consolidate its new military supply relationship with the Soviet Union. However, the role of the Carter administration in this connection has caused much debate. The most contentious issue has been the decision of the administration to further its attempt to improve relations with Somalia with an offer, in principle, of defensive arms, and the fact that the announcement coincided with the Somali invasion. On July 1, Cyrus Vance stated that the United States would consider military assistance to "states which are threatened by a build-up of foreign military equipment and advisers on their borders in the Horn and elsewhere in Africa,"[11] and on July 26, at virtually the same time as the skirmishes in the Ogaden were becoming full-fledged war, the State Department publicly announced the decision "in principle" to "grant military assistance" to Somalia.[12] In the meantime, Carter, pointing to the importance of policy towards the Horn of Africa in his overall conduct of the Cold War, told the Magazine Publishers Association that "my own inclination is to aggressively challenge, in a peaceful way of course, the Soviet Union and others for influence in areas of the world that we feel are crucial to us now or potentially crucial fifteen to twenty years from now. This includes places like Vietnam and places like Iraq and Somalia."[13] Notwithstanding his agenda, the president's announcement also provided evidence for those who sought to charge the Carter administration with complicity in the Ogaden incursion,

Consequently questions were raised. Among the more circumspect was an editorial in the *Los Angeles Times*, which noted that, although the announcement of the Carter administration stressed that the arms it offered were only so that Somalia could "defend its present territory," this was not, in fact, under threat.[14] A much more serious accusation came in an article that appeared in *Newsweek* on September 26, 1977, and directly charged the Carter administration with complicity in the Ogaden invasion. Written by Arnaud de Borchgrave, whose columns, it should be noted, appeared to reflect a right-wing bias and suggest that he was no friend to the Carter administration, it claimed that Dr. Kevin Cahill, Siad Barré's friend and personal physician, had delivered a secret message to the Somali leader that Washington was "not averse to further guerrilla pressure in the Ogaden," thereby implying that the U.S. would support the Somali incursion.[15] De Borchgrave also described an incident at a reception hosted by U.S. Ambassador Andrew Young at the United Nations in September, when Somali Ambassador Abdirizak Haji Hussen confronted Richard Moose, the assistant secretary of state for African affairs, and claimed that the Americans had let the Somalis down, as the prospect of American arms had prompted the Somali action.[16]

The Carter administration, however, insisted that these incidents were ill-timed coincidences, and an examination of the evidence, much of it from recently released primary sources, supports this view. The House Committee on International Relations, on examining the matter, concluded that the administration's decision to supply Somalia with defensive arms was "a foolish move at best."[17] Similarly, in an internal memo commenting on the administration's policy towards the Horn, Paul Henze remarked:

> There is only one step on which the president himself can be faulted: announcement of willingness to supply arms to Somalia just as the invasion of the Ogaden was getting under way. It has never been clear to me how this happened, but it shouldn't have. But it is wrong to say, as some critics have, that this announcement caused the invasion (a self-serving interpretation the Soviets like to encourage). The Somalis had planned to invade for a long time and may even have had incitement from some Soviets to do so. The oversupply of Soviet arms to Somalia in previous years was the real cause of the invasion.[18]

Although President Carter had told Siad Barré that the Horn nations should "have the capability to defend their existing territory,"[19] he had also insisted that Siad ought to make "every effort to promote peace and reconciliation in the Horn of Africa."[20] Tom Reston, deputy assistant secretary of state for public affairs, said at a press briefing that "I can categorically deny the implication that the United States encouraged in any way Somalia's support for the escalated fighting in the Ogaden,"[21] while Richard Moose of the State Department told critics that the American offers of military aid were "not of such a nature that a prudent man would have mounted an offensive on the basis of them."[22] Furthermore, in response to a letter from Dr. Albert Henn, who was with the Agency for International Development in Cameroon, Henze maintained:

> I can assure you that the Department of State did not use Dr. Cahill to send any message to President Siad Barré of Somalia.... At no time did we encourage Somali military action against Ethiopia as the *Newsweek* article alleges. Rather, we made it clear to them that any arms we might agree to give them would be defensive only in nature, could not be used outside their existing borders, and would be designed to fill any gaps which might develop in their territorial defense capabilities should Soviet supplies no longer be available.[23]

Perhaps the clearest indication that Carter had not intended the offer of military aid as an inducement for an invasion of the Ogaden was the fact that, as soon as the administration became aware of the extent of the Somali incursion into Ethiopia, the arms offer was withdrawn. State Department spokesman Hodding Carter stated that "we have decided that providing arms at this time would add fuel to a fire we are most interested in putting out."[24] Another administration official informed *U.S. News and World Report* that "we cannot supply weapons to a country that is attacking a neighbor."[25] Also, it must be noted that Somali officials were willing to admit that the invasion was not prompted by the Americans: Mohammed Aden, special aide to the Somali president, told a news conference that reports that the Carter administration had encouraged the invasion were "pure speculation," and the "Somalis never deluded ourselves about the U.S. attitude."[26]

Peaceful Resolution Through Negotiation

Although it appears that the Carter administration was not responsible for the war in the Ogaden, this did not mean that Jimmy Carter did not feel a responsibility towards the conflict. The president refused to support the Somali insurgency in Ethiopia for several reasons, not least of which was Carter's belief that there should be peaceful resolution of conflicts. He maintained that even if the Somali inhabitants of the Ogaden had the right to self-determination, the appropriate method for resolving the issue was negotiation and international mediation, rather than military conquest. Although Carter had some ideas as to the form that a negotiated settlement should take — for example, an autonomous Ogaden under Ethiopian protectorship — in general, the administration wished to avoid imposing an American solution on the African problem, and in August the president endorsed Brzezinski's recommendation that the United States "cannot intervene in the conflict between Ethiopia and Somalia."[27]

Indeed, Carter precluded any direct role for the United States, and instead limited the American involvement to support for negotiations. Initially he attempted to use his influence to persuade Siad to halt his act of aggression, and seek his goals through more peaceful and diplomatic means. On August 18 Carter wrote to the Somali leader expressing the "hope that your statesmanship and influence will help to bring about an early cessation of hostilities in the Ogaden and that a peaceful resolution of the dispute can be arranged."[28] Further administration policy was discussed at the Policy Review Committee of August 25 which decided that "we want to try to persuade other Africans to feel a sense of responsibility for what is happening between Ethiopia and Somalia,"[29] and resolved "to try to get as many African leaders as possible to participate in a call to all outside powers to refrain from supplying arms to fuel the Ethiopian-Somali confrontation so that there can be a cease-fire and an effort at mediation."[30]

In the administration's regionalist context, that African problems should have African solutions, the ideal forum to sponsor negotiations was the Organization of African Unity (OAU). The OAU officially became involved in the Ogaden War after the Ethiopian government demanded an emergency meeting to discuss the Somali aggression. The foreign ministers of eight African nations met in Libreville, Gabon, from August 5 to 9, 1977, but the prevalent opinion regarding the prospects for success was anything but optimistic. Diplomatic sources told the *New York Times* that the emergency meeting "would surely fail because of the deep antagonisms and fundamental differences between the two countries."[31] Indeed, it soon appeared that the diplomatic skepticism was well founded. The Ethiopian delegation insisted that they would never accept the "humiliation" of surrendering part of their territory, and refused to allow the Ogaden guerrillas to participate in the mediation talks.[32] This led to Somalia withdrawing from the negotiations; the Somali foreign minister, Abderahman Jama Barre, told reporters that "we are ready to enter into a dialogue with Ethiopia [only] if the persons concerned in Ogaden participate."[33] The special meeting of the OAU concluded with a call for a cessation of hostilities between Ethiopia and Somalia,[34] although because of the Somali withdrawal this announcement carried little weight. A month after the emergency session had ended, a spokesman for the Ethiopian government pointed out that Somalia had "shown no respect" for the resolution passed by the OAU and clearly "intended to pursue its aggression."[35]

The standpoint of the OAU was motivated, to a large degree, by the Cairo Resolution of 1964, which stated that existing territorial boundaries in Africa should be honored and not forcibly changed. The Carter administration also supported this position, not only because it was trying to improve the image of the United States in Africa, and therefore did not want to be seen going against the tenets of the OAU, but also because of the danger that changing borders by force might start a chain reaction on the African continent where so many international boundaries were artificially imposed. However, in response to the argument that the Somali incursion into Ethiopia breached both international law and the Cairo Resolution by violating territorial integrity, Siad claimed that the fighting in the Ogaden was an issue of self-determination, with the only Somalis involved being those who lived in Ethiopia, but had an ethnic Somali background. In an exclusive interview with *Newsweek* in June 1977, Siad insisted that "we are not responsible for the tactics of these Somali nationalists fighting for their freedom. We are helping them the same way we are helping freedom fighters in [Rhodesia] — with limited means. But we [Somalia] are not going to invade Ethiopia. That's the kind of nonsense you read in sensational Western papers."[36]

Rather than being "nonsense," Western journalists and analysts presented ample evidence that Somali regulars were actively involved in the Ogaden war. On August 12, 1977, the *New York Times* reported that among the diplomats in the Horn of Africa "there is almost a total rejection ... of what is viewed as the Somali charade that its regular forces are playing no part in the battles and that the Ethiopians are being engaged only by dissident Somalis living in Ethiopia."[37] Correspondents from the *Washington Post*, allowed to visit the combat zone by Ethiopia, reported that they had seen "the wreckage of a Soviet-built MiG jet fighter with Somali air force markings, two prisoners of war who said they were regular Somali troops and a large stockpile of captured Somali arms and ammunition."[38] Similarly, *Newsweek* journalists in Somalia filed reports in August 1977 on the:

> Many signs in Mogadishu that Somalia was mobilizing [for involvement in the war]. Recently one hundred and fifty construction workers building a Kuwaiti-financed dam at Desira were rounded up by Somali regulars and sent off to fight for the Liberation Front. Soldiers stopped other Somali men in the streets, and those who couldn't prove that they were steadily employed were carted away to the Ogaden.[39]

In September, *Newsweek* correspondent James Pringle joined a group of Western correspondents allowed by the Ethiopian government to visit the besieged city of Diredawa, and reported that he "had little doubt that the 2500 troops who attacked Diredawa were Somali regulars, not Ogaden freedom fighters."[40] Such reports bore out the intelligence received by the Carter administration. In a memo to the president on August 18, Brzezinski asserted that "there can be no doubt that the Somalis have launched an only very thinly disguised, premeditated invasion of Ethiopia."[41]

The concern felt by the Carter administration regarding the extent of official Somali participation in the war was compounded by concerns over the involvement of outside powers in the conflict. The Cabinet meeting of September 12 endorsed the standpoint of the OAU that "outside powers should not be 'fuelling' African territorial disputes," and reiterated the view that there should be an arms embargo to both sides for the duration of the conflict. [42] The main problem for the administration lay in the links of the Soviet Union and other countries of the communist bloc with the Horn region, and as the skirmishes in the Ogaden developed into full-fledged war, the risk increased that the extent of communist bloc support, particularly in the form of arms and equipment, would prolong the war and further destabilize the region. During the first few weeks of the war the Soviet Union continued to supply military aid to both Ethiopia and Somalia; on August 7, 1977, the *Washington Post* reported that "several Soviet ships loaded with war materiel have recently arrived [in Somalia] ... even as Moscow is pouring arms into neighboring Ethiopia."[43] The influx of military aid to Ethiopia culminated in a massive airlift during the fall of 1977, and articles in both the *Washington Post* and *New York Times* towards the end of September reported that MiG-21 jet fighters, T-55 tanks, and armored personnel carriers were arriving in Ethiopia from the Soviet Union by sea and air.[44]

However, it was not just those on the "other" side to the United States who had the potential to complicate the problems of the Horn. Carter's belief that the international community should provide the basis for agreement meant that he also had to deal with the inherent problems of global complexity. In the Horn of Africa this, in particular, meant dealing with the opposing interests of Israel and the Arab nations. As discussed in Chapter II, some of the more moderate Arab nations, led by Saudi Arabia, wished to prevent Soviet domination of the Horn region, arguably because of a concern that oil exports to the West might be impeded. David Lamb, the *Los Angeles Times* correspondent based in Nairobi, reported on August 1, 1977, that the "moderate Arab states ... [were] spending immense sums to impede the spread of communism."[45] Much of this was spent in support of Somalia, a Muslim country and member of the Arab League, in the hope that financial inducements could persuade the Somalis to break their ties with the USSR and ally itself more formally with the western bloc. However following the violation of territorial integrity and international law by the invasion of Ethiopia, the Arab League tempered its support for Somalia somewhat. Although Siad sought support for his actions from the Arab League, a meeting of the twenty-one-nation League that took place in Cairo in September 1977 refused the request of the Somali foreign minister for aid, and instead called on the two countries to "settle their dispute by peaceful means."[46]

Whereas Arab nations were concerned about Soviet domination of the Red Sea, Israel feared Arab domination of the region, and so lent its support to Ethiopia. The Carter administration was aware of the Israeli support for Mengistu: a letter sent from Douglas Bennett, assistant secretary for Congressional relations in the State Department, to Representative Lee Hamilton (D-In), chairman of the House Subcommittee on Europe and the Middle East, on October 6, 1977, acknowledged that "it is our understanding that Israel may have transferred small amounts of military equipment to Ethiopia and may have provided some military personnel and training assistance."[47] This apparent association of Israel and the Soviet Union in support of Ethiopia, although never formalized and probably always uneasy, serves to underscore the complexities of the world of the 1970s, and the problems that Carter faced in formulating Cold War foreign policy.

Unlike some of its allies and opponents, however, the Carter administration was determined to remain detached from the ongoing crisis in the Horn. Rather than react to the current conditions, it sought to adhere to its long-term policy aims, with regard to both Africa in particular and the Cold War in general. On August 26, 1977, Brzezinski suggested to the president that "we want to enhance our longer-range chances for increasing our influence in both Ethiopia and Somalia while doing what we can to ensure that the

Soviets gain as little as possible — or in fact lose — from their current involvement."[48] Brzezinski's wish that the USSR should "lose" is worthy of note,
although it must be said that his motives are not completely clear. While a
desire to remove Soviet influence would fit into a globalist perspective, perhaps suggesting the traditional Cold War notion of rollback, it also fits into
the regionalist view that African problems should have African solutions and
all outside influence should be removed.

One way of improving relations with Ethiopia was to attempt to repair
the formal diplomatic relations with the Mengistu regime that had been damaged earlier in the year. Within the administration the possibility of sending
an ambassador to Ethiopia was discussed, but the idea was postponed in case
such an action might impede the development of relations with Somalia. The
Policy Review Committee of August 15 decided that "to send an Ambassador
to Ethiopia now might lead the Somalis to conclude that we were tilting decisively against them."[49]

Additionally, the faint hope persisted within the administration that
Mengistu might be replaced as the Ethiopian head of state with someone
more amenable towards the United States. The United States could either wait
for this to happen on its own or, as Henze suggested to Brzezinski in August
1977, "consider whether we could hasten his fall and replacement by a person or group who could rally the country and set it back on the path to constructive political evolution in association with the Free World."[50] Henze
acknowledged, though, that one of the main problems for such a plan was
the reality of the situation in Ethiopia; there did not seem to be a resistance
movement for the United States to support. He remarked to Brzezinski that
"there is an astonishing dearth of evidence of serious plotting. Even in quiet
times under Haile Selassie, there was always a plot a month in Ethiopia."[51]
There were also signs that, although he continued his close relationship with
the Soviet Union, Mengistu's attitude towards the United States may be softening. On August 15, 1977, the *New York Times* reported:

> The formerly strident anti–American rhetoric so common here has abated sud-
> denly. There is a report that a new directive has been issued ordering all mass rev-
> olutionary organizations to discontinue using the terms "anti-imperialist" and
> "imperialist" which had previously formed general definitions here of good and
> evil. Even though there are still posters in Addis Ababa proclaiming "Yankee Go
> Home," there are also expressions being heard recalling the warmth of America's
> past relationship with this country.[52]

For various reasons then, not least of which may have been fears over the
American public's reaction to such covert activity in the post–Vietnam era,
the idea of an American-sponsored coup never got past the discussion stage.[53]

The long-term strategy of the Carter administration, and the restraint shown in limiting American involvement in the Ogaden War to diplomatic pressure won the administration an element of domestic support. An editorial in the *New York Times* commented that "the world's bloodiest war has been raging for several months in the Horn of East Africa. The Russians are deeply enmeshed in the conflict, which makes it all the more remarkable, and commendable, that the United States is not."[54] However, as with many of Carter's policies, there was also criticism. For some, Carter's new approach to the Cold War, and particularly the emphasis on peaceful resolution to conflicts, seemed inadequate. An editorial in the *Washington Post* on September 17 summarized a common position, declaring: "Did you know that the most 'modern' and destructive war ever fought between two states in black Africa is currently being waged? And that, aside from a little ineffective hand-wringing, nobody seems to be doing much to stop it?"[55] Others, including Representative Robert Sikes (D-Fla), were more concerned about the strategic implications. In a speech to the House of Representatives on October 25, 1977, Sikes described the refusal of the United States to aid the Somalis as "ineptness,"[56] and on November 29 he spoke again, arguing that "the United States will be derelict if we do not move quickly to take advantage of the potential" for replacing the Soviet Union in Somalia, particularly in the strategic naval base at Berbera.[57]

Despite such criticism, Carter remained resolute in his determination to pursue his foreign policy objectives in the Horn of Africa, and particularly his belief that world order should be based on global community. Thus although the Carter administration may have appeared relatively inactive with regard to the crisis in the Ogaden, such appearances were deceptive. In an address at Johns Hopkins University on October 27, Anthony Lake reminded the audience that an element of the administration's foreign policy strategy was "a recognition that we cannot rely on unilateral diplomacy,"[58] and members of the administration remained active in their attempts to engage the international community in their efforts. During a visit to the United Nations in October, Vance took the opportunity to once again reiterate the administration's view that the OAU was the proper forum to deal with the conflict between Ethiopia and Somalia, emphasizing to the African representatives "the solid support of the United States for their efforts through the Organization of African Unity to end this tragic episode."[59]

As well as endorsing the role of the OAU, while he was in New York Vance also pursued another option contemplated by the Carter administration in its search for a multilateral diplomatic effort; that of the United Nations itself. The secretary of state held a series of meetings with officials from both Ethiopia and Somalia and proposed a UN-supervised referendum to settle the conflict over the Ogaden.[60] This proposal was rejected by both sides, and in October both Ethiopia and Somalia also turned down mediation offers from UN Secretary General Kurt Waldheim.[61] There was, however, more success with a different element of the idea that the global community should act to address international crises; the International Red Cross instituted a war relief program in the Ogaden, to "give humanitarian assistance to the victims of the fighting," funded in part by a contribution of $450,000 from the United States.[62]

Whether because of the inherent problems and complexities of a global community, or because of the intractability of this particular conflict, the administration's hope that the Ogaden war could be ended by mediation and negotiation seemed unlikely to become reality. Despite early Somali military successes, the Ethiopians never gave any indication that they would accept a negotiated solution to the war. On September 19 Mengistu announced that peace could only come when all Somali forces had left the Ogaden, and expressed his commitment to the war "to throw out the invaders."[63] There were also hints that the Ethiopians wanted more than mere Somali withdrawal from their territory; a government official told the *New York Times* that the fighting in the Ogaden could turn from a "defensive war into an offensive one."[64] The Ethiopians, though, insisted that they had no intention of invading Somalia after reclaiming the Ogaden. In a speech marking the third anniversary of the overthrow of Emperor Haile Selassie, Mengistu declared that Ethiopia had not violated Somali territory during the current conflict and, he added, "never will."[65] Mengistu's assertion failed to reassure, however, and this issue would subsequently occupy the administration's foreign policy personnel, as we shall see.

Somalia, the Soviet Union and the United States

Despite displeasure over Somalia's role in the Ogaden, the Carter administration adhered to its long-term policy aims and maintained a dialogue with Siad Barré's regime, arguably because of the desire to eventually remove external influence (in the form of the Soviet Union and Cuba) from the region. This strategy appeared to be bearing fruit in November 1977 when, following a nineteen-hour government meeting, it was announced that Somalia was renouncing its treaty of friendship with the Soviet Union, ordering the expulsion of all Soviet military and civilian advisers, and closing the Soviet naval bases on the Indian Ocean, including the base at Berbera. Perhaps as a symbolic gesture, Siad allowed seven Soviet employees to remain at the Soviet Embassy, a figure that matched the size of the Somali Embassy staff in Moscow.[66] At the same time, Siad broke relations with the USSR's ally and perceived proxy, Cuba, and also expelled Cuban diplomats and advisers.[67]

Although the Somali action seemed to some to be precipitous — indeed, Vance described the decision to the Cabinet meeting of November 14 as "a major step,"[68] while *Newsweek* called it a "major gamble"[69] — it could be argued that Siad felt that he had very little choice. As discussed previously, the USSR had undertaken a massive airlift of supplies to Ethiopia, and manpower from both the Soviet Union and Cuba had also arrived to support Mengistu in the struggle with Somalia over the Ogaden. In addition, the Soviet leadership expressed open disapproval of the Somali incursion; on September 30, 1977, the *New York Times* reported that "Leonid I. Brezhnev, the Soviet leader, has criticized Somalia for supporting ethnic Somali guerrillas who have invaded Ethiopia."[70] The Soviets took their displeasure with Siad a step further when, towards the end of October, the USSR announced that it was halting all arms supplies to Somalia. The Soviet ambassador to Ethiopia, Anatoly Ratanov, told a news conference in Addis Ababa that Moscow had "officially and formally" terminated military aid to Somalia, but was providing Ethiopia with "defensive weapons" to counter the Somali invasion.[71] In addition, the communist bloc provided manpower to support the Ethiopian troops in the war; on November 5 the State Department estimated that about two hundred and fifty Cuban and Soviet military advisers were assisting Ethiopia in the fighting in both Eritrea and the Ogaden.[72] Siad therefore accepted that the Soviet Union was unlikely to support him in his military conquest of the Ogaden but realized that, if he were to face Ethiopian troops backed by Soviet and Cuban might, he too needed external support. This was most likely to come from the West, but presumably only if he no longer had ties with the communist bloc. The official government announcement that Siad was breaking these ties was couched in terms designed to elicit Western sympathies by emphasizing the Somali position that Soviet actions were assisting in the repression of freedom; Somali information minister Abdulkadir Salaad Hasan charged that the USSR was "brazenly" interfering "in the struggle of the peoples fighting for their liberation from the Ethiopian government."[73]

Although there does not appear to be any evidence that the United States played any direct role in the Somali decision, it is probable that the administration recognized that Siad Barré's ulterior motive in expelling the Soviets was a search for external support. Nevertheless, Carter continued to apply a regionalist policy and maintained the doctrine that outside powers should not fuel the Ogaden conflict. On November 15, the State Department spokesman, Hodding Carter, announced that, despite the Somali action, there would be no change in the administration's policy of refusing to supply arms to Somalia, and stated that the administration continued to believe that

"African problems should be solved by Africans themselves."[74] Another State Department spokesman, John Trattner, reiterated that "while the fighting continues in the Ogaden, the United States will supply no arms to either Ethiopia or Somalia."[75] Instead, the Carter administration limited its response to the Somali announcement to informal approval. In a meeting with the Somali minister and adviser on foreign affairs, Hussein Abdulkador Kassim, Brzezinski told him that the administration was "pleased the Somalis have broken with the Soviets,"[76] while on November 15 the *Washington Post* reported that the "United States applauded Somalia today for its decision this weekend to expel thousands of Soviet military advisers."[77]

The administration also had reason to be encouraged over the apparent continued improvement in relations with Ethiopia. In December, Mengistu granted an audience to a Congressional delegation, led by representatives Don Bonker (D-Wash) and Paul Tsongas (D-Mass)[78], who were visiting the region. The Ogaden War formed one of the main topics of conversation during the meeting, and the Congressmen once more confirmed American neutrality in the conflict, reiterating Carter's determination to "stick to its policy of refusing to supply arms to either Ethiopia or Somalia."[79] In return Mengistu warned the Americans that Carter's hope for peaceful resolution were likely to remain unfulfilled, commenting that the United States should not "expect the OAU to solve the problem." He insisted that the Somalis would not voluntarily withdraw from the Ogaden, and the only option therefore was to drive them out. As there was "no force at the disposal of the OAU," it was therefore the "duty of Ethiopia and its armed forces to expel the aggressors."[80] However, Mengistu also took pains to point out to Bonker and Tsongas that the Ethiopian position was one of nonalignment and that it was relying on the Soviet Union only out of military necessity due to the Somali invasion.[81]

Statements from the communist bloc seemed to support Mengistu's implication that the relationship between his country and the USSR should not concern the United States. Indeed, both the Soviet Union and Cuba sought to downplay their own military role in the Ogaden conflict. In his memoirs Vance recalled that "Gromyko and Carter ... had acerbic exchanges over Africa and human rights. The president underlined Soviet and Cuban involvement in Shaba and the Horn and pointed to the fact that our information indicated Soviet personnel were directing operations. Gromyko rejected [the information] as 'myth.'"[82] On November 6, 1977, the *New York Times* reported that "Cuba denied today that it has troops in Ethiopia, which is fighting against insurgents on two frontiers, including its western border with Somalia."[83]

In reality, though, communist bloc assistance for Ethiopia was increasing, and the administration had ample evidence that the denials from both the Soviet Union and Cuba were false. On December 13 Vance sent a telegram to several American Embassies around the world, including those in Africa, the Middle East, Moscow and London, confirming that the administration had "incontrovertible evidence of a massive, continuing Soviet airlift of equipment and personnel into Addis Ababa.... These deliveries include large quantities of modern weapons such as armor, artillery and sophisticated aircraft. Substantial seaborne deliveries continue as well."[84] Representatives Bonker and Tsongas told the House Committee on International Relations that during their visit in December they "personally saw Soviet MiGs being assembled at the Addis Ababa airport plus a sizeable number of Soviet transport planes."[85] State Department spokesman John Trattner acknowledged that published reports that the airport in Addis Ababa was "swamped with Soviet supplies" agreed with Washington's information on the airlift,[86] while the NSC weekly report to the president of December 16, 1977, noted that the Soviet airlift was taking into Ethiopia not only "large quantities of military equipment but sizeable new contingents of Soviet and Cuban advisers and more are expected."[87]

Despite the evidence that communist bloc involvement in the conflict was increasing, and could prove crucial to the outcome of the war, the administration maintained its support for a peaceful resolution, and therefore limited its response to diplomatic condemnation of this perceived unwarranted external involvement. During a discussion on the Horn in the Cabinet meeting of November 14, 1977, Brzezinski reported on the "scale of Cuban involvement in Africa, especially in Somalia and Angola," and Carter decided that "the United States will begin to express its frank criticism of the 'Cuban intrusion' into Africa."[88] Shortly afterwards, the president directed Andrew Young to make a speech in the UN deploring the Soviet and Cuban presence in Africa — once again reflecting Carter's belief in the importance of multilateral action in a world order based upon global community.[89] In addition, the telegram sent by Vance to various American embassies around the world on December 13, explained that the administration was:

> Deeply concerned about the Soviet airlift and, particularly, the obstacle it presents for the success of the OAU efforts to mediate this African problem. We are confining our response to this development to quiet diplomacy, including approaches to the Soviets and to key African states. We have decided on this course in an effort to prevent the situation from assuming the public appearance of a great power confrontation which would inevitably complicate any efforts the Africans themselves might wish to make to deal with this extra-continental interference in an African problem.[90]

The administration also expressed its concern directly to the Soviet Union and Cuba. In a meeting with Soviet foreign minister Gromyko in December Vance pointed out that the United States supported the OAU position that the major powers should disengage from the Ogaden conflict, and added that "it would be useful if the USSR did too."[91]

The administration's policy of continued non-involvement, especially in the face of the increasing role of the communist bloc, provoked some domestic support. An editorial in the *New York Times* on November 18 read:

> Unaccustomed as they are to watching international drama from the sidelines, Americans can be pleased with their recent role as onlookers of events in the African Horn. The events are rooted in long-standing local rivalries, but they have been made worse by extensive Soviet meddling and kept from becoming still worse by American restraint. As a result the United States may now have an opportunity to play the constructive role of peacemaker.[92]

However there was disapproval too. The report submitted to the House Committee on International Relations, following the visit of representatives Bonker and Tsongas to the Horn of Africa, put the conflict between Ethiopia and Somalia in the context of traditional Cold War rhetoric, arguing that nowhere on "the African Continent is there an area where the potential for East-West confrontation is greater, or strategic interests more important."[93] The report also likened the issue of territorial integrity to the Domino Theory, and warned of the dangers of appeasement:

> For Africans, the challenge of self-determination and the unraveling of established borders are at stake. What is happening in the Horn of Africa today is much more than a conflict between two African countries; it involves the potential of coastal areas and ports for military operations in and around the Red Sea and the Indian Ocean, and the control of naval and international commerce through this vital area. Soviet strategists have recognized the importance of the Horn of Africa and have shown their willingness to make substantial investments to secure Russia's interests, first in Somalia and now in Ethiopia. By undermining the fragile governments that exist in the Horn, Soviet influence could rapidly spread throughout the region and along the entire East Coast of Africa.... As long as there is turmoil and conflict in the Horn of Africa, the United States cannot afford to be complacent. To do so would risk possible Soviet domination of the whole Indian Ocean area and a consequent threat to fundamental Western interests.[94]

In his weekly report of November 18, 1977, Brzezinski, too, warned Carter that although:

> The various initiatives you have taken have been right, and individually correct, I feel that we are confronting a growing domestic problem involving public perception of the general character of that policy. To put it simply and quite bluntly, it is seen as "soft." ... Our critics ... will ask for some examples of "toughness," and exploit against us such things as ... the current Cuban activity in Africa.[95]

Although the degree of influence wielded by Brzezinski within the administration would apparently change as time passed, at this stage his views

did not always dominate and, as 1977 came to an end, the Carter administration adhered to its long-term policies that included an emphasis on the
importance of regionalism, and peaceful resolution of conflicts through negotiation. In December 1977, Siad Barré sent a goodwill mission to Washington, led by Hussein Abdulkador Kassim. The purpose of Kassim's visit, it was
believed, was to plead for American military assistance in the Ogaden conflict,
and when Brzezinski met with Kassim he repeated the administration's policy that "we can supply no arms because the Somalis have invaded Ethiopia."[96]
The determination of the administration to refrain from direct involvement
did not please the Somalis, however. At a news conference, Kassim declared
that "it is the feeling of my Government that the international community
has a responsibility to see that the plan of the Soviet Union to destabilize the
area is not carried out."[97] The same month Siad Barré called on the United
States to "fulfill its moral responsibility" to Somalia. He said he had gotten
"words, just words from the West" instead of material aid, even after expelling
the Soviets.[98]

The view of the Carter administration was somewhat different, though.
Its new approach to the Cold War, and emphasis on regionalism rather than
the global conflict, meant that it saw no reason why the Somalis should expect
to be rewarded just because they had expelled the Soviets. However, pursuant
to the administration's emphasis on the improvement of human rights and
the human condition, there was a willingness to provide economic, developmental and humanitarian aid to Somalia, despite the aggressive role of the
Somalis in the Ogaden War. At his meeting with Minister Kassim and Ambassador Addou in December 1977, Brzezinski told them that the president and
his administration "deplore the suffering that fighting in the Horn of Africa
is causing and therefore are prepared to give humanitarian and economic
aid."[99] The subsequent aid agreement, designed to help drought victims as
well as refugees displaced by the war, was worth $6 million, and in February
1978 the first consignment of food, including corn, rice and powdered milk
arrived in Mogadishu.[100]

Human rights in Ethiopia also concerned the members of the Carter
administration as 1977 ended. In his meeting with the Black Leaders Forum
in December, it was not the war in the Ogaden that President Carter focused
upon but the human rights problems prevalent throughout Africa.[101] Congressmen Bonker and Tsongas had just returned from their visit to Ethiopia
and reported that "there is no doubt that a reign of terror exists" in the
Ethiopian capital.[102] The congressmen expressed their concern for the
Ethiopian people, and recommended an "increase [in] economic and humanitarian aid to all parties" in the Horn of Africa.[103] This had been the position
of the administration even before the visit of the congressmen to the Horn;

the Policy Review Committee of August 25 decided that the administration would proceed "with two small aid projects in Ethiopia to show our concern for its people."[104] Indeed, as the Ogaden War progressed, and despite Soviet intervention there, the Carter administration continued to provide economic aid to Ethiopia, including $2 million in famine relief in December.[105]

A Long-Term Strategy

Despite the active role of the communist bloc in the Ogaden War, the Carter administration adhered to its long-term and neutral policy: that the United States should remain as uninvolved as possible and that the conflict should be resolved by negotiations arranged by the Africans themselves. In January 1978 State Department spokesman John Trattner told the *Washington Post* that "what we want both sides to do is to sit down and talk with each other and work out a negotiated solution."[106] Carter informed the Black Leaders' Forum that he and his administration "support the OAU mediation effort as a hopeful means to resolve these problems,"[107] and reiterated at a news conference on January 12 that the American role in the war should be to "offer our good services in support of the African nations who are responsible [and to] support the Organization of African Unity."[108]

However, hopes for peaceful resolution through negotiation appeared likely to remain unfulfilled. On January 18, 1978, the Ethiopian ambassador to the United States, Ayalew Mandefro, insisted that "we cannot negotiate on the Ogaden when the Somalis are still in the Ogaden." He told the *Washington Post* that Somalia had violated the most sensitive principle in the African continent, "acceptance of existing borders,"[109] and underscored that the "Ogaden is part of Ethiopia and is not a point of negotiation with Somalia."[110] Neither were the Somalis overly supportive or encouraging about the possible success of negotiations. In January 1978, Siad Barré gave an interview to West German television and claimed that there was no chance of a negotiated settlement with Ethiopia to end the war over the Ogaden.[111] Henze perhaps summed up the chances for successful negotiation best in a memo he sent to Brzezinski on January 12, 1978, commenting that "neither the Ethiopians nor the Somalis want negotiations now; how, then can you bring them to negotiate? Nor do the Russians and the Cubans want negotiations."[112] At the meeting of the Special Coordination Committee on February 21, Brzezinski remarked that it was "inevitable" that the OAU approach would not succeed, one reason being that it had no means of enforcement for its judgments.[113] The national security adviser had similar doubts regarding the prospects of success within the forum of the UN, informing the SCC that the "UN initiative was not propitious. The Ethiopians regard it as hostile and other Africans are unenthusiastic."[114]

Notwithstanding this lack of success, the administration continued to search for ways in which the war in the Ogaden could be resolved by negotiations. In January 1978, the United States sponsored and hosted an international conference to discuss the conflict in the Horn that was attended by Great Britain, France, West Germany and Italy. State Department spokesman John Trattner told the *New York Times* that the meeting "will examine ways to enhance the chances of achieving a peaceful settlement."[115] After an eight-hour meeting, the representatives concluded that "no lasting solution to the problem on the Horn of Africa can be found by force of arms,"[116] and asserted that "negotiation is the only means by which the fighting can be brought to an end and a durable settlement achieved."[117] The group expressed its support for the mediation committee of the Organization of African Unity, headed by Nigeria, and proposed that a negotiated solution should be "based on an autonomous Ogaden to reflect interests of inhabitants, combined with Somali government withdrawal from Ethiopian territory."[118]

The delegates also declared their support for the arms embargo initiated by the United States at the start of the Ogaden war, agreeing that "their governments would not give military supplies to either side so long as the conflict continued."[119] It should be noted, however, that at around the same time, the West Germans did make a grant of $11.8 million credits to Somalia. The grant was believed to be part of deal between West Germany and Somalia after a highjacked Lufthansa airline was successively liberated at Mogadishu airport.[120] Although the West German government claimed that the funds would not be used by the Somalis to buy weapons, officially the grant was unconditional, and led some diplomats to believe that the "aid would be used to help defray military costs of Somalia's six-month war with Ethiopia in the Ogaden region."[121]

In addition, the Carter administration continued in its efforts to persuade the international community in general to join it in its attempt to resolve the conflict between Ethiopia and Somalia by peaceful means. On a foreign trip over the New Year period, Carter took the opportunity to discuss the problem of the Horn of Africa with the Shah of Iran. At a state dinner in Tehran, Carter appealed for Iran to use its influence to bring about negotiations between Ethiopia and Somalia, adding that the Carter administration would be "glad to cooperate in any way that we can. We want peace to return."[122] In the same vein, Carter wrote to Marshal Tito, suggesting that the Yugoslav leader's "good relations with Ethiopia provide you with a channel of communication not available to us." Carter therefore requested that Tito indicate to Mengistu the American president's "own concern for a peaceful settlement" in the Horn.[123]

In spite of all Carter's efforts, neither the Ethiopians nor the Somalis showed any inclination to agree to a peaceful resolution of the Ogaden conflict. One reason for their intransigence was the involvement of the communist bloc, which, through the supply of men and materiel, provided the means with which the two sides in the Ogaden war could continue to fight. Despite persistent denials — for example on January 19, 1978, Major Birhanu Baye, a member of the Ethiopian Provisional Military Administrative Council, told a news conference that "there were no Soviet or Cuban military advisers, instructors or combat troops in his country"[124] — the Carter administration had overwhelming evidence to the contrary; in a recent interview Brzezinski commented that "the Soviets denied to us that they had any military presence whatsoever in Ethiopia, and we knew that was not true."[125] Indeed, the involvement of the Soviets and Cubans continued to increase, and on January 23 Henze informed Brzezinski that "between 2000 and 3000 more Cuban combat troops are scheduled to arrive in Ethiopia shortly and that planning is well advanced to commit them in the northern Ogaden.... The Cuban role is thus rapidly shifting from an advisory one to one of significant involvement in the fighting itself."[126] On February 23 Admiral Turner reported that "a Soviet General [Vasiliy I Petrov] is directing the Ethiopians in battle ... [and] nearly 10,000 Cubans are in Ethiopia now."[127] The amount of evidence amassed by the Carter administration of communist bloc involvement in the Ogaden conflict eventually forced the Ethiopians to acknowledge the Cuban presence and, in March 1978, Mengistu declared to a rally in Addis Ababa that "the Cubans, renowned for shedding their blood anywhere and at any time for a just struggle and cause, are bracing themselves with the Ethiopian people's army at the front line."[128]

In the same way that the opposition of the Carter administration to communist bloc involvement reflected the importance of the Cold War to the president, his justification for the removal of the Soviet and Cuban presence exemplified his new approach to the Cold War. The administration continued to emphasize that the Ogaden War was a regional conflict, and not a proxy war or Cold War battleground. In February 1978 Brzezinski told the *New York Times* that the Soviet and Cuban involvement was "clearly an external, foreign intrusion into a purely regional conflict."[129] Moreover, and perhaps reflecting a combination of traditional Cold War ideology as well as Carter's new approach, Brzezinski insisted that communist bloc involvement would make things worse. The national security adviser sent a letter to Representative Frederick Richmond (D-NY) in which he reiterated the official standpoint of the administration that "African political problems should be solved by Africans," such as the border dispute between Ethiopia and Somalia, and argued that "foreign military intervention further exacerbates these problems and leads to increased bloodshed."[130] In addition, Carter personally decried communist bloc involvement in the Horn on various occasions, including a question-and-answer session before a group of editors and news directors on November 11, a news conference on January 12, and in the text of the State of the Union message delivered to Congress on January 19, in which the president declared that "arms supplied by the Soviet Union now fuel both sides of a conflict in the Horn of Africa between Somalia and Ethiopia.... We deplore the fact that disagreements in this region have grown — with the assistance of outside powers — into bloody conflict."[131]

As the New Year began, the administration continued attempts to mobilize international opinion against Soviet and Cuban involvement in the Horn. At his news conference of January 12, Carter announced that he had shared his concern about the "Soviet Union's unwarranted involvement in Africa" with "the NATO alliance, and specifically with France, the Middle Eastern countries, and India."[132] On January 27, 1978, Carter sent a letter to President Valery Giscard d'Estaing of France, following a meeting the two leaders had had in Paris. Carter wrote that "I share your increasing concern about developments in the Horn of Africa. The growing military role of the Soviets and Cubans is transforming a local conflict into one with much graver implications."[133] On January 30 Carter sent a similar letter to Morarji Desai, prime minister of India, stating:

> We do not argue against legitimate Soviet and Cuban relations with Ethiopia or with any other country. We do, however, want to prevent the resurgence of great power competition in a region where it has in recent years been on the wane. Outside involvement in the conflict in the Horn should be aimed to reduce, not exacerbate, basic tensions in the area.[134]

Part of the plan to muster international support for the administration's position was to appeal to the Latin American countries, perhaps in the hope that this would influence Cuba. Consequently, official communiqués were sent from the United States to the leaders of various Latin American nations, including a letter from the American president to the president of Venezuela, Carlos Andres Perez. Carter pointed out that, despite American efforts to the contrary, "the Soviet Union and Cuba have become increasingly involved in the Horn, in a way that has transformed a conflict largely limited to regional powers, to one with broader implications and risks."[135] Carter requested that Perez use his influence to "condemn foreign intervention in the internal affairs of another country."[136] The following month Carter wrote to President Jose Lopez Portillo of Mexico expressing the "deep concern" of the United States over the situation in the Horn, and especially the Cuban involvement, and seeking the Mexican president's "advice on how we might persuade them to exercise more restraint."[137]

Furthermore, the administration continued to apply direct diplomatic pressure in the hope that it might influence the actions of the Soviet Union and Cuba. On January 25, Carter sent a letter to Brezhnev seeking Soviet support for a negotiated solution to the Ogaden conflict, based upon respect for territorial integrity, and the "immediate recall of both Soviet and Cuban military personnel from Ethiopia."[138] The following month a State Department telegram sent via the American Embassy in Cuba requested that the Cuban government also support OAU peace initiatives, pointing out that "continuing Soviet-Cuban involvement will not enhance prospects for such settlement." [139]

As well as the notable lack of attention that the Soviet Union and Cuba paid to the administration's requests, the Carter administration was faced with further problems in the "global community" as the complications caused by the opposing interests in the Horn of the Arab nations and Israel continued into 1978. Although the official stance of the Arab League was one of non-involvement in the Ogaden conflict, some nations, including Egypt and Saudi Arabia, continued to support Somalia. The latter was important both within the Arab League and also because of its oil supplies to the United States, and the fact that Saudi Arabia continued with clandestine arms supplies to Somalia caused a great deal of concern within the administration. The SCC met on February 21 to consider the interests and role of Saudi Arabia in the Horn region and agreed unanimously that the administration should express its concern about arms transfers from Saudi Arabia to Somalia. However, arguably because of the Saudis' importance to the American economy, the administration would not go so far as to condemn Saudi Arabian support for Somalia and indeed made it clear that there was no objection to "non-U.S. origin" weapons transfers.[140]

Egypt also openly sided with the Somalis. On February 7, 1978, the Egyptian president, Anwar el-Sadat, gave a news conference while on a state visit to the United States, in which he admitted sending military equipment to Somalia and suggested that Egyptian troops might be sent to fight alongside the Somalis.[141] On the same day, the Israeli foreign minister, Moshe Dayan, confirmed that Israel was "selling some arms to Ethiopia." Dayan added that "we have had cooperation with Ethiopia for years and years, never with Somalia. We want to retain the good relationship with Ethiopia. The fact that we are on the same side as the Soviets in this matter, well, that's another question."[142] The Arab/Israeli dimension to the conflict in the Horn of Africa posed a particular problem for the Carter administration because of another strand of the administration's foreign policy: Carter's desire to bring about peace in the Middle East. Hodding Carter, the State Department spokesman, admitted that the fact that Egypt and Israel were active on opposite sides in the Ogaden conflict was "not useful."[143] The main fear was that the Camp David talks might be compromised, exacerbated by an awareness that Sadat, especially, did not have overwhelming support at home for the idea of a peace treaty. The administration therefore wished to avoid any other issues that might increase the controversy faced by any of the participants in the peace process. In a memo to Brzezinski, Henze contended that "Egyptian ventures in the Horn/Red Sea have always become unpopular at home.... We don't want to encourage Sadat to get himself entangled in a situation in the Horn of such magnitude that his opponents can use it against him."[144]

The involvement in the Horn conflict of other nations, such as the members of the Arab League, further compounded the difficulties faced by the administration by intensifying pressure for greater American involvement. In a memo to Brzezinski in January 1978, Henze warned that the administration was facing calls from the international community for increased action:

> Our rich Middle Eastern allies, the Shah and the Saudis, want us to play more of a role, though they have proved to be relatively conservative and rational about the pitfalls and complications of the situation. The Africans would like to see us be more active in bringing the conflict to a halt because they have not found the courage or the means to be active themselves. The Soviets would like to implicate us in their own dilemmas and entangle us in the situation so that we cannot exploit it against them or improve our own position later.[145]

During his briefing for his forthcoming trip to Mexico, Vice President Mondale was advised that "our friends in the [Red Sea] area are deeply worried about the Soviet and Cubans establishing themselves permanently on both sides of the Red Sea (they are already entrenched in South Yemen) and are pressing us to do something."[146]

The administration also faced criticism of its passive role from American sources. A telegram sent from the United States Embassy in Moscow pointed to a flaw in the administration's regionalist orientation when it warned that "a basic fact we must bear in mind in all of this is that the Soviets are still playing a geopolitical 'zero-sum' game, and they have as yet shown little indication of a recognition that it would be to their long-range interest to reduce superpower involvement in the African continent."[147] On January 19, Representative Robert Sikes (D-Fla) told the House that "I find it exceedingly hard to comprehend an action of the U.S. Government which virtually gives the green light for the conquest of Somalia and Eritrea by Cuban forces under Russian control.... Arms for Somalia could have forced a negotiated settlement and kept the strategic Horn of Africa out of communist hands."[148] On February 8, Senator Thomas Eagleton (D-Mo) also expressed his concern about Soviet advances in the Horn, claiming that without U.S. help, "Somalia's relatively small and now-depleted military forces could not meet the military might of Ethiopia's Soviet backed forces, thus assuring a Soviet takeover in the Horn of Africa."[149]

Despite the adverse comments that were leveled at the administration, there might well have been as much, if not more, criticism if Carter had sought an overly active role for the United States. Certainly, the official policy reflected a sense of the post–Vietnam mood of the American public as well as a vision of a different sort of world order. Henze articulated this is a memo to Brzezinski on January 21 when he pointed out that "I am extremely skeptical that here at home we could ever get support for an active interventionist policy on the side of the Somalis against the Soviets and Cubans in the Horn."[150] Confirming this, Senator George McGovern (D-SD) told the Senate on March 16 that he commended "the U.S. administration for its restraint in not interfering in this border dispute between Somalia and Ethiopia."[151]

However, anxiety remained within the administration that the Horn might yet become an area for superpower conflict. Peter Tarnoff, executive secretary in the State Department, wrote to Brzezinski that the Ogaden War was of concern "because of the continuing bloodshed between the Ethiopian and Somali peoples and the danger that involvement by the Soviet Union and Cuba on the Ethiopian side may transform a localized conflict into one with global implications and risks."[152] Direct American involvement in opposition to the communist bloc in the Horn conflict would clearly exacerbate the risks referred to by Tarnoff; the administration, however, remained resolute in its determination to adhere to a long-term strategy, rather than react to the immediate situation. A memo sent to Brzezinski from Henze on January 16 summed up the general policy: "In the long term we want the Soviets (and Cubans) out of the Horn, and we want something like the status quo restored there under reasonably peaceful circumstances."[153]

In the short-term, however, and perhaps because it was only willing to use diplomatic pressure to achieve its long-term aims, there was an awareness that the administration must accept the presence of the Soviet Union in Ethiopia. Henze's memo of January 16 also stated:

> Much as we want the Soviets out, we are not going to get them out soon. We must reconcile ourselves to this. They will leave Ethiopia only (a) after exhaustion and frustration, as we did in Vietnam, or (b) because the Ethiopians kick them out. Neither is likely to happen in the near future, so our real policy expectations must be based on the assumption the Soviets are going to stay.[154]

It was still the case that Ethiopia was seen as the most important country in the Horn of Africa and consequently, despite Mengistu's close relationship with the Soviet Union, the Carter administration continued to focus upon the need to restore American influence. In his memo to Brzezinski, Henze insisted that "Ethiopia is too important to abandon to the Soviets. We need to maintain ties as long as we can to make clear to the Ethiopian people that we care about their country and will give it real help and support when we can do so again."[155]

As part of its long-term strategy, the Carter administration therefore continued with attempts to improve relations with the Ethiopian leader. This was arguably made easier now that Somalia had broken its ties with the Soviet Union. As previously discussed, prior American efforts in this area had been tempered by administration fears that Siad would react adversely and not cooperate in the improvement of relations between the United States and Somalia. The break between Siad and the Soviets, and Siad's subsequent near desperation for Western support, alleviated this concern somewhat and loosened constraints on policy towards Ethiopia. On January 19, Carter sent a message to Mengistu criticizing the Somali invasion of the Ogaden and contending that:

> The United States has never wavered from its long-standing position of support for the territorial integrity of all African countries and condemnation of use of force as a means of settling differences between nations. This has always been and continues to be the basis of our policy toward Ethiopia. We neither encouraged nor approved of the Somalis' incursion into the Ogaden, and we have told the Somalis that they can expect no military support from the United States as long as they are in Ethiopian territory. We would like to see all Somali presence in Ethiopian territory withdrawn.[156]

The administration also reconsidered the option of upgrading its diplomatic representation in Addis Ababa to ambassadorial level. Although Henze was adamant that the administration should maintain a relationship with Ethiopia, he counseled against the idea of raising the American diplomatic profile in Addis Ababa so substantially. On January 12, in a memo to Brzezinski discussing the situation in the Horn as the new year began, Henze argued:

> I come out in favor of maintaining our embassy in Addis Ababa, but I continue to be skeptical about the value of sending an ambassador: we both raise our visibility by doing so (and send a negative signal to the Somalis and others) and we make the expulsion of an ambassador a more attractive action if/when Mengistu decides or is persuaded by the Soviets to eliminate all American presence.[157]

However, there is little evidence of any support for Henze's position, and in general the members of the administration agreed with Vance who, as Henze reminded Brzezinski, had "consistently advocated sending an Ambassador to improve relations."[158] Thus, on January 26, 1978, the SCC concluded that, for the administration to pursue its goal in Ethiopia, an American presence at the ambassadorial level was desirable to "broaden contact and dialogue," and therefore a new Ambassador would shortly be sent to Addis Ababa.[159]

In February Mengistu provided further evidence that he was not averse to improving relations with the Carter administration when the Ethiopian leader agreed to meet with a presidential emissary to discuss future relations. Mengistu informed Carter that "Your Excellency's suggestion to send a senior emissary to Addis Ababa ... is most welcome. This, I believe, would contribute to a better understanding between our two governments and peoples."[160] The idea of a special emissary had been discussed in the SCC meeting of January 26, 1978, at the same time as approval was given for an Ambassadorial appointment as a second way in which the administration might improve the contact and dialogue with the Ethiopians.[161] Two weeks later, the SCC agreed that the deputy national security adviser, David Aaron, should go to Ethiopia.[162]

Aaron visited Mengistu in the middle of February and met with the Ethiopian leader for two and a half hours. Aaron later recalled that one of his priorities was to discuss the involvement of Cuba in Ethiopia:

> I went out there because we were deeply concerned with the advent of the Cuban intervention and that they would not just clear out the Ogaden, which they clearly had the capability to do, but also invade Somalia and take over the entire Horn. And my principal message out there was "don't do that."[163]

One of Aaron's most enduring memories of the meeting, however, appears to be of the lions that had belonged to Emperor Haile Selassie and were subsequently kept by Mengistu in an area directly beneath that in which the meeting took place. In a recent interview, Aaron remembered hearing the lions roar as he spoke with the Ethiopian leader, and admitted to a feeling of nervousness that Mengistu might take "extreme" action should the conversation displease him.[164]

Aaron's recollection of the discussion also provides an interesting insight into the role that regionalist issues were playing in international affairs. Aaron commented that Mengistu only said one thing of real interest to him:

> After I went through my long song and dance about how this would be a major mistake for him to ally himself with the Russians, and this would only ensure, you know, not just the enmity of the West but everybody else in the region, and he would isolate himself by that, and so forth and so on. He said, he leaned across and looked at me and said, "you don't understand. We're a Christian nation, surrounded by Muslims," and as far as he was concerned, all this other stuff was just, you know, sort of secondary.[165]

Following Mengistu's reasoning, it could be said that the Ethiopian leader was also attempting to pursue a regionalist policy, that traditional Cold War concerns were unimportant to him, and he would take any help, regardless of whether it came from the Western or communist sphere of influence, if it assisted him in resisting Muslim advances. It is also likely, of course, that

Mengistu had recognized the emphasis placed by the Carter administration on regionalism, or was seeking to exploit the president's commitment to Christianity, and was speaking in terms designed to impress Aaron. In either case, Mengistu's apparent lack of concern with the global Cold War would have encouraged those wishing to improve relations between the United States and Ethiopia.

Indeed, the initial reaction within the administration was that Aaron's meeting with Mengistu had gone well. On February 17, Brzezinski reported to the president that:

> None of the Derg members currently considered as hardliners were present. The mood of the meeting was temperate and serious with recognition on the Ethiopian side of its high-level nature and expressions of appreciation for your initiative. Much of the ground covered was as anticipated on both sides. Ethiopian criticisms of the U.S. past position toward their revolution were extensive but familiar and not particularly vindictive in tone. The concluding portion of the meeting was clearly upbeat and positive.[166]

Brzezinski also informed Carter that:

> In response to David's characterization of the destabilizing effect of Cuban and Soviet combat forces remaining in the region, Mengistu said he understood this concern and wished to reassure us that Ethiopia did not regard these forces as a permanent feature of the area, but as temporary though necessary forces to enable Ethiopia to overcome the effects of Somali aggression.[167]

Hodding Carter, the State Department spokesman, told the *Washington Post* that the meeting "accomplished the mission of improving relations." The most tangible indication of this improvement was Mengistu's decision, announced by the White House on February 21, to receive a new U.S. ambassador "in the near future."[168]

It appeared, then, that the administration was making good progress with the policy of improving relations throughout the Horn region. However, despite the fact that the goal of reducing Soviet influence in the Horn seemed to have been at least partially achieved by the expulsion of the USSR from Somalia, the Carter administration remained cautious with regard to its next step there. In a memo to Brzezinski in January, Henze pointed out that the Somalis "are not attractive as objects of a sustained campaign of sympathy: they brought the Soviets in in the first place, they committed bald aggression, they have lied and schemed; Siad's 'socialist' system is illiberal and has been repressive. These are not the kind of people the U.S. public can identify with for long."[169]

The activities of Siad in Ethiopia lent credence to Henze's recommendations, and there was no opposition within the administration to maintaining the policy of withholding military aid to Somalia, as long as the Ogaden war continued. On January 18, 1978, the *Washington Post* reported:

> The Carter administration yesterday rejected an appeal from Somalia for weapons and troops to repel what that country said was a planned invasion by Soviet-backed Ethiopian forces. As the war of words escalated to a higher pitch than the fighting in the Horn of Africa, a State Department spokesman said: "We will not contribute to a conflict ... by pouring gasoline on it."[170]

Vance reiterated the position that no arms would be supplied to either side in a news conference on February 10,[171] as did President Carter to representatives of Black Media Associations on February 16, 1978.[172] At the beginning of March 1978, Carter directed Ambassador John Loughran in Somalia to "tell Siad that we can maintain our commitment to seek Congressional authority to provide him with defensive arms only if he withdraws his forces immediately and completely from Ethiopian territory."[173]

Although the administration appeared resolute in its position that the Somalis could only be rewarded with military aid if they withdrew from Ethiopian territory, the Somalis persisted in their efforts to enlist U.S. support. Reflecting some of the criticism being directed at Carter within the United States, and perhaps in the hope that such critics might become his advocates, Siad invoked traditional Cold War themes. In an exclusive interview with *Newsweek* correspondents on February 13, Siad warned that the Carter administration should act because "Russia is outmaneuvering America."[174] In the same interview, an aide of Siad cautioned that "the Soviets can now see the day when they will control the oil supplies and the sea routes of the Western world."[175] However, at least within the administration, there was recognition that Siad's justification for American support had less to do with Cold War ideology, and more to do with practical necessity. In his memoirs Vance recalled: "the Somalis were increasingly desperate. Repeatedly, they appealed for U.S. military help as Cuban and Ethiopian pressure mounted. Each time we asked whether they were prepared to withdraw from the Ogaden. Their answer was no."[176]

Despite the early success enjoyed by the Somali insurgents in the Ogaden, the communist bloc support for Ethiopia had begun to change the military situation. Henze informed Brzezinski in January that "sometime this year, with all the Soviet weaponry and Cuban help they are getting, [the Ethiopians] are bound to push the Somalis back decisively."[177] On February 23, Admiral Turner gave an intelligence briefing to the National Security Council in which he reported on the Ethiopian build-up in the Ogaden and advised that a major push, in which the Cubans would be "deeply involved," should be expected in the next ten days.[178] Indeed, in February Ethiopian success was being reported throughout the American media. On February 8, Baalu Girma, the Ethiopian information minister, informed the *Los Angeles Times* that "we have taken a concerted action. We are now moving to drive the Somalis out."[179] Meanwhile, the Somali minister of information, Abdulkadir Salaad Hasan, told the *New York Times* that the Ethiopian counteroffensive meant that the "situation is very grave for Somalia."[180]

The desperation of the Somali position became more obvious when, on February 12, the *Washington Post* reported that "Somalia went on a full war footing last night as the government declared a state of emergency and announced it was formally committing its regular armed forces to the fighting with Ethiopia in the Ogaden desert."[181] The Somali government contended that because of the "failure of Western powers to assume the responsibility of confronting Soviet aggression, it has become incumbent for Somalia to defend itself against naked aggression and to increase its assistance to the Western Somali Liberation forces by dispatching units of its own regular army to the area."[182] This report was the first official announcement that Somali regulars were involved in the Ogaden conflict and, as we have seen, it bore out the intelligence long received by the Carter administration. In a memo of February 24, 1978, Peter Tarnoff of the State Department reminded Brzezinski that "since late July 1977 Somalia has involved itself heavily on the side of the Western Somali Liberation Front in an effort to achieve self-determination for the ethnic Somalis who predominate in the Ogaden."[183]

Regardless of the level of the Somali involvement in the Ogaden War, by February of 1978 the Carter administration apparently realized that it no longer need be concerned that Ethiopia's territorial integrity would be permanently violated. However, the course of the conflict meant that the threat to territorial integrity in the Horn of Africa as a whole was not over. One of the biggest fears within the administration was that once Ethiopia had expelled the Somalis from the Ogaden, the level of communist bloc support it had received would provide the means with which Mengistu could continue the conflict with an invasion of Somalia. In his memoirs Brzezinski recalled that "we were becoming increasingly concerned about ... the possibilities of expansion of the conflict beyond the borders of Ethiopia."[184] Indeed, the administration received many intelligence briefings warning of the danger, and on February 23, the issue was discussed in a meeting of the National Security Council where Turner stated that the intelligence community placed "considerable credence" in the reports of a possible Ethiopian invasion.[185]

However, the Ethiopians took pains to insist that this would not happen. On January 18, the Ethiopian permanent secretary for foreign affairs, Dawit Wolde-Georgis, told reporters that "we do not intend to fight a war inside Somalia."[186] As well as this public announcement, Mengistu also used more private diplomatic channels in an attempt to calm any fears that the administration might have. On February 22, Vance informed Carter that "Mengistu has conveyed to you his assurances that Ethiopia does not intend to cross the Somali frontier. Such assurances would appear to be fairly strong."[187] A similar message also reached Carter via the National Security Council, following the meeting between David Aaron and Mengistu in Ethiopia. Brzezinski informed the president:

> Mengistu asked that David personally convey to you his assurances that Ethiopia has no intention of crossing Somalia's border, nor has Ethiopia any intention of interfering in other countries' affairs. Further, Mengistu told David that Cuban and Soviet forces had come only to help Ethiopia and Ethiopia would not permit them to use Ethiopia as a base for intervention in neighboring countries.[188]

Brzezinski's last comment referred to the fact that it was not only potential Ethiopian actions that provided cause for concern. However, the Soviets, arguably the driving force behind Ethiopian military activities in the Ogaden, also insisted that there were no plans to invade Somalia. Soviet foreign minister Andrei Gromyko asserted to both Vance and Carter that, following high-level talks between the USSR and Ethiopia, the Soviet Union had received assurances that the Ethiopians would not cross the border into Somalia.[189] Additionally, Anatoly Dobrynin, the Soviet ambassador to Washington,[190] told both Vance and Brzezinski that the Soviets would not countenance the crossing of the border into Somalia, and added that Raul Castro "had also made it clear during his visit to Moscow that the Cuban forces had no intention of moving into Somali territory."[191] President Carter appeared reassured by the extent of the Ethiopian commitment to respect the border; at the Cabinet meeting of March 6, he asserted that "the Ethiopians have reaffirmed their commitment not to cross the Somali border."[192] When recently asked whether Ethiopia was likely to invade Somalia, Henze recalled that "there was never any serious evidence that that was the case."[193]

The Question of Linkage

In general, members of the Carter administration believed in the rhetoric that human rights should be a concern, that regionalist matters were important, and that the East-West dimension should not be allowed to dominate foreign policy. Nonetheless, they also accepted the reality of the world of the 1970s, and the fact that American national security concerns necessarily included the relationship with the Soviet Union. The debate that was to plague the administration, particularly in view of media coverage, arose from a difference of opinion over the balance between these two positions. In particular, press attention concentrated upon the relationship between Zbigniew

Brzezinski and Cyrus Vance, and although it should be noted that the media often overstated the level of antagonism between the two men, there were key areas in which they differed significantly in their foreign policy outlook. Brzezinski recently recalled that "we disagreed on a number of issues. We disagreed on Soviet expansionism, we disagreed on how hard we ought to press the Soviets on human rights. We disagreed specifically on the Soviet/Cuban role in Ethiopia and Somalia."[194] Of course, Carter's style of government, discussed in Chapter I, meant that he encouraged a free and frank discussion and exchange of views in policy deliberations, and therefore the fact that there were debates should not be viewed in itself as a negative. Nor should it be assumed that Brzezinski wished to change totally the foreign policy orientation of the Carter administration. However, it does seem clear that Brzezinski felt that the United States should be more concerned about, and consequently more active in response to, communist bloc involvement in the Horn.

Brzezinski viewed the Soviet Union as threatening and dangerous, and argued that Soviet actions in the Horn of Africa proved this. In the SCC meeting of March 2, 1978, Brzezinski contended that "the Soviets are demonstrating a predisposition to exploit a local conflict for larger purposes. They are frightening more countries in the region and they are creating a precedent for more involvement elsewhere."[195] In public Brzezinski may have supported the administration's regionalist policy, but in private memos, meetings, and later in his memoirs, it is clear that Brzezinski maintained a more globalist outlook. He argued that "the situation between the Ethiopians and the Somalis was more than a border conflict,"[196] and warned that Soviet success in the Horn could have serious repercussions around the world. Indeed, parroting classic Cold War rhetoric, Brzezinski's report to the president of February 9 maintained that the Soviet success in the African Horn demonstrated that "containment has now been fully breached."[197] On February 24, 1978, Brzezinski advised Carter that, unless the United States stood up to the Soviets in the Horn, "we will increasingly find Begin, Brezhnev, Vorster, Schmidt, Castro, Gaddafi, and a host of others thumbing their noses at us."[198] Ten days later Brzezinski sent a memo to Carter reflecting on the impact of Soviet success in the Horn of Africa:

> No one in the region will fail to notice that the Soviet Union acted assertively, energetically, and had its own way. This will have a significant effect on Soviet neighbors; I do not think anyone here appreciates the degree to which the neighbors of the Soviet Union are fearful of the Soviet Union and see themselves as entirely dependent on American resolution. I also do not believe that it is beating the drums of alarm to suggest that in the longer run there will be a ripple effect in Europe as well.[199]

In contrast to Brzezinski's globalist perspective, Vance reflected more closely Carter's emphasis on regionalism, and according to Brzezinski, "insisted that this issue [in the Ogaden] was purely a local one."[200] Vance argued that the administration should not place too much emphasis on Soviet activities in the Horn, and maintained that the Ogaden war had become a "daily crisis" because "we are stirring it up ourselves."[201] Although it would be wrong to say that Vance took a benign view of the Soviet Union, he did believe that it was possible for the administration to work with the USSR, and his priority, throughout his term of office as secretary of state, was always the Strategic Arms Limitations Talks. For Vance, nothing was more important, and he was determined that nothing should interfere with the talks; at the SCC meeting of March 2, 1978, he warned that losing SALT would be "the worst thing that could happen."[202] This led to debate within the administration as to the extent to which other issues should be allowed to impinge on Vance's priority, and the issue of "linkage" became a matter of contention. Brzezinski recalled that:

> Whether the African problem would be treated purely as an African issue disregarding the Cuban and Soviet involvement and on Rhodesia and South Africa there was agreement between NSC and State that this was a purely African problem. On Ethiopia, Somalia and Angola there was disagreement, the NSC feeling we cannot disregard that since it's part of a larger Soviet policy that therefore affects our larger strategy and the State Department feeling was strongly that now the two issues could somehow or other be compartmentalized.[203]

Notwithstanding internal discussion, the official administration standpoint was that there would be no linkage between various aspects of foreign policy. On February 21, 1978, the SCC "agreed unanimously that there is no direct linkage between Soviet or Cuban actions in the Horn and bilateral activities involving either country and the United States,"[204] and on March 2 Vance reiterated that he was "strongly opposed to any linkage with SALT."[205] Vance subsequently told a Congressional hearing that there was no linkage between events in the Horn and SALT. [206]

However, despite such categorical assertions, in reality the situation was much more complicated and, in practice, some elements of linkage could not be avoided. State Department spokesman Hodding Carter maintained that "as a matter of policy, there is no linkage," but it was inevitable that Soviet actions in the Horn were "going to have a spill over effect in Congress and in the nation as a whole."[207] President Carter told a news conference that the administration would never "initiate any linkage," but Soviet activities in the Horn might "lessen the confidence of the American people in the word and peaceful intentions of the Soviet Union, [and] would make it more difficult to ratify a SALT agreement or comprehensive test ban agreement if concluded, and therefore, the two are linked because of actions by the Soviets."[208] Even Vance accepted this fact. In a conversation with Averell Harriman, he acknowledged that "it would be very adverse to SALT if the Russians used the Cubans to drive the Somalis out by force."[209] At his news conference of February 10, 1978, Vance acknowledged that Soviet and Cuban involvement in the Horn "cannot help but have an effect upon the relationship between our two countries. It affects the political atmosphere between the United States and those two countries.... I am not suggesting any direct linkage, but I do suggest it affects the political atmosphere in which these discussions take place."[210]

Brzezinski was more blunt when considering the matter of linkage between Soviet activities in the Horn and other aspects of policy. At the SCC meeting of March 2, he asserted that "if there is an aggravation of tensions because of what the Soviets are doing in the Horn, there is going to be linkage. That is a statement of fact."[211] He also told the *Washington Post* that "if tensions were to rise because of the unwarranted intrusion of Soviet power" into the Ethiopian-Somali conflict, "that will inevitably complicate the process" of concluding a new strategic arms limitation talks (SALT) accord. This could affect "not only ... the negotiating process itself, but ... any ratification that would follow the successful conclusion of the (SALT) negotiations."[212] White House press secretary Jody Powell commented that Brzezinski "not only reflects the president's viewpoint, but reiterates simply a statement of the facts of life."[213] Indeed, on January 25, 1978, Carter sent a letter to Brezhnev arguing that Soviet involvement in the Horn "can only breed similar counter-reactions, with unavoidably negative effects on our bilateral relations."[214] In the presidential message sent to the heads of state in Sudan, Saudi Arabia, Iran and Egypt in January 1978, Carter stated that "we have again reminded the Soviets that if they persist in their intemperate actions in the Horn we will be forced to reduce efforts to work with them in other areas."[215]

The debates surrounding the deployment of a carrier task force to the Horn region also provided evidence of difference of opinions within the Carter administration. At the SCC meeting of February 21 the possibility was discussed, but the minutes noted that the "SCC was divided" over the issue.[216] Brzezinski argued that a task force should be sent because "it is important that regional powers not see the United States as passive in the face of Soviet and Cuban intervention in the Horn and in the potential invasion of Somalia — even if our support is, in the final analysis, only for the record."[217] However, Brzezinski met with united opposition; in his memoirs, Vance recalled, "every other member of the committee opposed the idea of deploying a carrier task force."[218] Brzezinski remembered that "Vance particularly was against any deployment of a carrier task force in the area of the Horn. For the first time in the course of our various meetings, he started to show impatience, to get red in the face, and to raise his voice. I could sense that personal tension was entering into our relationship."[219] In this matter, the majority of the SCC, supported by the president, held sway and the SCC meeting of March 2 noted that "an aircraft carrier will for the time being be kept in the area of Singapore."[220] For Brzezinski, this matter was a turning point in the life of the administration, as we shall see.

Ethiopia Retains the Ogaden

The way in which the Ogaden war officially came to an end bore out Henze's judgment that negotiations would not prove successful. At his news conference on March 9, President Carter announced, "last night, I was informed by President Siad Barré of Somalia that he was agreeing to withdraw his forces from the Ogaden area, the occupied areas of Ethiopia."[221] In fact, Siad had little choice in the matter; the might of Soviet and Cuban involvement on the side of Ethiopia in the Ogaden conflict had the inevitable result, and the "withdrawal" referred to by Siad was more like a rout. The Ethiopian ambassador to Kenya, Mengiste Desta, held a press conference and announced that the Somali troops were "being chased out from Ethiopian land by our troops." [222]

Jimmy Carter, of course, was delighted that peace appeared to be returning to the Horn of Africa; the president told his news conference that he welcomed Siad's announcement. [223] As well as ending the bloodshed, it appeared that the threat to the policy of regionalism had been reduced, and the administration's immediate post-war strategic plan once again proposed that Africans should take the lead. On March 10, the SCC agreed that the OAU should oversee the ceasefire arrangements,[224] and Carter expressed the "hope that the Organization of African Unity can move quickly to assist all parties to terminate hostilities, to agree quickly on rules that can be observed so that Somali forces can retire rapidly into their own territory and to ensure that peaceful conditions are restored among the civilian population."[225]

However, it was soon clear that the official Somali announcement of its withdrawal was not going to be the end of the problems in the Ogaden. A statement issued from Ethiopian embassies in Rome and London called for the Somali president to renounce all territorial claims, and pointed out that "the Ethiopian government considers that Somalia's offer to withdraw its forces in no way constitutes a permanent solution to the conflict between Ethiopia and Somalia, which has been going on for seventeen years."[226] A top-level official in Addis Ababa stated that "there is nothing to negotiate about the Ogaden. It is part of Ethiopia and there is nothing more to be said."[227] However, any student of the region would have realized that such capitulation from Siad Barré or the Somalis was unlikely; a solution had not yet been achieved for this "African problem," and the Carter administration would be faced with further complications in the Horn.

IV

Continuing Dilemmas
and Times of Transition

A Post-War Policy

As the Ogaden War drew to a close in March 1978, policy toward the Horn of Africa could once again be considered outside the framework of a crisis situation, and the emphasis returned to the priorities of January 1977. With the apparent end of the crisis, events in the Horn did not engage the attention of top-level U.S. officials to any great extent, such as the president, Brzezinski or Vance, but, at lower levels, members of the administration proceeded with efforts to implement the policy agenda previously set by Carter. These staffers continued to work towards improved relations with both Ethiopia and Somalia, and to aid the people of both countries by advancing human rights and related humanitarian concerns. Policy towards the Horn of Africa was not to be subordinated to the larger, East-West context, and although removing the influence of the communist bloc from the Horn region remained a goal, it was a long-term one. However, although these remained the proclaimed aims of the administration throughout 1978 and 1979, developments occurred during this period in both the United States and Africa that would ultimately subvert the declared objectives, and in 1980, a dramatic change in policy implementation would be effected.

Brzezinski and Vance

Perhaps the most obvious, and arguably the most significant, transition that occurred from March 1978 to December 1979 was the increasing dominance of the views and influence of Zbigniew Brzezinski. Despite reiterated official denials and statements, a tension between Brzezinski and Vance had existed since the earliest days of the administration;[1] Henze later claimed that Vance had "strongly opposed" Brzezinski's selection as national security adviser.[2] Handwritten notes by Vance, prepared for a meeting with Brzezinski in 1976, implied that he perceived the future national security adviser as a possible threat. Vance was determined that Brzezinski must recognize the primacy of the State Department in foreign policy, insisting that Brzezinski should "not see Ambassadors without my OK," that any input from Brzezinski on foreign policy matters should be discussed first with Vance, that all telegrams must be seen first by Vance, and that the National Security Council staff should not have access to the desk officer.[3] In the autobiographical *Hard Choices*, Vance recalled that he believed that it had been agreed that "only the president and his secretary of state were to have the responsibility for defining the administration's foreign policy." However, Vance wrote, "as time went on, there developed an increasingly serious breach of this understanding.... Brzezinski would attempt increasingly to take on the role of policy spokesman."[4]

The policy debate over issues pertinent to the Horn of Africa ultimately rested on the differences between the secretary of state and the national security adviser; Vance recollected in his memoirs that the debate over African policy was "essentially between Brzezinski and me." Vance believed that Brzezinski's view, that Soviet-Cuban actions should be a "major issue," was confrontational, and argued that:

> A policy of confrontation was not a winning strategy: Congress and the American people would not support direct U.S. military involvement (providing limited military aid to Zaire had been hard enough). By posing the issues in terms of an East-West controversy, we would be avoiding the underlying causes that produced these local conflicts.[5]

Underlying their differing perspectives, Brzezinski wrote in his memoirs:

> For Vance, the African matter was largely a local issue, and he was strongly backed by the State Department; I argued that the newly discovered Soviet-Cuban passion for the integrity of frontiers could hardly be analyzed in such narrow terms. Moreover, even if one allowed what seemed to me to be a preposterous notion, namely that the Soviets were acting out of some sort of strange territorial legalism, their presence so close to Saudi Arabia was bound to have strategic consequences, whatever the Soviet intent may have been.[6]

The relationship between Vance and Brzezinski prompted much media speculation. Indicative of much of the media coverage, *Newsweek* reported in February 1978 that "Russia's intervention in the Horn of Africa has provoked a major policy debate in Washington."[7] On March 3, Bernard Gwertzman, of the *New York Times*, commented that developments in the Horn of Africa demonstrated that:

> A perceptible difference has appeared between President Carter's foreign policy aides — Secretary of State Cyrus Vance and Zbigniew Brzezinski, the National Security Adviser — over the seriousness of the Soviet military role in Ethiopia and the extent to which it should be linked to the strategic arms negotiations.... The differences do not amount to what might be called a split, but they are being talked about openly.... Mr. Brzezinski has emphasized the Soviet Union's military role, its apparent lack of concern to American entreaties for slackening the buildup in Ethiopia, and the idea that the Russians may be testing American will in the Horn of Africa.... Mr. Vance believes that Mr. Brzezinski has gone too far in his comments, aides said.[8]

Although media commentary tended to focus on the conflict between Brzezinski and Vance, some noticed that the friction, rather than merely resulting from a personality clash between two Executive officials, appeared to reflect wider institutional divisions. In February 1978, David Ottaway of the *Washington Post* suggested that "a silent struggle is under way within the Carter administration between its global strategists and its 'Africanists' over how to respond to the growing Soviet-Cuban involvement in various conflicts throughout Africa, particularly in the trouble-ridden Horn." Ottaway reported that the Africanists, generally found in the State Department, were opposed by Brzezinski, who advocated a more globalist view, and led the way in "linking Cuban and Soviet activities in Africa to the larger issues of overall U.S.-Cuban and U.S.-Soviet relations."[9] There was also a degree of difference between Henze of the NSC and various members of the State Department with regards to the policy that each felt should be pursued in the Horn, as we shall see.

The First "Carter Doctrine"

An issue on which Brzezinski and Vance agreed was the inclusion of human rights as an important consideration in the formulation of foreign policy. In his State of the Union address of 1978, signaling the beginning of the second year of his four-year administration, Carter declared that "we are a confident nation. We've restored a moral basis for our foreign policy. The very heart of our identity as a nation is our firm commitment to human rights."[10] Indeed, Jimmy Carter's attempt to reorient foreign policy towards a moral basis, with its cornerstone of human rights, was dubbed by parts of the media during the early years of the administration as the "Carter Doctrine."[11] Why this definition of the Carter Doctrine did not persist is an interesting question, and one that will be discussed in the final chapter, because, in terms of public statements, this was the policy that the Carter administration publicly pursued for the majority of its term in office.

However, despite widespread agreement within the administration of the importance of human rights in general, designing and implementing specific policies proved to be much more contentious and problematic.[12] Taking the Universal Declaration of Human Rights as his model, Carter also defined human rights as: the right to be free of government violation of integrity of the person; economic and social rights; and civil and political liberties.[13] However, beyond this basic, and somewhat general, definition, there was a great deal of debate, both internally and externally, on the substantive content of these rights, whether all three of them must be respected to avoid sanctions, to what extent sanctions should be applied, and what other circumstances should be factored into the debate. Indeed, the administration faced allegations that it was applying double standards in its application of human rights policy, not all of which were unfounded. Notwithstanding, and despite the problems of application, there is little reason to believe that the president was insincere in his averred commitment; the administration continued to monitor human rights conditions worldwide, and was consequently aware that human rights problems persisted in Ethiopia. Not least of these was the violence, often government-sponsored, which pervaded the capital. On February 9, 1978, UPI correspondent Raymond Wilkenson, based in Addis Ababa, reported that he had "witnessed at first hand the grim wave of assassination and killings between pro- and anti-government forces," and advised that visitors to Ethiopia should not try to see the capital at night because of the terrorism, violence and "death on the streets."[14] John Darnton of the *New York Times* agreed that "the level of violence is worse than ever" in Addis Ababa.[15]

The repeated publicity surrounding the terrible conditions in Ethiopia caused a problem for the Carter administration in that it increased expectations for action, and stimulated domestic and international criticism of the administration if such action was seen to be lacking or ineffective. In addition to the ongoing problems with human rights, the continued presence of communist bloc countries in the Horn also aroused comment in the United States, thereby compounding public interest and anticipation. During his briefing for a visit to Mexico, Mondale was warned that "domestic pressures are also building on the Horn situation. Journalists and Congressmen are calling on the USG [United States Government] to do something."[16]

Henze, however, recommended that, rather than taking action to meet such criticism, the administration should instead downplay the situation in the Horn. In a memo to Brzezinski on January 12, 1978, Henze commented that:

> We have already put ourselves in the position of agitating about problems in the Horn but being seen as powerless to do much about them. The noise we make thus serves only to underscore our inability to have impact [*sic*] on the situation. By making noise we generate domestic and even foreign pressures for action that we may find difficult to cope with.[17]

Henze therefore recommended that "we should stop shouting" about the situation in the Horn, because "by condemning it we only underscore our inability to do anything to halt it or do much to limit it."[18] Instead, Henze proposed that the administration should seek to emphasize the positive aspects of policy towards the Horn, and stress that it was "rational — in terms of U.S. basic interests; moral — in the principles the U.S. stands for in the world; logical — we apply the same standards to all countries of the area; defensible — in terms of recognized international principles."[19] Henze's emphasis on the "moral" and "principle" aspects directly alluded to Carter's original approach, while his emphasis on the fact that the same standards were being applied to "all countries of the area" referred to the official administration policy that a regionalist, rather than an East-West dimension should direct policy; his sentence might have continued "regardless of the Soviet presence in Ethiopia." However, Henze's suggestions may well have reflected his pro–Ethiopian sympathies and his desire for a "soft" policy towards that country at best, as much as his attachment to the publicly proclaimed approach of the Carter administration.

Ethiopia and Eritrea

As the crisis in the Ogaden abated, the Carter administration was able to focus once again on long-term goals, including the desire to restore the position of influence that the United States had once enjoyed in Ethiopia, a policy that Henze was particularly keen on and active in promoting. The day after President Carter announced the official end of the Ogaden War, and the hope that peace and stability would return to the region, Henze proposed that, "using these statements as a starting point, we should orient our policy around the basic objective of getting the Russians and Cubans out (not necessarily this year or next) and restore/maintain our position and influence with the most significant and powerful countries in the region: Ethiopia, Kenya and the Sudan."[20]

The administration also continued with attempts to aid the Ethiopian people. The major areas of concern were the famine-hit areas of Wollo and

Tigre and the refugee problems in the Ogaden and Eritrea. One of the first measures pursued by the Carter administration after the Ogaden War was an attempt to secure multilateral humanitarian aid for the Ogaden,[21] and a State Department memo of March 7 recommended an increase in "humanitarian assistance to the thousands of Eritrean refugees who will flee the fighting in the area."[22] On May 23, Carter decreed that "$750,000 in funds appropriated under the United States Emergency Refugee and Migration Assistance Fund be made available for assistance" to refugees created "as a result of hostilities in the Horn of Africa."[23]

Indeed, although the conflict in the Ogaden appeared to have reached a conclusion, war in Ethiopia seemed unending. In the northern province of Eritrea secessionist groups continued to struggle for freedom as they had since 1962 when Eritrea lost its autonomous status and was officially incorporated into Ethiopia.[24] Keith Wauchope, the U.S. consul who had overseen the closure of the American base at Asmara and was now a member of the State Department, warned Richard Moose, assistant secretary of state for African affairs, that, following the conclusion of the Ogaden War, the "EPMG [Ethiopian Provisional Military Government] will inevitably turn the full weight of their military might on Eritrea."[25] Consequently Jimmy Carter told the Special Coordination Committee (SCC) meeting of March 10, 1978, that he wished "to have the Eritrean problem thoroughly examined" and policy options proposed.[26]

By the time the Carter administration came to power there were three main groups fighting for Eritrean independence. The details of the three groups were outlined in a State Department briefing prepared for a meeting of the SCC at the end of March. It described how, despite their common central goal, the three groups were riven by religious, ideological and personal differences. The largest of the three groups was the Eritrean Liberation Front (ELF), comprised of some six thousand troops led by Ahmed Mohamed Nasser. The ELF was predominantly Muslim, ideologically moderate, although with a minority radical element, and garnered support from conservative Arab countries, including Saudi Arabia. The Eritrean People's Liberation Front (EPLF), with some four thousand troops, was mainly Christian, although it had a minority of Muslims. It was a radical Marxist group, led by Isaias Afework, with a figurehead president, Ramadan Mohamed Nur, who attempted to gain the support of Muslim states. The third, and smallest of the groups, led by Osman Saleh Sabbe, was the Eritrean Liberation Front/Popular Liberation Front or ELF/PLF, with approximately two thousand troops. Ideologically the most conservative, this group was the most successful in gaining external Arab support, but had the least support within Eritrea.[27]

The ongoing conflict in Eritrea concerned members of the Carter administration, not only because of the suffering of any peoples beset by war but also because of larger regional implications. The Eritrean rebels had long received support from Arab nations; the State Department report claimed that Iraq, Syria, Iran, Egypt, Kuwait, Saudi Arabia, Morocco, North Yemen, and the Palestine Liberation Organization were all providing aid to the various rebel groups. In addition, Sudan, through which lay the main supply route to Eritrea, provided transshipment facilities and sanctuary.[28] Wauchope alerted Richard Moose to the possible dangers, asserting that a continuing military conflict would "further inflame the fears and concerns of the Arab nations in the region, and more particularly it will inevitably result in some form of hostile confrontation with Sudan."[29] Although somewhat more circumspect in tone, those attending the SCC meeting of March 27 also noted the wider ramifications of the insurgency, acknowledging that "as part of the attempt to pacify the Eritrean rebels the EPMG would be likely to establish control over much of the frontier with Sudan (the supply route to Eritrea)."[30]

As had happened in the Ogaden, the administration was therefore faced with a regional conflict, which potentially had larger implications; and, as with the Ogaden War, the Carter administration took the same stance of non-involvement, and cited the same reasons for doing so. The administration maintained support for the tenets of the OAU, which, according to the State Department report, did not "recognize the Eritrean liberation movements,"[31] and shared the official African view that to allow the Eritrean secessionist movement to succeed would violate the Cairo Resolution. In this aspect of policy, the views of the State Department advisers coincided with those from the NSC, providing further evidence for the argument that the "conflict" between Brzezinski and Vance, or the Department of State and the National Security Council, was not as clear-cut as the media often portrayed. Wauchope sent a memo to Moose arguing that the "U.S. can provide neither arms nor political support for the Eritreans without provoking charges of violating the principle of territorial integrity,"[32] and Henze commented to Brzezinski that "we [the United States] support Ethiopian territorial integrity, which includes Eritrea, and always have."[33] An interesting corollary to the support for territorial integrity is that this arguably represented the Domino Theory still alive and well in the 1970s, but now applied to Africa. In testimony before the House Subcommittee on Africa, Tom Farer alluded to the belief in this theory when he stated that "some enthusiasts for continued arms transfers to Ethiopia rest part of their case on the allegedly dangerous precedent of an Eritrean victory. It would, they insist, encourage latent secessionist movements throughout Africa. Countries would unravel at a terrible cost in blood and aborted development."[34]

Therefore, as with the war in the Ogaden, the Carter administration argued for the peaceful resolution of conflict through a negotiated settlement. In addition, pursuant to the commitment to regionalism, the administration continued to assert that African nations should take the lead in seeking solutions to the problems that beset their continent, with the United States providing only a supporting role. On March 7, Wauchope recommended that the administration should "encourage and support Nimeiri as president of the OAU and as a member in good standing of the Arab League to promote the formation of an Arab-African mediation group to seek a negotiated settlement," but did suggest that such a settlement should "give the Eritreans an acceptable degree of autonomy."[35] At a subsequent meeting of the SCC on March 27, those attending agreed that "the United States Government should take a public stand in favor of a negotiated solution and that we should continue to speak out against Soviet and Cuban support of an Ethiopian military solution."[36] When presented with these recommendations, Carter stated his desire that the administration "support a negotiated solution [even] more strongly."[37]

However, the divisions between the liberation groups posed a major problem for those who hoped to achieve a negotiated solution to the conflict in Eritrea; with no unified opposition, there was no one with whom the Ethiopian government could realistically negotiate. Wauchope commented on the extent of the division in a memo to Moose, pointing out that "even with doom staring them in the face (as when success seemed within their grasp), the two major Eritrean insurgent factions appear unable to unify their efforts or their forces against the Ethiopians."[38] The State Department briefing document issued to the members of the SCC pointed out that the "EPLF seems to have the strongest sense of Eritrean 'nationhood,' while the other two groups [ELF and PLF] seem more concerned with the preservation of traditional tribal authority," and commented that the divisions within the secessionist movements were prolonging the conflict by preventing victory over the government forces.[39] In addition to secessionist disunity complicating the prospects for negotiations, the Ethiopian government showed no inclination to solve the problem with any other than military means. The State Department briefing went on to acknowledge that "we see little prospect for a unified liberation movement negotiating front, and since Mengistu seems determined to solve the problem in terms of Ethiopian sovereignty, we believe that Ethiopia will step up the military pressure, and will campaign as long as necessary to bring the Eritreans to sue for peace on Ethiopian terms."[40]

The Eritrean insurgency was yet further complicated by the role and influence there of communist bloc countries. The extent of Cuban involvement, especially, raised many questions within the Carter administration, none of which, it seemed, could be satisfactorily answered. The State Department briefing paper argued that Castro's position was that "the dismemberment of Ethiopia would be 'intolerable.' Ethiopia, the USSR and Cuba are agreed that an independent Eritrea is out of the question,"[41] suggesting Cuban support for the Ethiopian government. However, when the House Subcommittee on Inter-American Affairs questioned John Bushnell, the deputy assistant secretary of state for inter-American affairs, in March 1978 about the extent of Cuban involvement on the side of the Eritreans, Bushnell acknowledged that the administration's information on the issue was incomplete but felt that "there has been Cuban artillery in the Eritrean area and some Cuban advisers.... The Cubans are involved with the support apparatus, supply and so forth."[42] Furthermore, in a meeting with Vance, Dobrynin denied any Soviet and Cuban direct involvement in the fighting in Eritrea, insisting that the "Soviets and Cubans did not intend to and preferred not to become involved in Eritrea."[43] Such incomplete and often contradictory information further complicated any chances of seeking a peaceful resolution for this conflict.

Somalia, Siad and Ethiopian Implications

The desire to establish better relations with Somalia remained one of the major long-term objectives for the Carter administration. It may have appeared that the reasons behind the determination to normalize relations with Somalia reflected traditional Cold War tactics: if a country was not friends with the Soviet Union, as Siad Barré had clearly demonstrated in November 1977, then it deserved American support, regardless of the ideology of its leadership or the nature of the governing regime. Indeed, it might be thought that there was no other reason for the Carter administration to provide support for the Somali president. Henze reflected a prevalent view within the administration when he told Brzezinski on March 16 that Siad "makes a poor hero by any standards acceptable in the West. He continues to engage in devious maneuvers."[44] Two weeks later, Henze further commented to Brzezinski that "Siad is a narrow, vain, intense, suspicious man. He has led his country into catastrophe. His limitations as a statesman include a lack of capacity to envision a goal for Somalia different from the one he has been pursuing.... Siad has nothing to offer his people but demands for more planes, tanks and artillery. He would go on keeping Somalia hopelessly at odds with all their neighbors."[45]

Why, then, following the conclusion of the Ogaden War, did the Carter administration reinstitute the policy of early 1977 to "get Somalia to be our friend"? In understanding this persistence, it is important to remember two elements of the administration's approach: the desire to apply long-term policies to countries regardless of their current leader or political orientation, and the determination to aid the cause of human rights.[46] The administration therefore resolved, as Henze put it to Brzezinski on March 10, to "avoid regarding Somalia and Siad as identical,"[47] and to pursue the goal of aiding the Somali people with economic and humanitarian aid. Henze asserted that "by persisting in humanitarian and economic aid efforts, we demonstrate a commitment to improving the well-being of the Somali people,"[48] and the SCC meeting of March 16 agreed that the United States should "seek to secure multilateral humanitarian assistance for the Ogaden and Somalia."[49] However, the administration's efforts were hampered by Siad's lack of cooperation. Henze reported to Brzezinski at the end of March that the Somali leader seemed to feel "little urgency about aid for refugees. It was impossible to get an accurate picture of the scope of the refugee problem."[50]

Siad Barré did feel urgency with respect to the issue of military aid, though. Although the Carter administration had offered him arms in principle in the summer of 1977, this offer had been rescinded as soon as the extent of the Ogaden incursion became clear. Throughout the war, the administration had repeatedly told Siad, who had continued to clamor for American support, that such aid could not be provided while Somalis remained in the Ogaden. However, with the official withdrawal of Somali troops from Ethiopia — and the end of the diplomatic complications that the war had entailed — it appeared that the administration could once again endeavor to pursue its policy ideas of early 1977, and resume its consideration of a military aid package as part of its attempts to forge a relationship with Somalia.

During March 1978 the topic dominated meetings on the Horn of Africa. The biggest support for the idea of military aid appeared to come from the State Department, where the assumption seemed to be that American credibility was at stake, and that the administration should carry out its pledge to provide defensive arms now that the American-imposed condition, of Somali withdrawal from the Ogaden, had been met. Henze reported to Brzezinski on a meeting he had attended at the Department of State in which Anthony Lake pointed out that "we have promised to try to get arms for Siad; we have to live up to that commitment and the Saudis expect us to. I don't care if Congress turns us down — we have to ask for it to show that we live up to commitments. If Congress doesn't like it and rejects it, I want the administration's position to be clear." Henze, however, criticized the State Department for this example of "inept political thinking," and commented to Brzezinski that "the last thing this administration needs now is to get itself rebuffed by Congress on a proposal of doubtful validity and efficacy."[51] On

March 16, Henze sent Brzezinski a memo insisting that there was "deep-seated and widespread Congressional opposition to arms programs."[52]

Henze also appeared disturbed by what he described as the State Department's "tendency to tilt toward Somalia — the idea that we should praise and reward Siad for withdrawing from the Ogaden."[53] As we have seen, Henze was no supporter of the Somali leader, and his perceived pro–Ethiopian bias occasionally drew comment from his colleagues in the administration.[54] On March 16, he now warned that the United States was in danger of "rushing into actions re Somalia which we may not only regret but which will complicate our policy in months ahead," and pleaded that the administration not provide military aid to Siad "until we have surveyed what Somalia's real defensive needs are."[55] However, demonstrating the apparent difference between Henze's views on policy and those of members of the State Department, Vance argued that military aid to Siad was important to achieve American long-term objectives in Somalia, promoting a non-aligned country and preserving the stability of the region. He contended that military aid to Siad was necessary "to consolidate our political position with Siad and Somalia; to restrain Somali irredentism; [and] to prohibit the Soviets from restoring their influence in Somalia."[56] This invocation of the Cold War by Vance, and Lake's intimation that American credibility should take priority over the possible humanitarian concerns related to the provision of military aid, also offers further evidence that the apparent split between Vance and the State Department, and Brzezinski and the NSC, was much more complex than is often suggested.

Notwithstanding Henze's objections, and after much internal debate, it was decided to inform Siad that the administration was "prepared to help meet his legitimate defense needs" with defensive equipment such as anti-tank weapons and ground surveillance radar. However, the members of the SCC also agreed that neither aircraft nor tanks would be provided, and "no offer of a specific military package would be made" until an American military survey team visited Somalia to ascertain Siad's needs.[57] Subsequently, Hodding Carter, the State Department spokesman, told the *Washington Post* that the administration was consulting with Congress with regard to the possibility of providing Somalia with defensive military equipment.[58] The Carter administration also continued its commitment to the ideal of global community by endeavoring to gain multilateral military aid for Somalia. The SCC meeting of March 16 concluded that the administration should "encourage the Arabs, Iranians and Europeans to provide defensive equipment to the Somalis."[59] More specifically, following a further SCC meeting two weeks later, it was decided to "talk to the Egyptians and possibly the Jordanians about supplying Siad with air-defense weapons."[60]

However, perhaps mindful of Henze's concerns, once again military aid was offered to Siad "in principle." In particular, the administration took pains to make it clear that any military aid to Somalia would only be provided once the government there had given definite guarantees to honor the principle of territorial integrity. At a news conference on March 16, President Carter insisted that the provision of American military aid would require "a renewed commitment [from Siad] not to dishonor the international boundaries of either Ethiopia or Kenya."[61] Henze later commented to Brzezinski that "the president showed a keen sense of both morality and practical politics when he answered the question about arms for Siad last week by setting a firm condition for Somalia to respect its neighbors' territorial integrity."[62]

An important step in the administration's attempt to establish better relations with Somalia was an official visit by Richard Moose, the assistant secretary of state, to Somalia. It should be noted, however, that the importance of Ethiopia in the Horn, and the desire to improve the relationship with Mengistu, remained uppermost. During the SCC meeting of March 16 it was agreed to "inform the Ethiopians immediately about Moose's mission and the purpose of the trip," to prevent any misunderstandings that might hamper the relationship between Ethiopia and the United States. Those present at the meeting also conferred upon the issues that Moose would discuss with Siad Barré, and the levels of aid that the administration was willing to provide. They decided that Moose should make it clear to Siad that conditions were attached to any military aid that the United States might supply, most prominently a guarantee that Somalia would abandon all territorial claims on Ethiopia, Kenya and Djibouti, and refrain from support for guerrilla movements or destabilization efforts in any of these countries.[63]

Richard Moose met with Siad Barré towards the end of March 1978 and the two undertook twelve hours of talks spread over six days, leading to, in Moose's opinion, "a new and positive phase" in relations between the United States and Somalia.[64] When he returned to the United States, Moose reported back to the SCC, and told them that, although Siad had "moved Somalia significantly toward the commitment we want," problems remained, mainly to do with the type of aid in which Siad was interested. Although Moose had offered Siad a package of "non-lethal military aid" worth some $10 million (for example, supply trucks and radar equipment), Siad had shown little interest in this, or in a visit by a military survey team.[65] Instead, Moose reported, "Siad left us with no doubt about the kind of American military support he really wants: tanks, airplanes and artillery."[66]

Following Moose's report of his meeting with Siad Barré, the administration held further discussions regarding subsequent policy to Somalia. The Moose mission was apparently perceived as a positive step in the improvement of relations and the SCC meeting of March 27, after hearing Moose's report, agreed to make "a further effort to develop a defensive military support relationship with Siad." Although it was decided to press ahead with the idea of sending "at least a small military presence to assess Somalia's immediate defensive needs,"[67] an air of caution nonetheless remained. The minutes of the SCC noted that "the letter Siad had given to Mr. Moose was not an adequate guarantee of Somalia's acceptance of limitations on use of military aid that might be provided," and in order to progress a supply relationship with Somalia the administration would therefore request a "more binding letter from Siad which clearly commits the Somali government to our conditions."[68]

Indeed, despite Siad's official announcement of March 9 that all Somali troops would be withdrawn from the Ogaden, the Carter administration received information suggesting that this was not the case. During a meeting with Vance on March 16, for example, Dobrynin insisted that Siad continued to support the irregular forces that remained in Ethiopia.[69] While, on their own, such claims from Soviet sources might have been perceived as an attempt to justify a continuing presence in Ethiopia, and therefore lacked credibility, the administration had further evidence that supported Dobrynin's assertion. A CIA report of April 18 confirmed that "the Somalis are stepping up their support for the guerrillas, are trying to improve their communications with them and that they are passing arms and materiel to them."[70]

Such a breach of trust from Siad in itself could have provided grounds to withhold military aid, but Henze suggested a further reason for caution. He sent a note to Brzezinski expressing his concerns about the increasing evidence of Somali activity in the Ogaden because of the potential uses for American military equipment. Henze pointed out that although the aid that the administration was considering sending was suitable for defense "if kept in Somalia's own territory," it was also "exactly the kinds of things of which guerrillas could make good use: mines, communications equipment, tents, field rations, etc." This possibility that American support could cause the situation in the Ogaden to further deteriorate, Henze warned Brzezinski, "has most serious implications for our efforts to provide defensive military assistance to the Somalis."[71]

A further complication with regard to the administration's consideration of military aid to Somalia was the way in which such a policy might impede efforts to improve relations with Ethiopia. Although a long-term objective, the hope remained that relations with Ethiopia would once again achieve the levels of 1953 to 1974, with the Soviet Union out of this main Horn country and the United States re-established. However, at the end of March, Henze warned Brzezinski that "any military aid we give to Siad makes it easier for the Russians and Cubans to justify their continued presence in Ethiopia and pushes the Ethiopians into dependence on them." He also pointed out that the "mere fact of our mission to Somalia may further delay Ethiopian acceptance of our Ambassador."[72] In April a meeting of the SCC discussed "what appears to be a downturn in our relations with the Ethiopian government." The meeting supported Vance's opinion that "for the immediate future we should avoid aggravating actions deriving from human rights complaints and compensation for nationalized property so as to keep open the possibility of an aid program and acceptance of an ambassador."[73]

The deprioritization of human rights in administration policy towards the Horn was evidence of the complicated nature of policy discussions during 1978 and 1979, but it should be noted that the human rights policy had not been completely abandoned. The emphasis appeared to have switched, however, from protesting governmental abuse of its citizens to providing humanitarian programs; a reorientation made possible by the ambiguity over the definition of human rights. Henze recommended that the administration "should continue to try to involve ourselves in humanitarian programs in the Ogaden and drought relief efforts in Wollo,"[74] although the main area of humanitarian concern was Eritrea and the ongoing guerrilla struggle there.

On humanitarian grounds then, as well as for the political reasons previously discussed, the administration continued to support the idea of a negotiated solution to the Eritrean insurgency. On April 7, the SCC decided that there would be "periodic statements by U.S. government spokesmen expressing concern for continued bloodshed in Eritrea and hope that Africans might exert themselves to bring about a negotiated solution." In addition, the administration would consult "Egyptians, Saudis and Sudanese on their support for the Eritrean insurgents and their perceptions of how negotiations can be encouraged."[75] During a visit to London in April, Vance reiterated that "the United States strongly supports the territorial integrity of all states in the region, including particularly Ethiopia, Djibouti, Somalia, and Kenya,"[76] and announced that "we seek the withdrawal of all foreign forces from Ethiopia and a peaceful resolution of the Eritrean dispute. It is clear to us that if the Eritrean issue is determined through the use of force by foreign troops, bloodshed and suffering will increase, no enduring solution will be found, and tensions in the region will only be heightened."[77]

The presence, or otherwise, of communist bloc forces in Eritrea provided the main topic for debate throughout April. On April 1, a White House official told the *Washington Post* that the administration believed that "Cuban troops are now fighting in Ethiopia against secessionist forces in the province of Eritrea."[78] In a memo to Brzezinski, Henze conversely suggested that there was no Cuban involvement as yet when he argued that "even with all the manpower and equipment they are concentrating in Eritrea, the Ethiopians are not likely to have an easy time. Where they falter badly, the Cubans will probably be compelled to come to their aid."[79] Perhaps unfortunately for the image of the Carter administration within the United States, the debate and confusion within its ranks over the extent of Cuban involvement in Eritrea was apparent. In April, Murray Marder, a staff writer for the *Washington Post*, commented that "the State Department spokesman was saying that there was 'no evidence that Cuban forces were engaged in Eritrea,' while the White House were saying just the opposite [*sic*]. No one offered to clarify the discrepancy, although the State Department spokesman inevitably deferred to the higher authority."[80]

Neither was the Carter administration's image helped by the domestic criticism of its acceptance of the continued presence of Soviet and Cuban forces in Ethiopia, and the perception that this represented American weakness in the face of Soviet aggression. Although in April 1978 Vance gave an interview to *Time* magazine in which he remarked that he did not believe that the Soviet Union was "deliberately trying to test the president,"[81] there was evidence that American public opinion was not totally convinced by the State Department line. On April 17 the *Washington Post* reported the results of a "Harris Survey" conducted on the communist bloc presence in the Horn of Africa, and the appropriate level of American response. The results reflected an interesting mix of the Vietnam Syndrome and traditional Cold War fears, with seventy-six percent agreeing that "once we get involved with military aid and advisers in Africa, we will soon find we are getting in too deep as we did in Vietnam." However, the survey also suggested that "there are real signs that Americans are increasingly worried about stepped up Cuban and Soviet military activity in Africa: ... [by] fifty to twenty-four percent ... [they feel] that unless the United States takes the lead in telling the Russians and Cubans they can't take over these countries, Africa will be taken over by communists."[82]

On Capitol Hill, Senator Bob Dole (R-Kan) commented on the issue and warned that the SALT negotiations were under threat "unless aggressive Soviet-Cuban military adventurism in Africa is halted." He declared:

> According to the latest intelligence estimates, Ethiopia has been saturated with more than sixteen thousand Cuban troops, and with Soviet military hardware including fifty MiG jet fighters and more than four hundred tanks. There is no way imaginable that the U.S. Senate could ignore this Soviet military presence in Africa in the context of our consideration of SALT II. Not only are the peaceful intentions of the Kremlin called into question by its aggressive African policies, but the credibility of Soviet pledges are cast into serious doubt as well.[83]

In May, Senator Barry Goldwater (R-Ariz) criticized the Carter administration for its policy towards the Horn, arguing that unless those in the administration "wake up, the African continent is going to be a communist enclave."[84] A week later Representative Robert Sikes (D-Fla) agreed, criticizing the administration for its "lack of a positive program to deal with Russian and Cuban activities on the continent of Africa," and arguing that policy towards Africa had "a very important bearing on America's future and that of the free world." He went on to insist:

> The sands of time are running out for the West in Africa. The Soviets and the Cubans have succeeded in installing Marxist governments in one nation after another. As many as 45,000 to 50,000 Cubans in sixteen countries do the bidding of Russia in these endeavors. Their major objectives are the Horn of Africa and the Cape. Control of these strategic locations would allow them to dominate shipping lanes where much of the world's oil and minerals must travel. Both oil and minerals are essential to the West. While the Russians are reaching for these goals, they continue to take advantage of opportunities to advance Marxism in other countries.[85]

The same month the Carter administration was faced with open criticism when thirty-six of the Senate's thirty-eight Republicans issued a statement which claimed that "in fifteen short months of incoherence, inconsistency and ineptitude our foreign policy and national security objectives are confused and we are being challenged around the globe by Soviet arrogance." The declaration cited Soviet military assistance to Angola and Ethiopia, and charged that the administration was "unwilling or unable to recognize or acknowledge that the Soviets and Cubans will continue to exploit situations of opportunity in Africa." It argued that the Soviet presence in the Horn of Africa "creates a pincer movement around our vital sources of Middle East oil and threatens the sea lanes through which supplies are routed."[86] As the campaign season for the mid-term elections approached, Republican criticism of the administration continued. Virginia governor John Dalton announced his intention in August 1978 to "send the message, all over this state that the Carter administration is soft on communism."[87]

More Violence in the Horn: Somali Coup and Eritrean War

Although, as discussed previously, the Carter administration apparently was unwilling to sponsor a coup against the Siad regime, others were not so reticent. The main development to take place in Somalia following the Ogaden War occurred on April 9 when the government-run radio station announced that "a few rebel officers and enlisted men" had attempted a coup against the government, but were quickly subdued by loyal members of the armed forces.[88] Although the official broadcast claimed that the coup had been influenced by foreign powers, the CIA review of the matter claimed that displeasure over Siad's failed attempt to annex the Ogaden lay at the cause. The report argued:

> Siad may have provided the catalyst for the abortive coup attempt of 9 April when he ordered the arrest and executions of a large number of officers who fought in the Ogaden campaign.... The leaders of the 9 April coup, the most important of whom were field grade officers and veteran Ogaden troop commanders, came from these very same clan elements: they were motivated at least as much by long-standing ethnic animosities toward Siad as by disenchantment with Siad in the aftermath of the Ogaden debacle, although they clearly hoped to capitalize on broader anti–Siad feeling. There is no evidence that Soviets or pro–Soviet Somali elements were involved in this coup attempt, but the logic of the situation, as well as open Cuban broadcasts, argues that the Soviets and Cubans are working to overthrow Siad.[89]

The administration, which noted the coup attempt but made no comment either officially or unofficially, continued to focus on its long-term policy aims towards Somalia. In May, Les Denend of the State Department wrote to Brzezinski, warning that they were nearing "the point where it will soon be our turn to demonstrate just what we mean by increasing cooperation with Somalia."[90] However, at the SCC meeting ten days later it was agreed "that we should move cautiously in establishing a military supply relationship with Siad in view of reports of renewed support for Ogaden separatism."[91] One problem, as Henze had already pointed out, and Denend now agreed, was that the types of defensive weapons requested by Siad were "perfect for insurgent operations."[92]

Some of the concerns appeared to be allayed when the administration received the guarantee from Siad that it had been seeking stating that he would honor Ethiopia's national integrity. Vance appeared before the Senate Subcommittee on African Affairs on May 12, and informed them of Siad's assurances that "he would respect the internationally recognized borders of his neighbors as a precondition for any U.S. military assistance."[93] However, although both Vance and Brzezinski agreed that a military survey team could now be sent to Somalia to assess Siad's needs, they also shared the opinion that the United States should not rush into a military supply relationship with Somalia. The minutes of the SCC meeting of May 15 noted that "Secretary Vance and Dr. Brzezinski felt that we should send the military survey team ... [but] the DOD [Department of Defense] recommendation to limit the survey team to discussion of communications, transportation items and light anti-tank weapons was accepted."[94]

However, any optimism, albeit cautious, felt within the administration was soon under threat. Virtually concurrent with Siad's pledge, the CIA provided an assessment which asserted that "there is a growing body of evidence that the Somalis are stepping up their support for the insurgents and are re-establishing the close command and support relationships that existed prior to the Somali evacuation of the Ogaden. Moreover, over the past few weeks, insurgent activity in the Ogaden has again begun to look as if it is an organized campaign rather than a series of isolated attacks." The report also suggested that a "Somali general has taken command of guerrilla operations.... and some arms and material support is being provided by Somalia to the insurgents, but this is limited by shortages in the Somali units themselves."[95] Towards the end of May, Henze further reported to Brzezinski that intelligence believed "that camps and staging areas have been established inside Somali territory, [and] that regular Somali officers are assigned to some guerrilla camps."[96]

Although the prospect of continued fighting in the Ogaden was undoubtedly serious, the Carter administration might have gained some comfort from the fact that, at this stage in the conflict, only Africans appeared to be involved in this region. In Eritrea, however, the administration argued that the situation was worsened by outside involvement from the communist bloc. A long-term aim of the Carter administration remained the removal of outside influence from Africa, and it directed its diplomatic efforts towards this endeavor. At a question and answer session with editors and news directors in May 1978, the president declared that the policy of the administration was to "point out that the military presence of the Cubans in Africa is inimicable to peaceful progress and is an unwarranted intrusion."[97] In a meeting with the Soviet foreign minister, Andrei Gromyko, on May 27 Carter expressed the hope that the dispute in Eritrea "could be resolved without Soviet or Cuban presence or involvement."[98] Meanwhile, in an interview for *Meet the Press* Brzezinski asserted:

> It seems to me essential for everyone to understand that in this day and age the intrusion of foreign military power to determine the outcome of specific and particular African conflicts is intolerable to international peace and is an insult to the Africans themselves. The Africans are intelligent and mature people. They have international organizations of their own. It seems to me that African problems ought to be solved by the Africans themselves and not by 40,000 Cuban troops armed and delivered by the Soviet Union.[99]

The conflict, the administration argued, should be brought to an end by African-sponsored negotiations, rather than external military force. Vance told the Subcommittee on African Affairs that, "insofar as Eritrea is concerned, as I indicated in my statement, we feel that that is a situation where there must be a negotiated solution, and we are urging that the OAU play a more active role in trying to bring about a negotiated solution."[100] Also in May, Hodding Carter told the *Washington Post* that "we [the administration] deplore the continuing, serious bloodshed. We are prepared to accept any solution mutually agreed to by the Ethiopians and the Eritreans."[101]

However, there remained a great deal of confusion over the extent of communist bloc involvement in Eritrea. For example, during a speech in May 1978, Mengistu claimed that "friends" of Ethiopia, which included the USSR, Cuba, South Yemen and East Germany, "are living with us, dying with us, and fighting with us, standing by the side of the broad masses of Ethiopia and their revolution after having traveled several thousand miles."[102] However evidence at this time began to suggest that, while Cuban troops remained in Ethiopia, they were playing no direct role in the fighting taking place in Eritrea. The SCC meeting of May 15 noted that there was "no evidence to date of Cuban participation in combat activities in Eritrea, although they are doing some planning."[103] When Gromyko met Carter in May, he was adamant that "there was not a single Cuban soldier fighting in Eritrea today."[104]

Castro's longstanding support for the various secessionist movements in Eritrea perhaps explains the reluctance of Cuba to involve itself in the fight against the insurgents. Although the Soviet Union had also provided support for the Eritrean guerrillas during the years before the Ethiopian revolution, the USSR then chose to prioritize its relationship with the Derg above that with the guerrillas, and Castro's refusal to do the same caused some displeasure in Addis Abba. At the end of May the *Washington Post* carried reports that relations between Ethiopia and Cuba had become so strained that the Cuban ambassador had left Addis Ababa, apparently because of a "falling out with the government on political and military issues."[105] A subsequent report noted that diplomatic sources in Addis Ababa attributed the departure to "Cuban reluctance to commit any of its 17,000 troops in Ethiopia to a current offensive against the rebels who have won control of most of northern Eritrea Province."[106]

A Summer of Conflict

The summer of 1978 saw the resurgence of media interest in the conflict between the secretary of state and the national security adviser. In June 1978, the deputy editor of *Newsweek*, Joseph Fromm, produced an article describing the "Tug of War Over Foreign Policy" in the Carter administration. Fromm argued that on one side was Zbigniew Brzezinski, who was "pushing for a tough response that could possibly involve the use of U.S. military forces in Africa. On the other side: Secretary of State Cyrus Vance. He maintains that nothing is more important that the signing of a 'sound' strategic-arms-limitation treaty with Moscow."[107] The article also commented upon the differences between the staff of the principals, thereby highlighting again the complexities of the inter-departmental relationships. The State Department was described as "dominated by professional arms controllers who were traumatized by the Vietnam experience," and accused of being "soft in dealing with Russia." Meanwhile a State Department official described the members of the National Security Council as "the weakest NSC staff in my memory," while another alleged that "staff work at the NSC is a shambles."[108] On June 20, Dan Oberdorfer of the *Washington Post* alluded to the inter-departmental differences when he commented that the statement given by Vance to the House International Relations Committee was "hard to square ... with tough, anti–Soviet declarations by presidential assistant Zbigniew Brzezinski."[109] In August, the *Washington Post* carried a report of a breakfast meeting in which it claimed:

> President Carter injected himself into the rivalry between Secretary of State Cyrus R Vance and White House national security affairs adviser Zbigniew Brzezinski, pointedly instructing his top officials that he wanted Vance to be his chief foreign policy spokesman. The president's action came after Vance had privately expressed his concern to Carter that recent public policy statements by Brzezinski were undercutting his ability to function effectively, according to informed sources.[110]

Although there undoubtedly was an element of truth to the stories regarding inter-departmental strife, as with many media stories, there was also a degree of exaggeration and overstatement.[111] The administration appeared more concerned with developments in the Ogaden than it was with addressing the speculation regarding its interpersonal relationships. The Somali government insisted that it was honoring Siad's pledge to stay out of the Ogaden region of Ethiopia. Indeed, Mohammed Warsama, the Somali ambassador to the United Nations, wrote to the *New York Times* in June insisting that "the allegations that there are Somali regular forces in Ogaden is absolutely baseless. They are profoundly astonishing in that they contradict the true fact and logic."[112] Notwithstanding, the administration continued to receive evidence of ongoing Somali-sponsored activity in the Ogaden. In June, Henze informed Brzezinski that "guerrilla activity in the Ogaden is again approaching the level of intensity that prevailed last year at this time," and went on to warn that "the CIA intelligence assessment is that Somali-supported guerrilla operations in the Ogaden are accelerating."[113] In addition to intelligence reports, there was also evidence of Somali activity in the Ogaden from more overt sources. David Lamb, reporter for the *Los Angeles Times* based in Mogadishu, stated that in Somalia "the national obsession to reunite all Somalis under a single flag burns as passionately as ever." A Somali civil servant told Lamb that "my children will be fighting the Abyssinians (Ethiopians) if that's what it takes to unite our people and our land. We will attack again and again, and we will fight for a thousand years even if a generation of Somalis must die." Lamb pointed out that the Somali government continued to support the Ogaden guerrillas, and quoted Omar Arteh Ghalib, a top adviser to Siad Barré, who insisted that "we have a moral obligation to support our brothers."[114] A Western diplomat in the Horn told Michael Kaufman, a *New York Times* reporter based in Nairobi, that Somali regular forces were once again in the Ogaden. The diplomat claimed that, "after the withdrawal, some of the soldiers shed their uniforms and put on desert robes and switched tactics," and added that "we believe they are getting the full support of the Mogadishu regime."[115]

The continued conflict in the Ogaden impacted on policy towards Somalia in a major way. As Henze took the opportunity of pointing out to Brzezinski in June, "if we stick to the principles the president enunciated in March, we cannot give arms to Somalia in face of hard and mounting evidence that Siad is increasing support for Ogaden guerrillas and willfully deceiving us."[116] Consequently, on June 3, a telegram was forwarded to Mogadishu insisting that "for fundamental policy reasons, the USG cannot enter into a military relationship with a state which is seen as involved in expansionist military adventures outside its own borders. As a practical matter, the Congress could not be expected to approve any military supply to Somalia as long as Somalia is involved in the Ogaden."[117]

However, public announcements made by members of the administration gave little or no sign of the extent of concern. On June 8 Hodding Carter, the State Department spokesman, told the *New York Times* that the administration had "no credible evidence that regular Somali forces have re-entered Ethiopia to support ethnic Somali guerrillas in the Ogaden region." But Hodding Carter went on to stress that the administration was "of course, watching the situation closely," and would withhold military aid if evidence should be forthcoming.[118] At the same time administration officials told the *New York Times* that an offer of military aid to Somalia had been made because they were satisfied that all Somali troops had been withdrawn from the Ogaden.[119] Subsequently, it was announced that the United States would shortly be sending a military survey team to Somalia as the first step "toward the supply of about $15 million in 'defensive' arms to that country."[120]

Arguably, one reason for the administration's efforts to press ahead with a military relationship with Somalia, despite evidence from the Ogaden, was its belief in the strategic importance of this region of Africa. On July 27, 1978, Henze sent a memo to Brzezinski pointing out that "the Horn remains an important area. Its proximity to the Arabian Peninsula, to the 'soft underbelly' of Asia and its relationship to the Indian Ocean, all contribute to its strategic significance. Africa and the Middle East meet here."[121] However, Henze stressed to Brzezinski that, despite the desire to develop better relations with Somalia, relations with Ethiopia should remain the priority of the administration, arguing that, "ranked in order of intrinsic importance (population, resources, strategic significance), Ethiopia remains the most important country in the Horn.... We should aim to reassert ourselves [there]." [122]

Indeed, there appeared to be more reason for optimism with regard to the improvement of the relationship with Ethiopia following developments in the spring and summer of 1978. One of the most telling signs that relations were becoming better was the decision of the Carter administration to send, and Mengistu's acceptance of, an American Ambassador to Addis Ababa. On May 31, 1978, Carter announced the nomination of a professional diplomat, Frederic L Chapin, as Ambassador to Ethiopia,[123] and on June 20 the Senate confirmed his nomination. The next day Henze remarked to Brzezinski that "Fred has prepared himself very carefully for his Ethiopian assignments. It is not going to be easy — but he seems to relish it. I can't think of many more difficult jobs in the foreign service than the one he is taking on."[124] Indeed, it appeared that the administration had high hopes that the arrival of a diplomat at the level of Ambassador would greatly help relations between Washington and Addis Ababa. Henze wrote to a friend of his, Professor Edward Ullendorff at Oxford University, commenting, "you have probably read that Mengistu has agreed to accept an ambassador from us. We ... hope, once he is in place, that our relations can return to a level of 'normalcy' where we at least have an established and recognized channel of regular communication with the Ethiopian government."[125]

One of the first actions of Ambassador Chapin was to recommend that the administration remain very cautious in its policy toward Somalia to ensure that this would not affect the chances of improving relations with Ethiopia. In June 1978, Henze sent a memo to Brzezinski arguing that "our ultimate aim in the Horn should be to get the Soviets out of Ethiopia [and] re-establish our own position there."[126] The same month Chapin attended a policy meeting of the SCC; the minutes noted that he expressed "a strong preference for a go-slow approach to the Somali survey team and on military aid to Somalia in general because he would like to have the opportunity, on arrival in Addis Ababa early next month, to start out his relationship with the Ethiopians unburdened by moves which the Ethiopians would interpret as a new U.S. tilt toward Somalia."[127] Chapin's concerns carried weight, and the Department of Defense decided that the military survey team's departure for Somalia would be postponed from the proposed date of June 15 until at least mid–July.[128]

The issue of military aid to Somalia provides us with further insight into the problems that existed between members of the NSC and State Department other than Brzezinski and Vance. On June 8, Henze sent a memo to Brzezinski in which he claimed that it was "some elements in State" that were the main advocates of rushing the survey team to Somalia, despite Chapin's objections.[129] In a second memo, Henze expressed his "disappointment" that the State Department had apparently inspired a story that appeared in the *Washington Post* reporting that the United States was already providing Somalia with arms, and claimed that "a clique in State and the Pentagon who are opposed to practically everything else you stand for persists in trying to demonstrate a dubious toughness and concern about Soviet actions in Africa by trying to justify shipping arms to Siad."[130]

Despite any such recommendations emanating from the State Department, in July the administration decided again to delay the visit of the military survey team to Somalia for at least two more weeks, because of the increase of Somali activity in the Ogaden.[131] On July 27, Henze informed Brzezinski that the latest intelligence from the region demonstrated that:

> Commitments and promises notwithstanding, Siad has consciously developed and expanded his support for Ogaden guerrillas since last March.... During recent weeks Siad has become bolder in his public commitment to the Ogaden guerrillas (e.g. at the Khartoum OAU summit) and all available intelligence indicates that he fully intends to continue support for them, employing various forms of prevarication and sophistry to confuse the United States and its friends.[132]

The briefing notes for the Policy Review Committee meeting of July 31 pointed out that "a high level of insurgent activity has in the meantime resumed in the Ogaden,"[133] and consequently the meeting reached the unanimous conclusion that "a military survey team should not be sent to Somalia at the present time, that it should not be regarded as ruled out for the future but that no date for sending it should be scheduled. The Somalis will be told that we cannot send it now because of their continued support for Ogaden guerrilla activity."[134]

Part of the reluctance in providing military aid to Somalia came, then, because of the fear that the conflict in the Ogaden would once again escalate to the level of all-out war; part came because of the administration's concerns over the possible Ethiopian reaction. The acceptance of an American ambassador by Mengistu suggested an improvement in relations between Ethiopia and the United States, but despite this apparently positive step, the Soviet and Cuban presence in Ethiopia remained as strong as ever, notwithstanding the repeated calls from the administration for the removal of external influences from Africa. In his speech before the graduating class at the U.S. Naval Academy in Annapolis on June 7, 1978, Carter declared:

In Africa we and our African friends want to see a continent that is free of the dominance of outside powers, free of the bitterness of racial injustice, free of conflict and free of the burdens of poverty and hunger and disease. We are convinced that the best way to work toward these objectives is through affirmative policies that recognize African realities and that recognize African aspirations. The persistent and increasing military involvement of the Soviet Union and Cuba in Africa could deny this hopeful vision. We are deeply concerned about the threat to regional peace and to the autonomy of countries within which these foreign troops seem permanently to be stationed.[135]

At his news conference on June 14, Carter again insisted that "it's time for the Cuban troops to withdraw from Ethiopia. Ethiopia has been heavily armed now by the rapid intrusion of Soviet weapons to them after Somalia did attack in the Ogaden area. I think Ethiopia is perfectly capable of defending themselves [*sic*] without Cuban troops, and it would certainly be contributory to world peace if Cuba would withdraw."[136] In an address in Atlantic City in June 1978, Vance pointed out that the problems between the Ethiopian government and the secessionist movements in Eritrea were exacerbated by "substantial quantities of Soviet arms and the continued presence of large numbers of Cuban troops," and argued that "peace and stability will not come to the region as long as Ethiopia and Somalia believe they can solve their problems through military means."[137]

The main area for debate regarding communist involvement in the Horn in the summer of 1978 remained the extent of Cuban participation in the ongoing fighting in Eritrea. In June the *Washington Post* reported on a broadcast from Addis Ababa radio in which Mengistu publicly denied that Cuba was taking part in fighting against secessionist forces in Eritrea. Mengistu admitted that Cuban forces had fought in the Ogaden war against Somali forces, but "allegations that they were participating in the Eritrean fighting were false."[138] Castro met with journalists in June and emphasized that the "long-standing Eritrean problem is Ethiopia's and not ours;" the *Washington Post* commented that the "Cuban government is determined, on both political and ideological grounds, to avoid direct military involvement in Ethiopia's war against Eritrean secessionists."[139] Evidence provided to the Carter administration appeared to bear out these assertions. Henze informed Brzezinski of intelligence reports that "about 2200 Cubans are currently involved in training and logistic support of Eritrean operations but there is no evidence of their use in combat roles."[140]

Concurrent with the news that Cuban involvement in Eritrea might not be as great as first feared, came reports that relations between Ethiopia and the United States might be improving in general. In July Henze told Brzezinski that "signs that Mengistu wants to keep openings to the West have multiplied."

Apparently eager to take advantage of the opportunity to portray the prospects for future U.S.-Ethiopian relations favorably, Henze went on to contend that "we have been on a consistent course in respect to Ethiopia since the Aaron Mission last February. Our new ambassador was quickly accepted and indications are that we will now have much more constructive dialogue with Mengistu and other senior officials. Our capacity to influence thinking and events in the country, still extremely limited, should gradually improve."[141] Indeed, early signs suggested that Chapin had made progress in improving relations, and Henze was keen to highlight this; in August he wrote to Harold Marcus, professor at Michigan State University and editor of *Ethiopianist Notes*, that "we have a new Ambassador in Addis Ababa, Fred Chapin, who has made a good beginning at warming up our relations a bit."[142]

There also appeared to be positive developments with respect to the administration's stated aim to provide the Horn peoples with economic and humanitarian aid, albeit in response to a crisis. During the summer of 1978 areas of Ethiopia were struck by famine; the state radio reported that "between 600,000 and one million people were starving in the northeastern province of Wollo."[143] On June 8, Henze reported on the progress that had been made in responding to the famine crisis, informing Brzezinski that "trucks to bring food into the Wollo-Tigre famine area are just being put into service, having been held up at Assab. There is adequate food on hand if it can be transported. Our contribution to famine and refugee relief is substantial and now totals well over $2 million."[144] On June 20, Vance told the fifty-eighth meeting of the U.S. Jaycees in Atlantic City that "a grave famine now threatens over a million Ethiopian people with starvation.... The United States has already contributed $1.5 million for relief operations in the famine area. We are also proceeding to provide assistance to the regional organization which is conducting the fight to curb the spread of locusts and save croplands."[145] An indication that Carter saw his new foreign policy approach as a way to fight the Cold War, discussed in detail in Chapter I, was reflected in Henze's comment to Brzezinski that "there is no evidence that the Soviets are providing any emergency aid whatsoever," and proposed that the administration "get this point across in the press."[146] The administration may have had no desire for direct military competition with the USSR, but it was apparently willing to compete in terms of morality and "good works."

In one particular area, however, there were grounds for concern about the administration's chances of improving relations with Ethiopia. Its efforts to aid the Ethiopian people, and perhaps resume better relations with the Ethiopian government, through the provision of economic and humanitarian aid, were complicated by Congressional legislation. The main problem was that, as a result of the Ethiopian revolution, some American businesses in the African country had been nationalized, and, unless the owners were compensated, American law, according to the Hickenlooper and Gonzalez Amendments, dictated that all U.S. aid to Ethiopia must be terminated.[147] On June 8, 1978, Henze sent Brzezinski a memo updating him on the situation:

> There have been some useful conversations with the Ethiopian finance minister which offer hope that the expropriation/compensation issue can be worked out without bringing on the Hickenlooper and Gonzalez amendments. Ambassador Designate Chapin has been directed by Vance to contact all affected American investors during the next three weeks and get claims clarified. The problem is that some of the smaller claimants do not want to make claims; they prefer to take tax losses and forget them. Some interpretations of the law would require that even in such cases aid must be cut off. No votes in international lending agencies are coming up in the immediate future, so we seem to have time to make some progress on this issue.[148]

Indeed, at the end of July, Henze noted with some satisfaction in a memo to Brzezinski that there were signs that "the problem of compensation for nationalized property may be amenable to settlement."[149]

In Somalia, the administration also pursued attempts to provide economic and developmental aid; on July 31, as the issue of military aid was facing problems because of evidence of Somali involvement in the Ogaden, the Policy Review Committee resolved that the "development assistance program [to Somalia] will be accelerated."[150] As part of this program, the administration supported the proposal made by Representative Robert Leggett (D-Calif) for a massive civil-aid program to be undertaken by the U.S. Corps of Engineers, financed by Saudi Arabia. The Policy Review Committee on July 31 decided that the Department of Defense should coordinate a preliminary feasibility study, although no commitment was made to go ahead at that stage.[151] However, the biggest problem faced by the administration in its attempt to aid the Somali people was Siad's disinterest in accepting economic or humanitarian aid. In July 1978 Henze informed Brzezinski that "Siad has shown little enthusiasm for the idea of concentration on economic development, toward which we and our European allies have tried to shift his interest."[152]

Instead, the Somali leader continued to appeal for military aid. A briefing memo for administration members attending the Policy Review Committee meeting of July 31, including Mondale, Vance, Turner and Brown, stated that "the Somalis have communicated their urgent desire for some tangible demonstration of U.S. support in the defense field. They have invited U.S. naval ship visits, the accreditation of a U.S. military attaché, etc."[153] The administration was also faced with international pressure, particularly from its Arab allies, to provide military aid to Somalia. The *Washington Post* had commented in March that the Carter administration was under "heavy pressure, particularly from Saudi Arabia, to do more for Somalia, including the provision of some arms to help compensate for the loss of Soviet military assistance."[154] At the Policy Review Committee meeting on July 31, it was reported that "we are under pressure from the Saudis, Egyptian President Sadat, and the Europeans to proceed with a military relationship with Somalia."[155] Siad Barré also attempted to persuade the Carter administration to be more forthcoming in the provision of military aid by implying that Somalia might once again turn to the Soviet Union. In a news conference in July 1978, Siad suggested that he was in danger of being deposed by pro–Soviet elements in Somalia, if the United States did not provide the $15 million worth of weapons it had promised.[156] However, Henze commented to Brzezinski that Siad was "the most pro–Soviet element in Somalia," and added that he had "tried to go back and they won't have him."[157]

Fall in the Horn: An Ambassador, an Aid Project, but Little Progress

Relations between Somalia and the United States appeared to take a step forward in September with the appointment of a new ambassador to Mogadishu. On September 21, 1978, Carter announced the nomination of Donald K. Petterson as ambassador extraordinary and plenipotentiary of the United States to the Somali Democratic Republic.[158] Paul Henze, never a fan of Siad or Somalia, commented that "anyone who wants the relatively thankless task of being ambassador to Somalia during the next couple of years and has basic qualifications for the job should be given a blessing and a liberal share of good wishes for modest success in the job. He will probably have to go through a couple of changes in government during his tour of duty but out of it all may come, eventually, an improved relationship with the U.S."[159]

To assist in the improvement of relations with Somalia, further talks were held on the Leggett proposal, involving a series of development and civil works to be undertaken by a unit from the American Corps of Engineers and financed by Saudi Arabia. In October, Peter Tarnoff of the State Department reported to Brzezinski that, following a feasibility study by the Defense Department, both the DOD and State Department recommended that discussions regarding the project take place with both the Saudis and the Somalis.[160] David McGiffert, assistant secretary of defense, commented to Aaron that:

> The program helps our relationship with Somalia and benefits it economically. Additionally, sending a Corps of Engineers survey team to Somalia would provide

us with an alternative for the military survey team which President Siad has requested. Finally the Saudis, who would like us to be more responsive to Somalia's military needs, are likely to appreciate the significance that a U.S. Army Corps of Engineers presence might have in Somalia.[161]

However, Henze argued that the project was unlikely to amount to anything much. He told Aaron in November that "Siad has never really shown any enthusiasm for the project, because he wants arms, and the Saudis on a couple of feeling-out approaches we have made to them to date have also been unenthusiastic." Henze also warned that actions by the Corps of Engineers in Somalia might easily be misinterpreted by both Ethiopia and Kenya as the beginning of a military relationship between Somalia and the United States, which could produce "far-reaching consequences," that the administration would not like, for example, a breakdown in relations between the United States and Ethiopia or Kenya.[162]

Although Henze and others in the administration still sought to restore the predominant position that the United States had once enjoyed in Ethiopia, all realized that they must overcome several obstacles in order to achieve this long-term aim. The most obvious of these, of course, was the presence of the Soviet Union in Ethiopia. Although hopes remained within the administration that relations between Mengistu and the USSR would deteriorate, evidence suggested that the opposite was true. In November, the American press carried reports that the relationship between the two countries was becoming stronger with the signature of a treaty of friendship and cooperation. Reporters based in Moscow described the developments in dispatches carried in many of the major American newspapers, including the *New York Times*, the *Washington Post* and the *Los Angeles Times*. The *New York Times* reported that the Soviet Union "solidified its relationship with Ethiopia by signing a treaty of friendship and cooperation that is expected to maintain or increase Soviet military involvement in the Horn of Africa."[163] Kevin Dlose, a *Washington Post* foreign correspondent based in Moscow, reported on November 22 that "the Soviet Union and Ethiopia yesterday disclosed a mutual pledge to collaborate in military, political and economic matters for the next twenty years under terms of a friendship and cooperation treaty." Dlose argued that "the accord intensifies the Soviet-Ethiopian military relationship, which has existed since Mengistu's government established a Marxist line following the overthrow of pro–Western Emperor Haile Selassie."[164]

Despite this development, Henze, in particular, remained optimistic that the Carter administration should not abandon its long-term goal to improve relations between the United States and Ethiopia. On December 8, he sent a memo to Brzezinski, in which he contended:

Difficult as it may be to reach it quickly, our goal in the Horn should continue to be to reduce, and eventually eliminate, Soviet predominance in Ethiopia, the most important country in the Horn and one of the most important in Africa. This will take time, patience and cleverness, as well as some luck. The Soviets know the value of Ethiopia and will assert themselves and go on paying a high price to stay there. But both Ethiopian nationalism and the inherent complexity of the country are against them.[165]

Henze went on to argue that the administration should remain positive because:

Ethiopia is a pluralist country in every sense. The Soviets cannot mould it into a model "socialist" state, but they can get themselves, and their Cubans, into a great deal of trouble by trying to do so. The best way for us to advance our interests is to try to help this process along and to hold ourselves and our friends ready to help the Ethiopians when they turn our way. This is what we have been doing since last January and the policy has already proven to be modestly successful.[166]

The continuing conflict in Eritrea posed a second obstacle to hopes of restoring the "special relationship" with Ethiopia. American concern over the refugees, and other victims of the conflict, as well as the pressure on the Ethiopian government to negotiate, sustained tensions between the administration and the Mengistu regime. The uprising also provided the Ethiopian leader with a reason to continue his military supply relationship with the Communist bloc. However, towards the end of 1978, evidence seemed to suggest that the insurgency might soon be over.

On May 17, the *New York Times* reported that Ethiopia had launched a major offensive against the rebels in Eritrea. Throughout the summer and fall, the government forces continued to press the rebels, and in November the *Washington Post* reported that "the sixteen-year-old Eritrean effort to gain independence from Ethiopia collapsed this week when upwards of 35,000 Ethiopian troops, backed by Soviet and Cuban advisers, drove the Eritreans from their last stronghold" at Keren, northwest of Asmara.[167] Henze commented to Brzezinski that the "Eritrean insurgency may well be finished as a major movement."[168] However, Thomas Reston, a State Department spokesman, told the *New York Times* that, despite Ethiopia's successes in reopening the road between Massawa and Asmara and the recapture of the city of Keren, "it is premature to conclude that the war is over or that the guerrilla movements in Eritrea have collapsed."[169] Indeed, as with most guerrilla wars, a large military victory was not enough; as they retreated from Keren, the Eritreans vowed to continue their guerrilla tactics.[170]

Also, as 1978 draw to a close, there was even less reason for American optimism regarding the Ogaden. Passing on information received from various sources, including the CIA, Brzezinski sent a memo to Mondale on

December 12, in which he informed the vice president that "Siad has steadily expanded guerrilla operations in the Ogaden, now estimated to involve 50,000 men. The Somali military system has been reoriented toward supporting them."[171] *New York Times* correspondent, John Darnton, reported from Mogadishu on interviews he had conducted with the leaders of two of the guerrilla groups in the Ogaden. The secretary general of the Western Somali Liberation Front, Abdullahi Hassan Muhamud, told Darnton that "today there are thousands of our troops in the country and the war is going on in every part of western Somalia," a term commonly used by the guerrillas to describe the disputed Ogaden region of Ethiopia. Darnton also interviewed Mohammed Ali Rube, the secretary general of the Somali Abo Liberation Front, and, although both commanders assured him that "not a single Somali regular is fighting alongside their forces," Darnton reported that this was unlikely.[172]

The administration was also faced with evidence that its efforts to improve human rights in both Ethiopia and Somalia had met with little success. Indeed, in Somalia it appeared that the situation might even be deteriorating. In the memo to Mondale, Brzezinski commented that "Siad has more people in jail now than he had before he broke with the Soviets; he executed a group of military plotters a few weeks ago and he has oppressed rival tribesmen in the military and among civil leaders."[173] Meanwhile, Amnesty International published a report in November on human rights conditions in Ethiopia, citing numerous violations. The report accused the Ethiopian government of "a consistent pattern of gross violations of fundamental human rights" and stated that "Ethiopia's military government is holding thousands of prisoners without trial in cramped, unsanitary conditions and has practiced torture and terror against its own citizens."[174] The official State Department report on the state of human rights in Ethiopia during 1978 stated that "individual human rights continue to be largely ignored by the government.... In the last year and a half, the PMGSE has launched extensive campaigns of repression against its internal enemies, most notably the 'Red Terror' drive of December 1977 to April 1978.... Although an abatement of the 'Red Terror' has occurred since March 1978, the human rights situation is not better than that which prevailed in mid–1977."[175]

1979: A Year of Setbacks

As 1978 became 1979, the Republicans did not ease up on their criticism of Carter's conduct of foreign policy. In his reply to the president's State of the Union message in January 1979, William Brock, the Republican

National Party chairman, declared that Carter "says that things are good around the world, and he refuses to admit that we have lost allies, that countries have fallen under communist control, that the world is in disarray, that this country has lost its ability to be a cause [sic] for peace." Meanwhile, House minority leader John Rhodes (R-Ariz) complained that "the deterioration in our foreign posture in the last two years is really hard to contemplate.... Look at the advances that the Russians have made around the globe.... You find all around the world the bastions of the United States for defending the free world in a position of crumbling [sic].... You've got to say that something very bad went wrong as far as foreign policy is concerned."[176]

In the face of such criticism, Richard Moose appeared before the House Subcommittee on Africa on February 4, to discuss government policy. He declared that the administration's goals in the Horn of Africa were "to maintain cordial relations with all the countries in this area; to assist within the limit of our resources in improving the well being of the people in these countries; to lend our support to the creation of an atmosphere that will eliminate the need for the large scale importation of military weapons."[177] In Ethiopia, Moose explained, "discussion is well underway of our bilateral problems, such as compensation for nationalized U.S. businesses and the settlement of issues involved in our past military program, which include payments due us by Ethiopia; the Soviet/Cuban presence remains in Ethiopia and does not make easier the negotiated settlements of its problems; we have several modest ongoing agricultural projects in Ethiopia totaling $1.7 million."[178] With regard to Somalia, Moose explained that the administration had "initiated economic assistance programs which will total over $50 million when completed, as well as a Public Law 480 food assistance program in fiscal year 1979 of $11 million; we have opened a defense attaché office in our Embassy and, after an interruption of nearly ten years, U.S. naval ships are again calling at Somali ports; we have remained firm in our resolve not to supply arms to Somalia because of its continuing high level of violence in the Ogaden." Moose acknowledged that the insurgency in the Ogaden was ongoing, but maintained that "Somali regular troops have withdrawn" from Ethiopia.[179]

Such apparent confidence seemed misplaced, however. Reports of guerrilla activity in the Ogaden continued throughout 1979. In February, the *Washington Post* reported that up to 30,000 "rebels in southeastern Ethiopia are tying down thousands of government troops in a campaign of hit-and-run attacks that is reviving the Ogaden war."[180] In March, William Campbell of UPI questioned Moose's categorical assertion to the House Subcommittee on Africa, claiming that the "Somali government has made no secret of its support for the guerrillas."[181] Indeed, it appeared that the private discussions within the administration belied Moose's public stance. During a meeting with Ambassador Addou in February, Henze indicated that he had evidence of ongoing Somali activity in the Ogaden. He confirmed to the Somali ambassador that military aid was "out of the question as long as Somalia stoked the Ogaden insurgency and helped keep the Cubans and Soviets in Ethiopia"; in reply, Addou replied that "Siad refused to make any concessions on the Ogaden and would go on supporting the insurgents."[182] Following this, Henze took the opportunity to reiterate his position that the United States should not pursue a relationship with Siad. In a memo to Brzezinski on March 16, Henze argued that "the essentials in the Horn remain what they have been since last year at this time. Siad has never reconciled himself to staying within his own borders and he has liberalized his own police state very little." He therefore recommended that "getting ourselves entangled with Siad under the illusion of strengthening our military position in the area would bring us into serious trouble later. We should resist this temptation, no matter what our own military and other miscellaneous enthusiasts of Siad advise."[183]

As well as the continuing dilemmas that surrounded the relationship with Somalia, as 1979 wore on the Carter administration was faced with ever-increasing problems with regard to its attempts to improve relations between the United States and Ethiopia, despite the apparent gains of 1978. In March, Brzezinski informed Carter that "Mengistu seems to be willingly moving closer and closer to the Soviets,"[184] and Carter raised the issue in his meeting with Brezhnev in June. The American president again deplored the presence of communist bloc troops in the Horn of Africa, telling his Soviet counterpart that the extensive activities of Cuba in areas of the world such as the Horn of Africa were "of deep concern," and as the administration regarded Cuba as "a proxy of the Soviet Union, a surrogate or at least an ally, which was being supported, financed and equipped by the Soviet Union," Carter hoped that Brezhnev would use his influence to promote withdrawal.[185] It should be noted, however, that Carter's comments were not well received. Although he did not challenge Carter's characterization of the Soviet-Cuban relationship, Brezhnev nevertheless replied that he "could cite genuine instances of U.S. interference in the affairs of other countries and, of course, he could draw on them to cause tensions in U.S.-Soviet relations. But the Soviet Union had no desire to do so."[186]

Furthermore, the role and position of Fred Chapin, the ambassador to Ethiopia, appeared under threat. During a meeting of the working group on the Horn of Africa, Gordon Beyer, the East Africa director for the State Department, reported that the State Department felt that Chapin "was not relating well to Ethiopians and was personally antagonizing many of the officials with whom he was dealing. He was becoming frustrated and disillusioned at not being able to solve the complicated legal issues affecting aid programs."[187] A few days later, Henze expressed increasing concerns over Chapin's actions in Ethiopia in a memo to Brzezinski:

> I am now convinced that left to their own State and Fred Chapin are going to undermine what little we have left of a position in Ethiopia. Chapin, angered by the Ethiopians' lack of response to his intense effort to work out the compensation-/aid-cut-off issue, has adopted a punitive, worse-the-better position and has made considerable headway in selling it to Moose and Newsom. I am not sure that Chapin is not deliberately trying to worsen the situation to the point where the Ethiopians retaliate by PNG'ing him or breaking relations. This would be unfortunate, not only for our position in Ethiopia, but for the larger framework of our Horn and Middle Eastern policy in relation to Soviets and Cubans. And it might simply be playing into Soviet hands.[188]

Henze's implications regarding the actions of some members of the State Department, as well as the discrepancies between the public announcements made by Moose and the discussions within the NSC over the Ogaden, offer further evidence of lack of collegiality within the executive branch. However, inter-departmental tensions were perhaps the least of Carter's worries when it came to implementing policy. Congress remained determined to enforce the Hickenlooper and Gonzalez Amendments, which would require the administration to halt any aid provisions to Ethiopia. In an effort to prevent this, Gorden Beyer from the State Department was sent to Ethiopia in July. Part of his mission, Henze reported to Brzezinski, was to visit "Addis Ababa to make a last-ditch effort to persuade the Ethiopians to make some gestures that will enable us to reverse the decision to cut off aid."[189] Unfortunately for the administration, this failed, and that month economic and development aid from the United States to Ethiopia was suspended, as Henze later recalled, "to comply with laws prohibiting aid to countries that nationalize American investments without compensation."[190] That month, the administration's aid program to Somalia also appeared to be stalling. The plan to send an American unit of engineers to Somalia to undertake civil construction projects financed by Saudi Arabia had still not been carried out because of the administration's concern over the Ethiopian reaction and, evidence suggests, because of diminishing Saudi interest in the scheme.[191]

A Time of Transition

Despite these setbacks, it appeared that some senior members of the administration felt that the policy framework chosen in 1977 was still appropriate in the Horn of Africa as 1979 drew to a close. Brzezinski informed

Peter Tarnoff in the State Department that "the NSC Interdepartmental Group for Africa met on September 28, 1979, to review U.S. policy in the Horn of Africa.... The conclusion of the meeting was that the main outline of U.S. policy remains valid and that there is no need to engage senior officials in deliberations at the PRC or SCC level."[192]

However, in the time since the Carter administration had assumed office it appeared that little had changed in Ethiopia or Somalia. Perhaps most important for a Cold War president was the fact that there was still extensive communist bloc involvement in the region. In an appearance before the House Subcommittee on Africa, David Newsom, under secretary of state for political affairs, reported that, at the end of 1978, the administration believed that nearly 40,000 communist bloc personnel were in Ethiopia, of whom 35,800 were military personnel.[193] If anything, communist support for Ethiopia was increasing. In November 1979, the *New York Times* reported that:

> President Erich Honecker left for Ethiopia today on his second trip to Africa this year. During the four-day state visit, Mr. Honecker is expected to sign a treaty of friendship and cooperation with the Ethiopian government of President Mengistu Haile Mariam. Ethiopia already is a recipient of military aid and other support from East Germany. Behind the Soviet Union and Cuba, East Germany is the most active member of the communist bloc in promoting cooperation with African countries.[194]

Equally important for an administration that had pledged itself to principles such as global community and peaceful resolution of conflict, was the fact that, as Henze commented to Brzezinski, essentially nothing had changed in the Ogaden. In a memo of October 24, 1979, Henze reported that "fighting in the Ogaden has not decreased and there can be no doubt about Siad's control over the WSLF [Western Somali Liberation Front]—periodic cosmetic adjustments notwithstanding."[195] Henze later recalled that from the end of the Ogaden War through the summer of 1979, the administration was provided with "excellent" intelligence and therefore it knew "exactly what was happening" as "Siad gradually increased support for his guerrillas and introduced more and more regulars." Despite the administration informing Siad that it was aware of the truth, this "had no deterrent effect whatever" on the actions of the Somali leader.[196] Moreover, Siad's actions were public knowledge; *Newsweek* reported in December that "Somalia is not about to abandon its centuries-old claim that the Ogaden belongs to the Somalis. Reliable Western sources maintain that Siad Barré's regime is still funneling arms and ammunition to the Ogaden guerrillas."[197] Hence there was no objection within the administration when, in the late summer of 1979, a working group on the Horn of Africa chaired by Henze "concluded that Siad's behavior and Somalia's predicament continued to make an effort to initiate a military relationship undesirable."[198]

The condition of the peoples of the Horn region also appeared to have undergone little improvement, despite the emphasis of the Carter administration on human rights, and related humanitarian concerns. Wars in the region had created a tremendous refugee problem. At the end of October the *New York Times* reported that some 350,000 refugees from the Ogaden were housed in twenty-one camps in Somalia, with approximately a thousand more arriving daily.[199] Also, Gregory Jaynes, the *New York Times* correspondent based in Somalia, reported that "with 357,000 refugees in camps and another 650,000 assimilated into villages and towns, Somalia has the worst refugee problem in Africa and the country's officials are begging for world concern."[200]

In September 1979, in his weekly report to the president, Brzezinski addressed the lack of progress in the Horn of Africa, as well as the criticism that had been directed at Carter throughout his administration. The national security adviser argued that:

> Both in tone and occasionally in substance, we have been excessively acquiescent, and that the country craves, and our national security needs, both a more assertive tone and a more assertive substance to our foreign policy. I believe that both for international reasons as well as for domestic political reasons you ought to deliberately toughen both the tone and the substance of our foreign policy. The country associates assertiveness with leadership, and the world at large expects American leadership insofar as the Soviet challenge is concerned. That challenge is real.

To counter this perception, Brzezinski recommended that the administration should have "less hesitation in explicitly condemning Soviet/Cuban exploitation of Third World turbulence. This means occasionally a very tough-minded remark by you and your instructions to the Secretary of State, to me, and to others at least to echo or perhaps to go a touch beyond you."[201]

Brzezinski's words were to prove almost prophetic. Although the situation in the Horn of Africa remained the same during 1980 as it had during the first three years of the administration — Somali troops in the Ogaden, human rights violations, communist bloc troops in Ethiopia — the response of Carter and his administration was to prove radically different.

V

1980: Cold War Resurgent

International Developments and Policy Reorientation

On November 4, 1979, Iranian students seized the American Embassy in Tehran and took 90 American citizens hostage.[1] The day after Christmas the Soviet Union invaded Afghanistan. Faced with these twin crises, with religious fundamentalist terrorism and communist advancement by military force, the Carter administration, which had been engaging in debates for two years over the direction and implementation techniques of foreign policy, halted its equivocation. Although Carter did not abandon his commitment to human rights, the issue was accorded a much lower priority in policy formulation, and no longer used as a major weapon with which to wage the Cold War. Instead, the official administration posture reflected a more traditional Cold War style with the main emphasis on American military power. In addition, a globalist perspective of the international environment began to dominate over a regionalist outlook, with the related increased importance of the Soviet Union and East-West issues.

Several factors prompted this reorientation of foreign policy, not least of which was the perception that the invasion of Afghanistan represented a new approach by the Soviets; Carter would later describe the invasion as "quite a change in their basic policy."[2] For some in the administration, notably Brzezinski, the invasion of Afghanistan by the USSR provided the necessary evidence supporting their view that Soviet aggression posed a real threat, and, when added to the developments in Iran, not to mention the domestic pressures and criticism in an election year, required a tough response from the Carter administration.[3] In his memoirs, Henze commented that, in addition to the events in Iran and Afghanistan, "the perception that the U.S. had suffered a defeat in the Horn contributed to the conclusion within the administration that the U.S. had to act urgently to protect its interests in the Middle East/Indian Ocean region. This concern was not irrational."[4]

The new approach resulted in a profound change of attitude toward the Horn of Africa. Until 1980 the official stance of the administration had been that the Horn region as a whole had strategic value, and it had sought to maintain or improve relations with all the countries of the area, and, as specifically discussed here, with both Ethiopia and Somalia, regardless of political orientation or external influence therein. However, as Henze argued in his book on the Horn of Africa, "strategic value is a flexible concept."[5] Asmara, for example, had been strategically important to the United States when Kagnew Station was needed as a communications facility, but the advances in satellite technology had rendered it strategically unimportant; more recently, it could perhaps be argued that the strategic importance of Britain or Germany to the United States has diminished since the end of the Cold War.

The flexibility in assigning strategic importance, referred to by Henze, was demonstrated in the Horn in 1980 when, rather than continuing with attempts to develop good relations with both Ethiopia and Somalia, the administration chose to focus only on the latter. The reason lay in the perceived need to project an American military presence into the Middle East and Indian Ocean. In order to do this, the United States required access to bases from which military operations could be directed and supported. The Horn region was one of several that the administration decided was geographically suitable for American military facilities, but the circumstances of the relationship between the United States and Ethiopia by November 1979, coupled with the communist bloc presence in Ethiopia, meant that Mengistu was unlikely to grant access to the Americans, should they consider such a request. Siad Barré, on the other hand, had been desperate for extended American support, and the former Soviet military base at Berbera was there for the taking. As Henze later recalled, for strategic reasons the administration "was ready to turn a blind eye on internal conditions in Somalia," and moved to consolidate the relationship between the United States and Siad's regime.[6] A corollary of this decision was the acceptance that establishing such a military agreement with Somalia would reduce the hope of improving U.S.-Ethiopian relations and securing the diminution of Soviet and Cuban influence in Ethiopia. The decision of the administration to pursue such an agreement therefore represented an implicit downgrading of such objectives, suggesting a deprioritization of regionalist issues, as well as a more pragmatic and realistic approach to foreign affairs.

As well as prompting a reorientation of the substance of foreign policy, the developments in the Middle East also impinged on the processes of policy formulation. When considering any aspect of American foreign policy in 1980 it is absolutely vital to remember the overall context. The hostage crisis in Iran dominated everything, and while serious situations occurred elsewhere in the world, they were very often dealt with at a lower level than might have been the case before the American Embassy was seized. In his memoirs Carter recalled that "the first week of November 1979 marked the beginning of the most difficult period of my life. The safety and well-being of the American hostages became a constant concern for me, no matter what other duties I was performing as president."[7] Other members of the administration have similar recollections. Stansfield Turner commented that "the hostages just overwhelmed us. Seventy percent of my time was put on the hostages, for six months anyway. Somebody was following the Ogaden, Somalia and Ethiopia, but it wasn't getting discussed in the National Security Council. It wasn't getting my personal attention because it never heated up enough and the forecasts were never dire enough to interrupt the concentration first on Iran and then on Afghanistan."[8] David Aaron recalled that "we were obsessed with Iran. There wasn't much room for anything else,"[9] while Henze remembered that the attention of the senior staff was "almost entirely" on Iran and Afghanistan.[10]

The "Real" Carter Doctrine

Within this context Jimmy Carter appeared before Congress on January 22, 1980, to deliver his annual message on the State of the Union.[11] During the speech he articulated his new approach to foreign policy when he declared that "an attempt by any outside force to gain control of the Persian Gulf region will be regarded as an assault on the vital interests of the United States of America, and such an assault will be repelled by any means necessary, including military force."[12] The president's announcement was quickly dubbed the "Carter Doctrine" and this time the appellation endured. As mentioned at the beginning of Chapter IV, Carter's emphasis on human rights had also been termed the "Carter Doctrine" by elements of the American press, but to no lasting effect. The reason why the president's 1980 declaration is remembered as his "Doctrine" arguably lies in the generally accepted definition of the phrase. John Dumbrell has contended that presidential declarations are termed doctrines when they are "unilateral warnings to enemies, often designed primarily to mobilize opinion at home.... Most have been exemplifications or applications of (usually anti-communist containment) 'grand strategy.'"[13] While Carter's emphasis on human rights may have been designed to appeal to American public opinion, it could hardly be deemed a serious "warning to enemies," or an effective example of anti-communist containment. Thus, Dumbrell's definition of the criteria for a presidential doctrine suggests why the 1980 approach, as opposed to the 1977 approach, is remembered as the "Carter Doctrine."

The reorientation articulated by Carter in his State of the Union message did not go unnoticed. An article in *Congressional Quarterly* commented that "President Carter's responses to turmoil in the Middle East appear to abandon some foreign policy goals that had received great emphasis early in his administration.... The Carter administration's early hopes for negotiating with Moscow an agreement to demilitarize the Indian Ocean — which long had been dead in the water — were sunk without a trace."[14] *Washington Post* staff writer, Don Oberdorfer, remarked that the "Carter Doctrine" represented "a policy shift of great significance. For the first time since the high point of involvement in the Vietnam War a decade ago, the United States is increasing its military forces and security commitment in a far-away region rather than reducing them."[15] An article in *U.S. News & World Report* compared the Soviet invasion of Afghanistan to communist aggression in Korea and Vietnam, observing that "for the third time since World War II, the U.S. is taking up the burden of resisting Soviet expansion," and argued that the "face-off with Russia represents a total reversal of a U.S. foreign policy that, for nearly three years, downgraded the Russian threat and de-emphasized the role of American military power. Top priority is being given to preventing the Russians from extending their aggression beyond Afghanistan."[16] Oberdorfer's article in the *Post* also highlighted a second shift when he commented on the ascendancy of Brzezinski and the NSC, pointing out that "Brzezinski and his NSC staff have played the central role in new policy toward the Persian Gulf-Indian Ocean."[17] Brzezinski later claimed in his memoirs that the State of the Union address was "the culmination of a longer process ... which had started about a year earlier. By late 1978, I began to press the 'arc of crisis' thesis, and on 28th February, 1979, I submitted a memo to the president urging a new 'security framework' to reassert U.S. power and influence in the region."[18]

The Carter Administration Seeks Military Facilities

Although Carter announced his tougher approach to the American people toward the end of January, the reorientation of foreign policy had been decided upon as soon as it was realized that the situation in Iran was indeed a crisis. In Somalia, Siad Barré also realized that the changes in the international environment might further his chances to develop a military relationship with the administration, and offered the United States access to the former Soviet naval base of Berbera, on the Arabian Sea.[19] A Congressional delegation led by Representative Samuel S. Stratton (D-NY) visited Somalia at Siad's invitation and urged the administration to accept the Somali leader's offer, reporting that the Berbera complex had been "the most comprehensive naval support facility available to the Soviets anywhere outside the Soviet homeland, including Cuba."[20]

Within the administration, Admiral Turner argued that at least military access, if not permanent bases, was necessary if the United States was to project power in the region of the Persian Gulf and Indian Ocean. Research conducted by the CIA suggested that the Omanis were willing to allow the United States access to Masire Island, off the coast of Oman, the Kenyans would permit the use of facilities in Mombassa, and the "desperate Somalis" had offered Berbera.[21] The National Security Council met on December 4 to discuss these options and, in a decision endorsed by Brzezinski, Vance and Harold Brown, recommended to the president that access to military facilities in all three countries should be sought. Carter agreed, and on December 14 ordered the immediate departure of a group comprised of State and Defense Department staff to investigate the possible facilities in Oman, Kenya and Somalia.[22] The officials told the *New York Times* that their objective was "permission for the use of bases from which the United States could project military power." [23] On January 7, during an interview with John Chancellor of NBC, when asked about the decision, Carter hinted at the themes to come in his State of the Union message. He explained that his administration was attempting to effect agreements for American access to military facilities in the Gulf region because it "is important to our nation to prepare for the long-range meeting of any threat to the peace in the Mideast-Persian Gulf-northern Indian Ocean area."[24] Meanwhile the *Los Angeles Times* commented that the decision of the Carter administration to seek "long-term air and naval facilities in Oman and Somalia on the Arabian Sea and to lift the embargo on arms sales to Pakistan" came as part of the concern of the administration "for the drift of events in the oil-rich area in which American national security interests are vital."[25]

By mid–January the officials from the state and defense departments had completed a preliminary survey of potential sites for military facilities in the region of the Persian Gulf and Indian Ocean. The three sites chosen as most appropriate for the administration's needs were indeed the island of Masire off the coast of Oman, the port and associated airfield at Mombassa in Kenya, and the port-airfield complex at Berbera in Somalia.[26] Administration officials told the *New York Times* that their main concern had been to "find air and naval sites to handle the expected increase in port calls by the naval carrier forces that will be on virtually permanent station in future in the Arabian Sea and Indian Ocean."[27]

It should be noted however that, despite the apparent radical change in the official policy of the Carter administration toward the Horn of Africa, there was a degree of dissent within the ranks. Henze, in particular, was vocal in his opposition to any deal with Somalia. On January 16 he sent a memo to his NSC colleague, Fritz Ermath, expressing his doubts over the advisability of a relationship with Somalia:

> Any arrangement with Siad which goes beyond small-scale utilization of Somali ports and airfields on a short-term and essentially ad hoc basis is likely to lead us eventually into unmanageable politico-military problems. Any commitment of arms to Somalia will make us responsible (which we are not now) for containing/stopping Somali attacks on Ethiopia through the Ogaden — and will contribute to consolidation of Soviet/Cuban presence and the oppressive regime which they underwrite in Ethiopia — thus postponing the day when Ethiopian nationalism will generate a break with the Soviets, our ultimate policy objective. Anything other than a severely limited basing agreement with Somalia will embarrass us with the rest of Africa — which can never accept Somali irredentism.[28]

Henze also questioned the strategic need for a base in Berbera. On January 22 he commented to Ermath that:

> The real issue in all this is how badly, militarily, we need Berbera. I find it difficult to escape the feeling that a major component of the motivation that has led to a decision to seek facilities there is the psychological appeal of our taking over a former Soviet base and being able to trumpet to the world, in an election year, that we have not been set back in the Horn as badly as some say — because, look, we are in Berbera now![29]

Henze has held to this view in the years since he served in the Carter administration. In an interview in 2000 he repeated his opinion that the United States had been so interested in Berbera because "we needed to demonstrate that we'd taken something away from the Soviets."[30] Such a perception demonstrates once again the return to a more traditional Cold War orientation in the foreign policy of the Carter administration. However, rather than suggesting that Henze disagreed with the reformulation of policy, it is more likely that his opposition to a closer relationship with Somalia was connected to his repeatedly demonstrated pro–Ethiopian proclivity.

Not everyone shared Henze's opinion regarding the significance of an American occupation of Berbera, though; some argued for the importance of the base on purely strategic grounds. General William Odom, military adviser to the National Security Council, for example, took great pains to point to the geographical location of Berbera: situated near the mouth of the Red Sea, opposite a Soviet base across the Gulf of Aden and within flying range of the Persian Gulf. Odom insisted that "my motives, and I think my motives reflect the planners I was dealing with at the Pentagon ... couldn't care less that it was an ex–Soviet base. The psychological effect was not one we gave a damn about.... The issue was whether we could get that thing operable rapidly enough to be an important staging base. All you have to do is start looking at airplane ranges and you'll see why you need some bases [in that region]."[31] An administration official told the *New York Times* that the Soviet intervention in Afghanistan has "changed our whole military posture in that part of the world" and a military relationship with Somalia was now appropriate despite the concerns raised by Henze, such as possible complications regarding the Ogaden. The official stated that "once a decision is made that you need greater access for ships and aircraft in that part of the world, Somalia becomes a logical candidate. If you look at the map you find that you don't have a lot of choice as to where you go." [32]

However, the issue of Somali involvement in the Ogaden was not overlooked, perhaps due to the influence of administration members such as Henze. Even during the preliminary discussions the American delegates warned Siad that any agreement would not mean "automatic support for that country's claims to the Ogaden region held by Ethiopia."[33] Also, in the early weeks of the talks, a degree of hope flickered among some in the administration that an agreement between the United States and Somalia might allow the Americans to pressurize Siad into reducing his support for those fighting in the Ogaden. Although Ambassador Petterson warned Vance that "we cannot expect Siad to cease the support his government has been giving to the Ogadeni guerrillas," he went on to suggest that the administration could make it clear "that the scope of our security assistance will be directly related to the effort Somalia makes to reduce the fighting in the Ogaden and create a better atmosphere for the possibility of a negotiated settlement." Petterson acknowledged the strategic need of the United States but pointed out that Siad's need for an agreement with the United States was equally strong, giving the administration a degree of influence that it should use. The Ambassador told Vance that:

> Siad needs us; he very much wants to see a U.S. military presence in Somalia. He has assiduously sought the closest kind of relationship with the U.S. Siad has emphasized to me that even a modest amount of U.S. military aid would provide him with sufficient symbolic and political support to placate those in the Somali military who he says claim that his move toward the West has endangered Somalia's security. Moreover, the idea of a U.S. military presence in Somalia is immensely popular with the Somali public.[34]

Indeed, on February 3, the *Los Angeles Times* quoted a Somali official who commented that "we want the Americans here. The Americans want to be here. So where is the problem?"[35]

Nowhere, it seemed. Perhaps encouraged by this positive outlook, negotiations continued with Siad Barré, as well as with the governments of Oman and Kenya, and on February 12 it was announced that agreement had been reached. Administration officials told the *New York Times* that "leaders in the three countries accepted proposals that would allow American forces to pay regular visits to military bases and use them to store equipment and fuel" in return for military aid. [36] A senior administration aide remarked that the accord on access to facilities in Oman, Kenya and Somalia was "the beginning of a significant reversal of our strategic decline in that part of the world."[37]

The United States and Ethiopia

As the United States moved toward a closer relationship with Somalia, it was perhaps no coincidence that the administration began to give more publicity to the deplorable conditions in Ethiopia. The annual State Department report to Congress on human rights practices around the world in February 1980 contended that the Ethiopian government still "tortures political and military prisoners to extract information or confessions ... [and] arbitrary arrests occur frequently."[38] However, perhaps the most significant aspect of the report, and one that reflected the new attitudes within the Carter administration, was the fact that no mention was made of Somalia, even though the administration had evidence of persistent human rights abuses in that country occurring as recently as December 1979.

In addition, the administration appeared to change its position regarding the unresolved issue of Ethiopian compensation for nationalized industries. Whereas, in 1979, efforts had been made to limit Congressional action, now the administration appeared to be drawing attention to the issue thereby further hardening attitudes towards this former ally. The deputy assistant secretary of state for African affairs, William Harrop, appeared before the House Subcommittee on Africa in February, and reminded them that Ethiopia's "refusal to make significant progress toward compensation to the sixteen American claimants who claim to have lost some $22 million" from the nationalization of industries had resulted in Congressional legislation suspending economic aid in 1979. Harrop informed the Subcommittee that there was little prospect that the situation would be rectified in the near future and that "five years after these nationalizations began and despite assurance that it would pay, Ethiopia has not yet paid a single claimant, Ethiopian or foreign. We do not know when this question will be settled."[39]

The reorientation of policy toward the Horn of Africa also led to a change of attitude with regard to the communist bloc presence in Ethiopia. After spending three years insisting that the relationship between Ethiopia and the Soviet Union was a temporary inconvenience, the administration began to portray the relationship in a more negative light. Harrop told the Subcommittee on Africa that:

> The provisional military government of Socialist Ethiopia is pursuing pro–Soviet and anti–American foreign policies. It has supported the Soviet invasion of Afghanistan and it is one of the three African countries to vote with the Soviets on that resolution in New York. It has signed treaties of friendship and cooperation with the German Democratic Republic and the Peoples Republic of Yemen in addition to a similar agreement in 1978 with the USSR itself.[40]

The corollary was that a re-establishment of a close relationship between the United States and Ethiopia was unlikely. Harrop stated that "as long as Ethiopia relies so heavily on Soviet material assistance to fight its wars and therefore is subject to heavy Soviet influence, we see little prospect for improving our bilateral relations."[41]

Progress on Negotiations with Somalia

Having reached a preliminary agreement with Somalia over the use of military facilities at Berbera, the Carter administration proceeded with the technical requirements to consolidate the deal. Perhaps the most challenging task was the need to gain Congressional endorsement of the necessary expenditure. The administration was well aware that there was unlikely to be overwhelming support for its proposal, despite the recent setbacks in Iran and Afghanistan. Vance told Carter that "we can expect some Congressional opposition to the establishment of a security assistance relationship with Somalia because of Somalia's past record in the Ogaden, concern over the need for adequate assurances against misuse of U.S. equipment, and the danger of U.S. involvement in a conflict between Somalia and one of its neighbors. Advance consultation with the Congress will be essential if these concerns are to be met."[42] Similarly, Madeleine Albright, then a member of the National Security Council staff, sent a memo to Brzezinski noting that "we can expect some problems from the Hill on this. Pell, Glenn and Javits want to be assured that whatever weapons we send are defensive. Hamilton and Solarz have similar views."[43]

Consequently, Franklin Kramer, principal deputy assistant secretary of defense for international security affairs, appeared before the House Subcommittee on African Affairs to put forward the administration's case for a military relationship with Somalia and to attempt to alleviate Congressional fears. He focused upon the strong communist presence in the Horn region, implying that American access to military facilities in the area was necessary to withstand Soviet aggression, and argued that:

> In our view the Soviet and Cuban military presence in Ethiopia and within the People's Democratic Republic of Yemen just across the Gulf are disturbing elements of concern to us and of concern to friendly regimes in the area. They are particularly disturbing after the Soviet invasion of Afghanistan which ... manifests Soviet willingness to use force in the third world.[44]

Fortunately for the ease of Kramer's task, some members of Congress seemed to share the view that international developments required an increased American response. At the hearings held by the Subcommittee on Africa to discuss economic and security assistance programs for FY81 [Fiscal Year 1981], Representative Stephen Solarz, chairman of the Subcommittee, commented that the "question of U.S. capability in the Indian Ocean region has taken on increased importance following the Soviet invasion of Afghanistan."[45]

Notwithstanding agreement between the White House and Capitol Hill that the United States needed to take some sort of direct action to counter Soviet adventurism, there was still much concern over the implications of a relationship with Somalia. During his appearance before the House Subcommittee on Africa, Harrop took the opportunity to emphasize that the administration was aware of the possible complications that a military supply relationship with Somalia might engender, and consequently was imposing limitations and conditions on the deal. He told the Subcommittee that "the Somali government has a keen sense of the Soviet threat to the region. We appreciate its willingness to provide access to its facilities in support of our activities in the Persian Gulf. In return we recognize that we should also be responsive to legitimate Somali security concerns." However, Harrop insisted that the administration had made it clear that the border dispute with Ethiopia did not fall into this category, and "intend[ed] to build our relationship with Somalia in ways which do not contribute to the fighting in the Ogaden." The administration, Harrop continued, had "told the Somalis that in the future as we enter into a new relationship with them that any arms we sell must be defensive in nature and cannot be used in or against Ethiopian territory."[46] Kramer also took pains to emphasize the administration's determination to avoid exacerbating military conflict in the Horn region. He told the Subcommittee, "let me underscore what Mr. Harrop said. We have no intention of creating a Somali capability to be used in the Ogaden."[47]

Nonetheless, the question of American responsibility, should the conflict in the Ogaden flare up, remained the main area of concern. During the hearings, Subcommittee Chairman Solarz engaged in a lengthy questioning session with Harrop on the possibility that a military relationship with Somalia would necessitate American involvement if the skirmishes in the Ogaden became full-fledged war. The State Department official assured Solarz that the administration had "no contemplation of any kind of security guarantee of that nature," and emphasized that:

> We have tried very hard and will continue to make clear to the Somali government that any growing relationship we have with them is in no sense an endorsement of what they are doing in the Ogaden, and in fact clearly no defensive equipment which resulted from this new relationship could be used in the Ogaden or anywhere else outside of Somalia. We have also tried very hard to explain, and will continue, to the Ethiopians that our activities in Somalia and that part of the world are not an endorsement or support for anything which may happen in the Ogaden.[48]

The issue of Somali involvement in the Ogaden provided perhaps the best evidence of the new orientation in the official stance of the Carter administration with regard to Horn policy. Notwithstanding administration assurances that the United States would never support the Ogadeni guerrillas, some of the official announcements began to include subtle changes. Indeed, in his appearance before the Subcommittee on Africa, at the same time as he was insisting that the United States would never be involved in the Ogaden, William Harrop appeared to be justifying and even excusing Somali support for the Ogaden guerrillas. He stated that the support of the Somali government for the Western Somali Liberation Front was the "continuation of the relationships which have existed there for a long time. It is probably very difficult for any leader of Somalia to withdraw from the Ogaden. The majority of the ethnic groups and population of Somalia are very much attached to the notion of the self-determination of the people there."[49]

The reorientation in the official attitude of the Carter administration was also apparent in its response to Ethiopian concerns regarding a deal between the United States and Somalia, and the possible implications for the Ogaden. According to the *New York Times*, Ethiopian diplomats warned the United States that American military aid to Somalia could lead to an "Ethiopian invasion of Somalia that might involve an attack on military facilities there that the United States hopes to use."[50] In response, a State Department official stressed that the Ethiopian government had been assured that "the modest military relationship" contemplated with Somalia was in no way directed against Ethiopia. According to another official, the Ethiopian government had been told that the administration would never "condone any Somalian activity in the Ogaden. We regard the Ogaden as part of Ethiopia, and you can be certain that any military aid we give Somalia will have conditions attached, restricting its use."[51] Notwithstanding such apparent appeasement, administration personnel readily admitted to the *New York Times* that any agreement with Somalia could further alienate the Soviet-backed revolutionary government of Ethiopia, but added that this was a risk that the administration had decided must be taken.[52] In addition, the State Department response to Ethiopian concerns clearly demonstrated that globalist, and not regionalist, issues were the administration's priority. State Department officials asserted that they had "tried to persuade the Ethiopians that their nation was not threatened, and that countering the Soviet threat to the Persian Gulf region was more important that Ethiopian objections."[53]

Mengistu, though, was not mollified by such assurances, and indeed it seemed that Ethiopian fears regarding an escalation of hostilities in the Ogaden were not groundless. On February 28, Henze sent a memo to Brzezinski notifying him that intelligence reports indicated that "Siad has no intention of reducing support to the Ogaden insurgency. He promised a recent meeting of guerrilla leaders that, even if Somalia signs an agreement with the U.S., Somali Government support for them will not be reduced."[54] Similarly Vance informed the president that although Siad had officially agreed to withdraw Somali troops from the Ogaden in March 1978, he had "reintroduced regular units in the Ogaden by November 1979 and has expanded their use and the scale of military activity since then," although the Somali leader continued to officially deny his involvement.[55] Dennis Mullin, correspondent for *U.S. News & World Report* based in the Horn, spent time with the Ogaden guerrillas and was told by a guerrilla leader, Hussein Mohamed Nur, that the deal between the United States and Somalia for the use of Berbera was a great psychological boost. Nur commented that "the Americans in Berbera will be a definite advantage for us. It will make Somalia more secure psychologically, and this will enable us to get more aid from Mogadishu."[56] The implication, of course, was that the Somali government must have been providing some level of support in order to be able to provide more.

Similarly, the Carter administration was aware that its other reason for previously refusing to enter into a military supply relationship with Siad Barré, his record of human rights abuses, had not improved. Vance informed Carter that "the Somali government has continued to subordinate individual liberties to its political and economic goals. It is an authoritarian, one party, military regime." [57] However, as with Somali involvement in the Ogaden, this was deemed less important than the national security concerns and the need to establish the use of military facilities in the region.

Thus the administration continued with the legal and practical requirements to further its aims. On February 25, in a briefing memo to the president, Vance reminded Carter that his decision to "seek agreement from the Government of Somalia for extended U.S. access to Somali military facilities, and to initiate a cooperative security arrangement with Somalia, including the provision of security assistance" would require a "Presidential Determination that the sale of defense articles and defense services under the Arms

Export control Act will 'strengthen the security of the United States and promote world peace.' Such a Determination would also permit the transfer to Somalia of U.S.-origin military equipment previously provided under FMS [Foreign Military Sales] to third countries."[58]

Accordingly, on March 3, 1980, Jimmy Carter issued a Presidential Determination justifying the establishment of a military relationship between the United States and Somalia. The president declared that "pursuant to the authority vested in my by Section 3(a)(1) of the Arms Control Export Act, I hereby find that the sale of defense articles and defense services to the Government of Somalia will strengthen the security of the United States and promote world peace." The reasons cited by Carter were that:

> The sale of U.S.-origin defense articles and services to Somalia would strengthen a number of United States security interests in the region. Somalia is strategically situated in the Horn of Africa at the entrance of the Bab el-Mandeb Straits, which is a major access route to petroleum supplies for Western Europe and Israel. Recently, Somalia has developed close ties with Saudi Arabia and other states of the area, as it has drawn away from dependence on the Soviet Union. Somalia has continued its traditionally close ties with Egypt in spite of Arab League opposition to the Middle East peace process. By providing Somalia with defense material to bolster its confidence in its security arrangements, the United States would support the maintenance of a non-aligned government which occupies an important crossroads position in Africa.... Located in an area of extreme political volatility, Somalia needs external assistance to develop a credible defense posture. Somalia desires assistance from Western nations. It is in the interest of the United States, with the cooperation of our European allies and Arab friends, to help Somalia improve its ability to defend itself.[59]

The interesting thing about the Presidential Determination was that the reasons cited had existed since 1977, but the administration had felt that Somali involvement in the Ogaden and humans rights abuses in Somalia provided grounds for avoiding a military relationship. It was the international developments of late 1979 and 1980 that prompted the reorientation of the administration's foreign policy. Indeed in an interview in 2000, Henze maintained that the deal with Somalia took place "because of Iran and Afghanistan. That's the only factor [sic]."[60] David Aaron agreed that the developments in Iran were the main motivation behind the administration actions in making arrangements with Somalia, despite the problems with human rights and in the Ogaden.[61]

Ogaden Complications

The possible involvement of Somalia in the Ogaden continued to provide the greatest threat to the consolidation of the relationship between Siad Barré's regime and the United States. Pat Malone, of the White House press office, contacted Paul Henze on March 13, asking if it was true that the Somalis had military units inside Ethiopia and that the Ogaden war was increasing in tempo. In the authorized response that was to be released to the media, it should be noted that Henze avoided the question, but took pains to re-state the official administration position:

> We have made clear to the Somalis in every discussion we have had with them that we will not support military activities directed against Ethiopia. We favor peaceful resolution of the difficulties between Somalia and Ethiopia. In any case, we are prepared to give Somalia only military material that can be used defensively. We continue to be interested in modest military facilities in Somalia and we believe that these will be in the interest of both Somalia and the United States, and in the interest of peace in the whole region. We are still negotiating with the Somalis about these arrangements. We have made clear to them that we do not support Somali military intervention against Ethiopia. If regular Somali troops continue to be used in Ethiopia, we may have to delay our plans for establishing military facilities in Berbera.[62]

Indeed, by the end of March, the administration appeared to be increasingly encountering problems as it attempted to finalize the arrangements for the use of military facilities in Somalia. One of the main problems appeared to be reaching agreement on the levels of aid to be provided in return for American access to the facilities at Berbera; according to *New York Times* correspondent Richard Halloran, Siad had "asked for more than the administration is prepared to give."[63] Toward the end of April, Government officials acknowledged that, although agreement had been reached for the use of military facilities in Oman and Kenya, negotiations with Somalia had "run into problems." The main stumbling blocks, they admitted, were Somalia's request for $2 billion in military and economic aid and for support for the conflict with Ethiopia. The administration, in contrast, had offered an aid package in the region of $100 million, and categorically refused to endorse Somali activities in the Ogaden.[64] The Somali incursion continued to cause concern for Carter's advisers; the SCC meeting of April 7 noted that "it was becoming increasingly clear that our efforts to secure facilities in Somalia entailed the danger of entanglement in the Ogaden War." In an attempt to ascertain the possible ramifications, Henze sent a memo requesting that the CIA "make a preliminary assessment of the longer-term implications of present trends in the Horn."[65]

The administration also faced problems with regard to its relationship with Ethiopia. Although relations with Ethiopia had clearly taken second place to those with Somalia, the Carter administration had shown no inclination to break contact completely with the Mengistu regime, and perhaps still retained the long-term hope that the situation with Ethiopia would one day improve. However, on April 3, Henze, who was the strongest advocate of maintaining relations with Ethiopia, wrote to Brzezinski noting his "surprise" at a communication he had just received from Ambassador Chapin:

> From it you will see that he has been informed by Dick Moose that he will be recalled this summer and the embassy in Addis Ababa will be downgraded to chargé level. Were you or anyone else here consulted on this "decision"? This is the first either Jerry Funk or I have heard of it. We both consider it a serious mistake.... We regularized our position in Ethiopia in July 1978, when Fred Chapin arrived. No great claims can be made for accomplishments there since, but I find it remarkable evidence of Ethiopian desire to maintain relations at full ambassadorial level that they have not even intimated action against him as a result of our "facilities" negotiations with Somalia. Having and keeping an ambassador in Addis gives us an important card for the future, when the political situation there may give us more room for maneuver than we seem to have now.[66]

Perhaps in an attempt to win Brzezinski over to his point of view, Henze concluded with the argument that downgrading the American presence in Ethiopia would "give comfort to the Soviets and Cubans who will be happy to see us so willingly consigning ourselves to a secondary role."[67] Henze's memo regarding Chapin's tenure in Addis Ababa is interesting also for its implicit references to the inter-departmental tension between the National Security Council and the Department of State, and provides further evidence that the conflict between the two agencies resulted from more than a personality clash between the respective section heads, Brzezinski and Vance.

A Change at State

Of course, the most significant event for the Carter administration in April was the failed attempt to rescue the hostages in Iran, and the resignation of secretary of state Cyrus Vance in protest.[68] However, Vance's opposition to the disastrous effort was the final event in a chain of confrontations that had plagued the secretary of state throughout his term in office and brought him to this decision that he described as "one of the most painful days of my life."[69]

Media coverage of Vance's departure was extensive, and a common theme dominated the analyses of his decision to resign. Once again, the apparent struggle with Brzezinski for foreign policy supremacy occupied the attention of reporters. *Time* devoted several pages in its edition of May 12 to the change in leadership at the State Department and recalled one of the clashes as being when the administration discussed its response to the escalation of Soviet and Cuban involvement in Ethiopia in early 1978:

> Brzezinski urged a show of force; Vance argued that it was not the right time or place to draw the line. For one thing, contended Vance, the Ethiopian government had

asked for Soviet-Cuban assistance in repelling an invasion by Somalia. That made it harder to charge Moscow with aggression. Vance won that round. To this day Brzezinski believes that if he had prevailed two years ago and the U.S. had stood up to the Kremlin over Ethiopia, the Carter administration would have impressed congressional hard-liners, chastened the Soviet leaders, preserved détente and secured enough support for the ratification of SALT II.[70]

A similar report in *Newsweek*, analyzing Vance's decision to resign, contended that, although relations between Vance and Brzezinski were perhaps not as bad as the media might have liked to suggest, their fundamental differences with regard to policy toward the Soviet Union in particular had placed Vance in an untenable position by 1980:

> In the early days of the administration, both emphasized the importance of détente. But with Soviet-Cuban adventurism in the Horn of Africa and, later, Moscow's invasion of Afghanistan, Vance's influence waned. Brzezinski favored a more combative approach, while Vance thought that the tougher response ought to be tempered by a continuing dialogue with Moscow.... Given the president's change of heart, Cyrus Vance, with his gentle ways and strict adherence to quiet diplomacy, had grown increasingly out of tune not only with Brzezinski but with a president who had reluctantly turned away from much of the world view he shared with Vance when his administration began.[71]

Whatever the reasons for Vance's departure, he was gone, and Carter chose Senator Edmund Muskie of Maine to replace him. The son of a Polish immigrant,[72] Muskie added to his degree in history and government from Bates College, Maine, with a law degree from Cornell University Law School in 1939. He began his career as a public servant in 1946 when he was elected as a member of Maine's House of Representatives, then ran successfully for Governor in 1954. Muskie joined the federal government in 1958 when he was elected to the U.S. Senate for the first of four terms. Once there, he became known as a skilled legislator, with specialist knowledge of environmental affairs. He was the Democratic vice presidential candidate in 1968, and campaigned briefly for the presidential nomination in 1972. Back in the Senate he assumed the chairmanship of the newly formed Budget Committee in 1975, where he became known as a fiscal conservative. Oklahoman Senator, Henry Bellmon, ranking Republican on the Budget Committee, described his colleague as "an enormously able person, a pragmatist without many ideological hang-ups."[73] Bellmon's assessment of Muskie is interesting for its resemblance to various portrayals of Brzezinski, highlighting once again the supremacy of the National Security Adviser's approach to foreign policy by 1980.

Muskie also had some experience of foreign affairs.[74] In 1967 he had participated in the U.S. mission to observe the elections in South Vietnam, and shortly afterwards became active in opposing the war there. In 1970 he joined the calls for arms control and from 1971 to 1974 served on the Senate Committee on Foreign Relations and traveled in an official capacity to Western Europe, the Soviet Union and the Middle East. In 1979 he once again served on the Foreign Relations Committee, until he resigned his Senate seat to accept Carter's invitation to head the Department of State.

Carter's decision may be attributed to several factors, only one of which was Muskie's foreign policy experience. The Carter administration had not had good relations with Congress during its first three years of office, and it was perhaps hoped that Muskie's reputation as one of the most influential and highly respected members of the Senate would help to rectify this. Muskie's reputation might also help the image of the administration with some of its allies; an editorial in *U.S. News & World Report* commented that "foreign leaders, such as Britain's Prime Minister Margaret Thatcher and West Germany's Chancellor Helmut Schmidt, are bound to be impressed by a hard-headed American politician with strong links both to Capitol Hill and the White House."[75] *Time* pointed to another reason for the president's choice when it remarked upon the "personal rapport" between Muskie and Jimmy Carter, claiming that Carter had long admired the Maine senator and had briefly considered him as a running mate in 1976. The two shared similar views on fiscal policy; as Chairman of the Senate Budget Committee, Muskie had supported Carter's programs.[76] The battles in the Democratic primaries with Ted Kennedy may well have figured in Carter's mind when he made his decision. Campaign director Robert Strauss stated that "Muskie was Carter's first and only choice. The president felt Muskie's judgment was good, his mind tough, and he thought Muskie could balance his team."[77]

While an advocate of arms control talks, Muskie also appeared to reflect the administration's desire to stand up to the USSR. He described the Soviet invasion of Afghanistan as a "single act of international cannibalism" and warned that, unless nations such as the United States stood firm, "the potential for future Soviet ... adventurism will greatly increase and will alter the foreign policy of every nation in the area, including the oil-producing countries of the Middle East."[78] However, the media appeared less interested in the new Secretary's views on foreign affairs than in his relationship with Zbigniew Brzezinski. The major article in *Time* on the transition in the State Department reported that Vance's outgoing words to Carter included the comment that "there has absolutely got to be an end to the confusion over who speaks for you."[79] Indeed, it appeared that Muskie shared this view. On April 30, immediately after accepting the appointment, Muskie declared that "the challenge is to establish the role of Secretary of State as the number one voice. The president made it clear to me that's what he wants his Secretary of State to do. I took this job not to be second in foreign policy, but to be first." However, commentators recalled that Carter had given Vance similar assurances in 1978, with little obvious effect.[80]

Indeed, the relationship between the Department of State and the National Security Council appeared destined to fare little better after Vance's departure. In a memo eerily reminiscent of a note penned by Vance at the beginning of the Carter administration,[81] Leon Billings, Muskie's chief of staff, suggested that Muskie must insist on "clearance with you on overseas travel by members of the NSC staff.... Prior coordination with appropriate people here on the subject matter, visits, etc. associated with such travel ... [and] participation of your people in any meetings between NSC staff and representatives of foreign governments — at home or abroad."[82] However, despite the behind-the-scenes tension, Muskie, like his predecessor, took pains to emphasize publicly that there was no conflict between the NSC and State. He told a press conference that he and Brzezinski were "both Poles, you know — we are not poles apart. We get along fine on a personal basis.... He has a different slant on things than I do, from time to time, but our differences of opinion are discussed and debated in a civilized way. Sometimes I win, sometimes I persuade him and sometimes he persuades me."[83]

Negotiations Continue with Somalia

Meanwhile, as Muskie settled into the State Department, negotiations continued on the use of military facilities in Somalia. However, Somali actions, particularly in the Ogaden, were making it increasingly difficult for the United States to consummate the relationship. In June, Henze informed Brzezinski that evidence was increasing that Somali regulars were involved in the Ogaden. He told the national security adviser that:

> For the third time in the last three years, Siad has unleashed a major military effort in Ethiopia using Somali regular forces.... Rather than a reduction in Ogaden operations, we have had a steady expansion with more and more direct regular Somali military participation. This had reached its natural culmination over the past ten days in serious military engagements between regular Ethiopian and Somali forces, with both sides now reinforcing the units already engaged. The prospect is for further escalation, expanded Ethiopian air retaliation against Somali territory and perhaps Ethiopian attacks onto Somali territory.[84]

The problems caused by Somali involvement in the Ogaden led to a reconsideration of the advisability of forming a military relationship with Siad Barré. While on a visit to Turkey to attend the North Atlantic Treaty Organization ministerial meeting at the end of June, Muskie admitted that the administration was now "re-thinking whether to pursue an agreement to obtain military facilities in Somalia."[85] Henze continued to argue against the plan, contending that "a serious assessment of American strategic interests in the region would underscore the unwisdom [sic] of proceeding further with Siad.... While the Somalis escalate the fighting in Ethiopia, our effort to gain facilities there should be put on the shelf."[86] He was supported by some, mainly in the State Department, who were concerned that Siad would use American support as encouragement for his activities in the Ogaden, thereby increasing both the seriousness of the conflict and of the refugee problem. However, there also remained a wealth of support for the opposing view. Some echoed Brzezinski's argument that the United States should continue to press for the facilities as a demonstration of American power in the region following the Soviet intervention in Afghanistan; others, such as General William Odom, pointed to the strategic necessity of the base for an American presence in the region.[87] Reflecting public support for Odom's reasoning, *New York Times* correspondent Christopher Wren, based in Mogadishu, commented that the "United States wants the air base [at Berbera] because the runway could put American B-52 bombers within strategic range of almost any trouble spot in the region." [88]

Carter's previous assurances to Muskie notwithstanding, Brzezinski's influence in foreign policy formulation seemed to predominate in discussions regarding future relations between the United States and Somalia. Following the national security adviser's lead, it seemed that those within the administration who were arguing that an American presence was necessary in Somalia were having their way. Indeed, some sought to downplay the possible complications of a closer relationship. On July 2, Odom advised Brzezinski of his opinion that an agreement between the United States and Somalia, even one that included military provisions, was unlikely to entangle the Americans in the problems in the Ogaden, therefore obviating the main area for concern. Odom argued that:

> Closer examination of the intelligence on Ethiopian offensive capabilities indicates that we have been grossly misled about the imminence of hostilities toward Hargeisa-Berbera. In fact, the Ethiopian predicament is such that an offensive with good prospects is not possible in the foreseeable future — months, maybe years. Furthermore, Somali operations in the Ogaden seem to be constrained by logistic problems; not fear of Ethiopian retaliation. Thus, a U.S. presence in Berbera will not likely lead to a greater Somali effort in the Ogaden.... In sum, the probabilities of our entanglement in an Ethiopian-Somali war in the next couple of years through an access agreement seem very very small.

Odom therefore suggested that negotiations for the use of Berbera should continue, and the American ambassador in Somalia, Donald Petterson, be

briefed on the American offer. However, Odom proposed that the administration should not abandon all caution and that the offer and terms of the
agreement "should be identical to the present one with the exception of a new
section on our security commitment. Our security commitment should explicitly exclude Ethiopian retaliatory attacks for Somali operations in the
Ogaden."[89]

Following a meeting of the SCC discussing Odom's proposals, a telegram
was sent to Petterson in Mogadishu asking that he seek a meeting with Siad
to make a series of points with regard to the negotiations. Petterson was
instructed to inform Siad that:

> The U.S. remains interested in concluding an agreement, and reaffirms its offer to
> assist Somalia in providing for its legitimate defense requirements. For this pur-
> pose and subject to appropriate congressional action, we would allocate over the
> next two years ... $40 million in credits on favorable repayment terms. Details of
> equipment that would be supplied can be worked out with Somali military officials,
> but we would expect to concentrate on air defense as a priority. In addition, sub-
> ject to Congressional action, the U.S. would make available $5 million in grant
> economic support funds in the coming year, and $300,000 in military training.

Petterson was also urged to emphasize that the United States had evidence that Somali regulars were involved in the Ogaden conflict, and warn
Siad that the administration's position regarding Somali involvement in the
Ogaden had not changed. The ambassador would have to make it clear that
"U.S. equipment or material would be provided to Somalia only for the legitimate defense of the internationally recognized territory of Somalia. The U.S.
cannot provide equipment to replace items used or transferred by Somalia for
use against the territory of any neighboring state, or to permit Somali equipment to be diverted to such use." Siad should also be told that "any increase
in Somali activities in the Ogaden and in any case the use of Somali regular
forces could jeopardize our efforts to enter into a military access relationship
with Somalia." The telegram concluded by asking Petterson to ascertain if
these terms were acceptable to the Somali government.[90]

Although within the administration there appeared to be a general
acceptance that strategic interests outweighed any complications that a deal
with Somalia might bring, some members of Congress were not yet convinced. This, of course, was important because of the need for Congressional
endorsement of any agreement. Representative Solarz, chairman of the House
Subcommittee on Africa, expressed the feelings of members of both cham-
bers in an editorial for the *New York Times*. He articulated his concerns that
a military relationship with Somalia might drag the United States into a border war in the Horn, and contended that the United States would then face
two choices:

Either we would rush to Somalia's assistance at great cost to our relations with economically and politically important African states, and with the danger of being drawn into a major military involvement in a peripheral area where the regional balance of powers would be weighed against us, or we would refuse to help Somalia, raising new doubts about our international credibility and jeopardizing our relationship with Somalia itself.

Solarz asserted, therefore, that "it would appear to be the better part of wisdom to forego the acquisition of a marginally useful military facility in Somalia that would pose great risks for our African diplomacy, our overall international credibility, and our relationship with the Somalis themselves."[91] But not everyone in Congress shared Solarz's view. Congressman Samuel Stratton (D-NY) expressed his support for the administration's argument of strategic necessity, contending:

> Mr. Solarz forgets that seven months after Afghanistan we still do not have that capability [to put rapid-deployment forces into the very regions where a Soviet "lunge" could spell economic disaster for the whole free world] because we lack adequate facilities from which to project our power.... To suggest so airily that the facilities at Berbera are "neither unique nor essential to the achievement of U.S. military objectives" betrays a shocking ignorance of the strategic and geopolitical realities involved in trying to deter Soviet military moves in the Soviet Union's own backyard and in the face of current Soviet superiority in almost every category of military power.[92]

As it appeared that the United States would finally consolidate its relationship with Somalia, the administration appeared to accept that the maintenance of relations with Ethiopia, not to mention its earlier desire to improve the relationship, were necessary casualties. There was little protest or outrage when, at the end of July, Ethiopia expelled the American ambassador, Fred Chapin. In the official announcement, State Department spokesman John Trattner declared that, following the request of the Ethiopian government, Chapin had left Addis Ababa on July 29, but that twenty-two other staff members remained and the facility would stay open. As the Ethiopian Ambassador to Washington had been recalled in 1978, both countries would now be represented only by chargés d'affaires. Trattner also reminded reporters that Ethiopia owed "twenty-two U.S. business claimants about $30 million for properties it has seized, and since 1976 it has failed to meet its installment payments on $4.5 million in military debts to the United States."[93] Henze later recalled that "Chapin left Addis Ababa in 1980 disillusioned and convinced that Mengistu wanted a hostile relationship with the U.S. to help draw the Soviets more fully into backing him."[94]

Agreement is Reached

On August 13 the Democratic National Convention confirmed that Jimmy Carter would once again be the Democrat candidate in the forthcoming presidential election. There is no question that Carter wanted to remain in the White House after November, but it appears he did not want to hold on to his job at any cost. Stansfield Turner contended that he did "not believe that President Carter made decisions ... with respect to how it affected his electoral chances. I think he was very careful to do what was best for the country"[95]; similarly, Brzezinski was adamant that "not on any score" did the forthcoming election factor into policy decisions.[96] Notwithstanding, Carter wanted to win in November, and therefore some plans had to be made. Hamilton Jordan left his role as chief of staff to work full-time on re-election, and early in August Brzezinski produced a report discussing the role of foreign policy in the upcoming presidential campaign. The national security adviser pointed out to Carter that "foreign policy should offer you the greatest opportunity for the exercise of presidential leadership, in a manner that could significantly influence the outcome of the elections." Despite the current international situation, Brzezinski felt that the president had reason to be proud, arguing that "the most distinctive hallmark of your foreign policy is that you have blended together two elements that traditionally have been seen in America as being in conflict: concern for moral principle and recognition of the importance of American power.... You have managed to combine the two in order to shape a foreign policy that has been both moral and realistic."[97] In the large context of the administration's foreign policy as a whole it is reasonable to argue that Brzezinski had a point — and certainly it is difficult to disagree with the view that foreign policy matters would contribute greatly to the result in November.

Meanwhile, in the Horn of Africa, an event took place that perhaps contributed to, or even prompted, Brzezinski's optimism. After months of negotiations it appeared that the United States and Somalia were nearing agreement over the use of military facilities at Berbera. On August 12, a State Department spokesman announced that a delegation from Somalia was expected shortly to finalize the details of the arrangement,[98] and they duly arrived a week later, led by General Suleyman Abdullah, the commandant of the National Security Service.[99] Richard Moose, the assistant secretary of state for African affairs, and Robert Pelletreau of the Pentagon's Office of International Security Affairs, led the American delegation to the meeting and they soon reported a breakthrough in negotiations. A State Department spokesman subsequently announced that Somalia had accepted the administration's offer and was ready to let the American Navy and Air Force use its facilities at the port of Berbera in the Gulf of Aden in return for military and economic aid.[100]

Having previously refused to form an alliance with Somalia because of Siad's violations of human rights and international law, the United States, in

August 1980, reached an agreement for use of Somali military facilities in Berbera, despite the fact that the Somali leader's internal and external policies had not changed. On August 22, 1980, the State Department announced that:

> The United States and the Somalia Democratic Republic [*sic*] exchanged diplomatic notes [today] providing for expanded cooperation between Somalia and the United States in both the civil and military spheres. The implementation of this agreement will be a matter of mutual and continuing consultation between the two governments as we work together toward an expanded relationship across a broad range of mutual interests, including the development of programs of security assistance and economic cooperation. This exchange of notes allows the United States increased access to Somalia's air and port facilities. The provisions of this agreement are defensive in nature and are aimed at the promotion of stability in the general area; they are not directed against any particular nation or group of nations.[101]

In return for granting the Americans access to military facilities at Berbera, the United States agreed to provide economic and military aid to Siad Barré. The total aid package, to be given to Somalia by the United States over the next two years, seemed impressive, especially given the complexities of the situation in the Horn of Africa. Totaling some $103.3 million, it included $20 million for arms credits in 1980, $20 million for arms credits in 1981, $300,000 for training Somali military personnel in 1981, $53 million in economic development aid during 1980 and 1981 and $5 million in both 1980 and 1981 for economic support financing of grain shipments.[102] However, this still represented substantially less than the $2 billion in military and economic aid that Siad had been insisting upon previously. Perhaps most impressive, though, and certainly from a diplomatic point of view, was Siad's retreat from his demand that the United States must back his claims to the Ogaden.[103]

The official announcement concluded by pointing out that the agreement with Somalia, combined with similar agreements reached previously with Oman and Kenya, would provide the United States with access to strategic locations that would enable American forces to move into the Persian Gulf region should a crisis arise.[104] State Department officials explained that the deal meant that "American forces will have access to airfields and port facilities at Mogadishu in the Indian Ocean, at Berbera in the Gulf of Aden and possibly other locations."[105] In addition, they contended that "the agreement with Somalia, coupled with recent similar accords with Kenya and Oman and arrangements for more limited use by American forces of port facilities in Djibouti, would help achieve President Carter's goal of enhanced security for the region."[106] Within the administration Henze commented to Jerry Funk that, although other events, such as the scandal with Billy Carter and the Democratic convention, might have deflected attention from Somalia, there was indeed some capital to be gained from "entering into an agreement and thereby achieving another 'foreign policy success' and shouting and waving it about too — since the Somalis, unlike the Kenyans and the Omanis, are not averse to publicity."[107]

A few days after the official announcement, Moose appeared before the Subcommittee on Africa to discuss the accord, which needed Congressional endorsement of the military aid provisions. The assistant secretary of state declared that the administration had "undertaken these negotiations and this agreement in furtherance of a global strategic objective," but went on to argue that efforts to acquire access to facilities on the Indian Ocean, including those in Somalia and Kenya, "do not represent any basic change in the policy established by this administration toward Africa. We continue to believe that conflicts on the African continent should be resolved peacefully and that economic development remains the primary task with which we should associate ourselves."[108]

However, the problems in the Ogaden remained uppermost in the minds of all those associated with the agreement with Somalia. Moose told the House Subcommittee on African Affairs that the negotiations:

> Have given us the opportunity to discuss problems which could arise from the continuing dispute between Somalia and Ethiopia over the Ogaden region. We believe that we have made abundantly clear to the Somalis the limitations imposed by our laws on the use of materiel which might be supplied in the future under foreign military sales agreements and the possible consequences of their violation of these provisions. We are confident that the Somalis understand our views on the activities in the Ogaden.[109]

When questioned by Chairman Solarz as to the extent of the Somali incursion into the Ogaden, Moose replied that "I do not believe there is any significant body of Somali forces in the Ogaden.... I doubt there are any Somali battalions. It's very possible there are Somali patrols."[110] Moose also told the Subcommittee that the United States had received assurances "orally and in writing that the Somalis will not introduce regular forces into the Ogaden" in the future.[111] A high-ranking State Department official told the *New York Times* that "the Somalis have told us they will avoid the Ogaden with their regular forces and have given us very explicit assurances that they will not use American military equipment outside their own territory." He added that "it would be contrary to the letter and spirit of the assurances the Somalis have given us if they used arms we provided in the Ogaden."[112]

Unfortunately for the administration, the State Department announcements and assurances quickly appeared to be premature. U.S. negotiators had told reporters that while the Somali government had agreed in writing not to use American-supplied equipment to fight in Ethiopia, they were unsure of the reliability of such assurances, in view of the proven and long-standing Somali determination to reclaim the Ogaden.[113] Indeed the administration soon had evidence that Somali military involvement in Ethiopia, rather than diminishing, was in fact increasing. On September 3, Henze informed Brzezinski that "intelligence reports this week indicate that they [the Somalis] may be intensifying operations in the Ogaden and may be introducing new troops."[114] One of the problems, Henze pointed out to Brzezinski, was that "unfortunately, we did not get a firm commitment from the Somalis on desisting from Ogaden operations as part of our deal with them."[115]

Even more unfortunate, from the administration's point of view, was the fact that the Somali involvement in the Ogaden was common knowledge in the United States. Within days of the announcement of the agreement between Somalia and the United States, administration officials conceded to the *New York Times* that "they could not give assurances that Somali troops were not fighting in the Ogaden region in eastern Ethiopia, despite an agreement with the United States not to fight."[116] Moreover, CIA reports suggested that there was extensive Somali involvement with the Ogadeni guerrillas. Members of the CIA told the House Subcommittee on African Affairs that elements of three Somali regular battalions were still in the Ogaden, and CIA sources told the *Washington Post* that from three hundred to one thousand Somali regulars were serving as "volunteers" with the insurgents trying to annex the Ogaden to Somalia. Although Solarz would not confirm the figures quoted to him by CIA personnel when questioned by *Post* reporters, he admitted that there was "a sharp difference" between the CIA testimony and the official State Department reports, including those given in open session to the Subcommittee by Moose.[117]

At the beginning of September Henze highlighted the difficulties that the publicity surrounding Somali activity in the Ogaden could cause for the administration. He warned Brzezinski that "the problem of Ogaden fighting and Ethio-Somali tension is going to remain alive in the U.S. and world press. Under such circumstances, Congress is not going to be easily persuaded that the agreement the administration has signed is a good idea."[118] Nor were Henze's fears groundless. The matter aroused much discussion among the members of the House Subcommittee on African Affairs, provoking seven of the eight members to send a letter to Muskie, expressing their deep opposition to the agreement with Somalia. The members argued that administration plans to provide $20 million in arms credits to Somalia in 1980 "would increase the dangers of United States involvement" in fighting between Somalia and Ethiopia. The letter went on, "it is our understanding that, despite its written and verbal assurance to the contrary, Somalia remains deeply and intimately involved in the armed struggle which continues to rage in the Ethiopian Ogaden." Therefore, the Congressmen argued, "new U.S. military commitments in Somalia could very well exacerbate the ongoing military conflict between Ethiopia and Somalia over the Ogaden, increase the dangers of U.S. involvement in the conflict, and estrange the U.S. from important African states who overwhelmingly oppose Somalia's efforts in the Ogaden."[119]

Although members of the Subcommittee on African Affairs protested the administration's action, this particular subcommittee had no power to thwart the decision of the Carter administration to allow military equipment to be sent to Somalia. Nonetheless, Solarz declared that he expected the administration to heed the Subcommittee's objections, because "if they don't, the Congress is likely to restrict in the future the reprogramming flexibility the administration currently enjoys." [120] However, while the views of the Subcommittee on Africa were merely advisory, the House Appropriations Subcommittee on Foreign Operations did have the power to block the arms-for-bases deal with Somalia, and held its own hearings on September 16 to discuss the reprogramming of foreign military sales funds to Somalia. Matthew Nimetz, under secretary of state for security assistance, testified before the Subcommittee to argue the administration's case. The obvious care and attention to detail that had gone into his statement reflected the importance that the Carter administration attached to the deal. Nimetz first described the context that had prompted the administration's action, his comments reflecting the traditional approach to Cold War foreign policy that had predominated since the beginning of the year:

> The pattern of increased Soviet activity in and around the Indian Ocean has intensified during the past few years. It includes both substantial Soviet naval and air deployments as well as a major effort to expand Soviet influence through political and subversive techniques. Parallel with that Soviet thrust, new internal stresses and tensions developed in key states of the region, some of them rooted in the massive inflow of wealth flowing from oil production. The effects of Soviet activity were most apparent in Ethiopia and in South Yemen, but also in the attitudes of other important nations. The cataclysm in Iran also had a dramatic and destabilizing effect on the region as a whole.... The Soviet invasion of Afghanistan was the latest and most direct Soviet effort in this region.[121]

These events, Nimetz argued, had led the administration to seek access to military facilities in Oman, Kenya and Somalia in order to develop "an enhanced capacity to deal with specific threats ... [and] to begin the long-term process of protecting our interests and those of our friends and allies in the Indian Ocean and Persian Gulf." [122]

Nimetz then took pains to stress the official administration position with regard to Siad's territorial ambitions and reassure the Subcommittee that there were no dangers inherent in the agreement with Somalia:

> We do not believe that the limited supplies of defensive equipment we are prepared to sell Somalia will be decisive or even greatly relevant to the balance of power in the area which substantially favors Ethiopia, and Somalia has assured us that they understand our laws which require in no uncertain terms that military equipment acquired through the FMS [Foreign Military Sales] program can only be used for legitimate self-defense.... The $20 million will be used for defensive military equipment. We have not yet sat down with the Somali officials to discuss what they will use it for, but under our system we have to approve anything they acquire, and we expect it to be defensive equipment.[123]

However, Stephen Solarz also appeared as a witness before the Subcommittee and commented on the situation in the Ogaden:

> I have to tell you that when our Subcommittee took testimony on this question a few weeks ago, I had never heard a greater discrepancy between the testimony that we received in public session and the testimony that we received in executive session in my six years in the Congress. I gather, Mr. Chairman, that you will be hearing later today from representatives of the Central Intelligence Agency, and it is not for me in public session to disclose what I am confident you will hear at that time. Suffice it to say, however, that in spite of the public written and verbal assurances which we appear to have received from the Somalis that they are no longer involved in the Ogaden, it was the judgment of seven of the eight members of the Subcommittee on Africa after hearing all of the testimony that the Somalis remain deeply and intimately involved in the Ogaden.[124]

With such conflicting evidence regarding the advisability of a military relationship between the United States and Somalia, it was perhaps not surprising that the result of the hearings was not good for the Carter administration. The Appropriations Subcommittee informed Muskie that the administration's case for providing military aid to Somalia was "not sufficiently strong," and refused to endorse the request of $20 million for Somalia in the next fiscal year. Although Clarence Long (D-Md), the Subcommittee chairman, offered to hold further hearings "if the administration wishes to rejustify the proposal," any agreement had to be reached before the end of the current fiscal year on September 30.[125] The reality was that the administration would be unable to resubmit the request until after the election in November. John Felton of *Congressional Quarterly* described the action by the Subcommittee as a "slap at President Carter."[126]

Notwithstanding, there was some support for the Carter administration on Capitol Hill. On September 16 and 17 the Senate passed military construction bills related to the administration's plans for building or improving military facilities in Kenya, Oman and Somalia.[127] Also, at the beginning of October, there were signs that attitudes were softening on the south side of the Capitol, when Stephen Solarz (D-NY) and the Congressional Black Caucus relented in their opposition to the arrangements. Likewise, the House Appropriations Subcommittee on Foreign Operations, which had claimed that the administration had not made a strong enough case for funding, notified Muskie that it had subsequently decided to approve the administration's request for $20 million in arms sales to Somalia, although it retained the condition that "no specific equipment will be agreed to or delivered until it has received verified assurances that all regular Somali forces are completely removed from the Ogaden."[128] In the same way that developments in Afghanistan and Iran had prompted the reorientation of the administration's approach, it appeared that similar international developments had brought about the congressional change of heart — in this case, the outbreak of war between Iran and Iraq on September 21.[129]

Concurrent with the battle with Capitol Hill, the Carter administration was faced with opposition to its agreement with Somalia from Ethiopia. On August 30 Mengistu sent a letter to Jimmy Carter expressing his serious displeasure at the developments between the United States and Somalia. Mengistu complained that the agreement, especially the establishment of military facilities at Berbera, was a matter of grave concern to the Ethiopian government, because:

> As a result of the latest accord between Washington and Mogadishu, your administration has openly and actively associated itself with the misguided policy of a country that has been fanatically obsessed with the dream of the so-called "Greater Somalia" since the very day of its emergence to independence.... It is regrettable that the U.S. should have found it fit and proper to provide Somalia a firm backing [sic] at a time when that country's aggressive policy has been condemned by African and many other countries. The agreement on the Berbera base is neither useful to U.S. African policy nor helpful to the promotion of peace and stability in our region.[130]

Proof of the re-orientation of the foreign policy of the Carter administration was reflected in the discussions following receipt of Mengistu's letter of protest. For three years the administration had tempered its policy toward Somalia because of concerns about the Ethiopian reaction. However, by September 1980 the general opinion was that Mengistu's concerns should be ignored. Even Henze, who had repeatedly and consistently demonstrated his tendency to favor the maintenance of relations with Ethiopia almost at any cost, told Brzezinski that "my own judgment continues to be against a reply or at least against a reply with much substance.... There are, of course, contrary views, and these should perhaps be given consideration. If we really want a dialogue with Mengistu now as part of a larger Horn strategy, then there is a case for a substantive presidential letter. I do not have the impression that we want a dialogue."[131]

In fact, a letter to Mengistu was approved at the end of September, but the contents would have done little to reassure the Ethiopian leader. In it, Carter insisted that "we continue to support the integrity of internationally recognized boundaries; we recognize and respect the sovereignty and independence of Ethiopia, Somalia, and all other states in the region; and we strongly advocate the resolution of conflict by peaceful means. My government is not hostile to Ethiopia and stands ready to resolve outstanding bilateral problems." However, the president also made it plain that he was determined to press ahead with the agreement with Somalia. He argued that his "purpose in reaching agreement with Somalia, and with a number of other nations in the region, is to enhance the peace and security of the Indian Ocean region in the face of commonly perceived danger resulting from aggressive Soviet activities there. I believe the U.S. presence is in the interest of any regional state which seeks to preserve its independence and sovereignty from Soviet domination."[132]

The letter epitomized the foreign policy of the Carter administration in 1980. Carter had not abandoned his interest in improving the human condition but his priority as president was clearly the Cold War; a war that was to be fought with traditional methods based upon American military power.

The Legacy of the Carter Administration

In November, the American people were given the opportunity to comment upon the incumbent administration. Overwhelmingly, the well-intentioned but often politically ineffectual Southerner was repudiated, as Ronald Reagan won the presidential election by a landslide.[133] The reasons for Carter's defeat, which have been well documented by historical commentators on the administration,[134] included domestic issues such as the energy crisis and poor economy, with high unemployment and high inflation, as well as foreign policy matters such as the impression that Carter had "given away" the Panama Canal, weakness in the face of Soviet adventurism and, arguably most important, his seeming inability to resolve the ongoing hostage crisis in Iran.

The situation in the Horn of Africa also suggested that there was little about which the administration could boast. There had been no peaceful resolution to the conflicts in the region, with continuing military activity in the Ogaden and Eritrea. On November 19, in a report eerily reminiscent of commentaries of early 1977, the Ogaden was described as "a focal point that could erupt into a major crisis between the United States and the Soviet Union, both vying for influence in the region."[135] A Western diplomat in Addis Ababa claimed that "it is a no-win situation for both sides. The Ethiopians can't give it up because to do so would set a precedent for other regions of the country where ethnic groups are demanding independence," such as the Eritreans in the north. "The Somalis won't give it up," the diplomat added. "To reclaim traditional homelands is a driving force among the Somalis and any leader who renounced it wouldn't last in power very long. This has been going on for five hundred years. It certainly isn't going to end tomorrow or in the foreseeable future."[136]

Furthermore, the conditions faced by the people of Ethiopia and Somalia did not seem to have improved. Human rights continued to be violated in both countries, and, as Henze informed Brzezinski in December 1980, "the Ogaden refugee situation is now probably the worst in the world and not improving."[137] Perhaps most significantly, the arms-for-bases deal with Somalia had required that the administration abandon the principles that it had adhered to for three years, by agreeing to a military supply relationship with Siad Barré's regime despite ongoing activity in the Ogaden and continued human rights violations. Paul Henze, never a fan of Somalia, later reflected bitterly that, "by embracing Somalia in 1980, the U.S. helped prolong an odious regime which has killed — proportionately — as many of its citizens as Mengistu's regime has and has forced even larger numbers — proportionately — to flee."[138] Similarly, Brzezinski acknowledged in his memoirs that "events later on, notably growing Soviet self-assertiveness, did deflect the administration from some of its original goals."[139]

Arguably, the most visible of these had been the emphasis upon human rights in policy formulation, and this issue certainly demonstrated the "deflection" referred to by Brzezinski. As discussed in Chapter I, the administration had chosen to emphasize human rights matters for several reasons: it provided a way to fight the Cold War in the era of the Vietnam Syndrome by attacking the Soviet Union and communism on a moral level; it was designed to increase the standing and prestige of the United States in the eyes of the world, after involvement in Vietnam had destroyed or diminished that standing; and for Carter, the Christian and moralist, it had seemed the right thing to do. However, the events of 1980 had prompted a new approach within the administration. Now, the Cold War should be fought, and American international prestige improved, by more traditional methods in which American power and might were emphasized. Indeed, in December 1980, Muskie sent a memo to Jimmy Carter, setting out the foreign policy accomplishments of the administration. The secretary of state claimed that the summation of achievements was "truly impressive" and headed the list with "building America's military strength." However, eighth and last on the list came "asserting our national commitment to human rights."[140]

Notwithstanding the radical change in the direction of the public face of foreign policy toward the Horn of Africa and elsewhere in 1980—and the charges of hypocrisy that this has brought, arguably with some justification — the Carter administration does not deserve a totally negative evaluation. Although the administration had accepted that practical necessity often reduced the emphasis that could be placed on human rights matters by a presidential administration,[141] and the extent to which it could be the principal weapon in fighting the Cold War, the fact remains that the publicity given to human rights at that level integrated the issue into policy formulation at the highest echelons—a place that it has retained today. Human rights issues may not drive policy formulation, as the Carter administration had originally hoped that they might, but they cannot be ignored. In his memoirs, Brzezinski was right to claim that the administration deserved credit for its success in that "it established a climate of global concern that encouraged improvements in human rights conditions and inhibited as well as exhibited the gross violations."[142]

Despite the pressing problems caused by developments in the international arena in 1980, it should be noted that Jimmy Carter retained a degree of commitment to the importance of human rights. In a speech to the Asian/Pacific Democratic Caucus in May, the president declared that "there's a hunger for the realization of human rights, a hunger and a demand for the right of each human being in many nations on Earth now to control one's own destiny, to have the elements of the rudiments of democracy, the benefits of freedom." Developing the argument that "the worldwide problem of refugees is caused by the deprivation of freedom," Carter linked human rights with humanitarian concerns, and went on:

> In the world today, there are probably three million refugees, eight or nine hundred thousand refugees who've escaped from Afghanistan, most into Pakistan, some into Iran. Hundreds of thousands of refugees have escaped from the Ethiopian area into Somalia and into other countries that border on Ethiopia. There's a potential flood of refugees trying to escape from the Castro regime in Cuba, hundreds of thousands of refugees escaping from the domination by the Vietnamese, the people in Kampuchea.

However, the new orientation in the administration's foreign policy was also reflected as Carter continued, "in almost every instance, the escapees are trying to get away from communism, sponsored by, condoned by, supported by, financed by the Soviet Union."[143]

By 1980, therefore, while still important, the issue of human rights was less of a priority for the administration as it struggled to cope with the many crises of that year. However, the administration's impact in bringing the matter to the fore in policy debate was already in effect. Although the administration could no longer devote as much attention to human rights problems, and related humanitarian concerns such as the predicament of refugees, as it might have wished, Carter might well have been gratified to see other bodies, particularly Congress and the media, continue to highlight, and attempt to address, these matters. Indeed, despite the personal bitterness that existed between Carter and his chief rival for the Democratic nomination for president, Senator Edward Kennedy (D-Mass), the two men were agreed on this issue. On January 24, 1980, Kennedy announced to the Senate:

> I am introducing legislation today to provide emergency authority to respond to the growing needs of Afghanistan and Somalian refugees. A massive human crisis is developing in these two nations of major importance to the United States. In Pakistan, over a half million Afghan refugees have now flooded into its northern provinces, and in Somalia some 600,000 refugees have fled from Ethiopia. It would be a tragic error if we were to focus solely on the military and security issues along this so-called "crescent of crisis," when there is also a human crisis equally compelling — and one that not only poses grave humanitarian problems, but also threatens the area's political and economic stability.[144]

On the other side of the Capitol, Representative Thomas Petri (R-Wis) demonstrated that human rights issues and related humanitarian concerns transcended partisan politics. Expressing his deep sadness at the "tragic overwhelming refugee problem" in Somalia, he went on to explain:

> That small country of 3.4 million people has 474,000 refugees in camps. The Somali government itself estimates that, for every one refugee in camps, two others roam the countryside in need of food, clothing and medicine. That means there are almost 1.5 million refugees, or over one-third of Somali's total normal population. No other nation on earth has such a high proportion of refugees in country [sic].

Petri also praised the House Subcommittee on Africa, which was shortly to hold hearings on the refugee problem in Africa in order to consider emergency aid that could be provided by the United States, and called for action throughout America at every level. He argued that "it is clear that, on purely humanitarian grounds, we must support Somalia in its effort to provide the 1.5 million refugees with food, shelter, clothing and medicine. We should also consider directing America's surplus grain, and our surplus dry milk supplies, to the people of this needy area."[145]

The House Subcommittee on Foreign Agricultural Policy discussed relief measures and recommended that an additional 34,000 tons of food aid be provided to Somalia under Public Law 480. On May 13, Representative Andrew Maguire (D-NJ) urged support for this proposal, arguing that "Somalia's refugee problem is getting bigger, not smaller.... Of Somalia's many needs, the food deficit is the most pressing.... If we are to avert disaster later this summer, quick passage of Public Law 480 supplemental appropriations is imperative."[146]

Meanwhile, human rights abuses in Ethiopia were highlighted by Senator William Proxmire (D-Wis), who called for action to prevent the genocide practiced by Ethiopia in the Ogaden against the ethnic Somalia inhabitants. On April 2 he declared that "this brutal campaign, which includes such tactics as poisoning water-holes, strafing villages, and attacking them by air with napalm has been quietly underway for the past six months" and had resulted in "thousands of casualties." He insisted that the Senate must "speak out on behalf of the millions of innocent people who have been murdered. We must take concrete action to let the world know where we stand."[147] Neither did the Senate forget the other countries of the Horn. On April 23, Senator George McGovern (D-SD) warned that "as concerns of national security lead us to focus increasing attention upon African countries bordering the Indian Ocean, a human tragedy is developing in this region which we cannot allow to go unnoticed or unaddressed." He went on to urge "my colleagues in both the Senate and the House to make the securing of additional food aid for Somalia a top priority."[148]

Notwithstanding the concern expressed by government officials at both ends of Pennsylvania Avenue, reports throughout 1980 suggested that there was little evidence of any improvement in the situation in the Horn. On May 22, Edward Cody, the correspondent for the *Washington Post* based in the Ogaden, indicated that the increase in activity from Somali guerrillas in the Ogaden has "generated a gigantic stream of refugees into Somalia."[149] In August, Robert Knight reported from Mozambique for *U.S. News & World Report* that "from Ethiopia to South Africa, the twin specters of drought and war are threatening millions of people in East Africa with starvation.... The five-year conflict between Somalia and Ethiopia over Ethiopia's Ogaden region has spawned about 1.5 million refugees. Nearly half of them live in twenty-five shanty camps in Somalia. The rest try to eke out a nomadic existence. Thousands have died for lack of food and medicines, and thousands more may share their fate."[150] Furthermore, on October 12, Joseph Kennedy, director of international development for Africa, told the *New York Times* that "Somalia is a disaster zone. Every fourth person is a refugee. The strain on the economy, the water, the grass, the trees is destroying everything in the country." The plight of the refugees worsened when Iraq, Somalia's sole supplier of oil, cut off shipments because of the war with Iran, thus denying relief agencies the fuel they needed to transport humanitarian aid to the refugee camps.[151]

Perhaps spurred on by the media reports, members of Congress attempted to take concrete action that might help to alleviate the plight of the Somali refugees. In September a report assessing the refugee situation in Somalia was prepared for the Senate Foreign Relations Committee under the chairmanship of Frank Church (D-Idaho). The report began by pointing out that, not only did the Committee have oversight responsibility for U.S. refugee assistance, it also had a moral responsibility and "an abiding humanitarian concern for those who have been forced to flee their homes as a result of natural or manmade disasters." Although the report acknowledged that emergency aid, over half of which had been supplied by the United States, had helped half a million refugees in Somalia, often making the difference between "starvation and continued existence," much more needed to be done. Thus, the report recommended that:

> The Auditor General of AID undertake, immediately, an audit of the disposition of food which the United States has provided to Somalia for refugee relief, ... that AID immediately increase its staff in Somalia, ... that the U.S. AID mission, in cooperation with international organizations, immediately develop contingency plans to provide assistance in the event that a large influx of refugees move across the border from the Ogaden or food supplies are disrupted for any other reason ... [and] that the Committee and the U.S. Department of State carefully review the response of the U.S. system to the refugee problem in Somalia.[152]

In the House, Representative Andrew Maguire (D-NJ) called in August for support for a resolution providing aid to Somali refugees "not only for food but for the purchase of medical supplies as well.... I urge members of Congress to join in sponsoring this important statement of conscience on behalf of Somalia's refugees."[153] The bill remained active and was one of the last matters to be dealt with by the 96th Congress. On November 12, Representative Robert Dornan (R-Calif) addressed the House. He stated that "there are not too many positive things we can accomplish in this remaining session. But we will have a bill, HR 7854 before us for aid to halt the famine in Somalia."[154] Dornan argued that the "fallout" of the war in the Ogaden, "as in every war, is the death, disease, and starvation of the civilian population. As a result of the constant fighting and a drought in the region, the people of the Horn of Africa are confronting a terrible famine.... I ask all of my colleagues to reflect on this terrible suffering and to support the hunger relief measures found in HR 7854."[155]

The Carter administration may have been forced by practical necessity and the realities of the international environment to reconsider its policy priorities, and the way in which those policies were implemented, but the legacy of the administration was already being demonstrated: a commitment to human rights and related humanitarian concerns that endures today. Thus, the Carter administration's foreign policy towards the Horn of Africa does not deserve a totally negative evaluation. Although, ultimately, Carter was forced to allow practical necessity and the realities of the international environment to predominate in his foreign policy formulation, his attempts to reorient foreign policy would have some lasting impact in the enduring emphasis placed upon human rights in policy formulation at every level in the United States, and throughout the world.

Conclusion:
History Does Matter

As we have seen, an analysis of the policy towards the Horn of Africa can provide an excellent case study in comprehending American diplomatic history during the years of the Carter administration. By gaining an understanding of the policy and decision-making process with regards to Ethiopia and Somalia, we can apply that knowledge to the administration's policy as a whole and thereby gain a greater appreciation of it. This in turn provides further insight into the many debates that still surround the Carter administration, and facilitates an evaluation of Jimmy Carter's four-year term as president. In particular, there are three main areas of interest: the importance of the Horn of Africa in the history of détente; Carter's role and ability as a Cold War president; and the style of his presidency.

The Horn of Africa and the Demise of Détente

Jimmy Carter's reorientation of foreign policy, from one which focused upon regionalism and human rights, to one which emphasized more traditional Cold War themes such as globalism and containment, seemed, to some historians, to signal the demise of détente and the onset of a second Cold War. Although, as previously discussed, various viewpoints are put forward as explanations for the demise of détente,[1] a common theme throughout is the importance of events in the developing world, particularly in the swathe of countries that stretched from the Indian subcontinent, through the Middle East, to the Horn of Africa — a region collectively dubbed the Arc of Crisis.[2]

Zbigniew Brzezinski certainly shared this view. In his memoirs, Carter's national security adviser claimed that American foreign policy towards the Horn of Africa was directly responsible for the failure of the SALT agreement, the cooling of relations between the United States and the Soviet Union, and ultimately the collapse of détente. He wrote:

> In March 1980, as we were reacting to the Soviet invasion of Afghanistan, I wrote in my journal: "I have been reflecting on when did things begin genuinely to go wrong in the U.S.-Soviet relationship. My view is that it was on the day sometime in ... 1978 when at the SCC meeting I advocated that we send in a carrier task force in reaction to the Soviet deployment of the Cubans in Ethiopia. At that meeting not only was I opposed by Vance, but Harold Brown asked why, for what reason, without taking into account that that is a question that should perplex the Soviets rather than us. The president backed the others rather than me, we did not react. Subsequently, as the Soviets became more emboldened, we overreacted, particularly in the Cuban Soviet brigade fiasco of last fall. That derailed SALT, the momentum of SALT was lost, and the final nail in the coffin was the Soviet invasion of Afghanistan. In brief underreaction then bred overreaction." That is why I have used occasionally the phrase, "SALT lies buried in the sands of the Ogaden."[3]

Brzezinski's allusion to the Munich analogy, and the danger that appeasement would encourage aggression and adventurism, is clear. Equally apparent is the acceptability of the principle of his argument. World leaders and policy-makers continue to adhere to such a doctrine; indeed, the war on terror, waged since September 11, 2001, is based upon the principle that a lack of resistance to acts of terrorism would serve to encourage others to commit similar atrocities.

However, although the principles of Brzezinski's argument are convincing, it is far from certain that Brzezinski was right to attribute American policy towards the Horn of Africa with such significance. By doing so, the national security adviser seemed to be making one of two assumptions. Either he appeared to have forgotten the lessons of Vietnam, and overlooked the difference, as Richard Nixon had pointed out when attempting to extricate the United States from South East Asia, between areas of strategic and peripheral interest. Or Brzezinski considered the Horn of Africa to be of strategic interest.

It seems unlikely, though, that a man of Brzezinski's obvious analytical abilities would have reverted to the simplistic perspective of the early Cold War, especially when the recognition given to the issue of global complexity by the Carter administration is taken into account. Therefore, for Brzezinski to be correct — for failure to react to a relatively insignificant incident in a frequently overlooked region of the world to have had such momentous consequences — the Horn of Africa would have had to be the pivotal area in the global arena for both the United States and the Soviet Union. Although, as we have seen, the Horn does have some strategic importance, particularly with regard to its geographical proximity to the oil-rich Middle East, it would be wrong to over-emphasize its significance in international relations. According to Peter Schraeder, in *United States Foreign Policy Toward Africa: Incrementalism, Crisis and Change*, the increased importance placed upon Africa as a whole by the Carter administration in 1977 meant that although it thereafter accounted for eleven percent of foreign policy behavior, it still ranked last behind other regions of the world, and over the next three years it decreased in importance by nearly fifty percent. Indeed, in their memoirs although Brzezinski and Vance devoted a few pages to events in the Horn, Carter only made passing reference to Africa as a whole.[4]

So even if Brzezinski is correct in his assertion that détente collapsed because of American weakness, then areas of the world that were much more in the public eye than Ethiopia and Somalia should be of much more importance in creating the perception of such weakness. The most obvious example would be the situation in Iran, and the perceived inability and powerlessness of the Carter administration to free the American hostages held there. There are no grounds to suggest that the policy of the Carter administration towards the Horn of Africa prompted the crisis in Iran — it was undoubtedly an issue of religious fundamentalism and the legacy of American support for the Shah. Notwithstanding, Carter's association with the hostage crisis has tainted his legacy. Despite the fact that the deal that secured the release of the fifty-two hostages was brokered by the Carter administration, the fact that the men were not allowed to leave Iranian territory until Ronald Reagan took the presidential oath, and Carter had left the office, remains the enduring image. Thus it appears much more likely that, if the Soviet Union were motivated by the image of American weakness, it would have been weakness in Iran, rather than in the Horn of Africa, that gave rise to this.

The decision of the Carter administration to offer full diplomatic recognition to China, and consent to the seating of the People's Republic in the United Nations and on the UN Security Council, is also worthy of consideration as an inducement for Soviet adventurism. Fears within the Kremlin that Soviet influence might be waning in Asia, resulting from the forging of still closer relations between the United States and China, may well have played a part in the Soviet decision that direct action was needed to bolster its position in other countries in that region, thereby prompting the 1979 invasion of Afghanistan in support of the pro-communist government. Indeed, in his biography of Cyrus Vance, David McLellan argues that it was Soviet suspicion and concern over the growing Sino-U.S. closeness, and the implications for Soviet interests in southwest Asia, that prompted Soviet action in Afghanistan.[5] Again, Carter's policy to China was unconnected to his African policy, throwing further doubt on Brzezinski's claim.

Additional testimony that Brzezinski's connection between the collapse of détente and the administration's policy in the Horn of Africa was flawed can by found in the words of participants in the events of the time. Anatoly Dobrynin, the Soviet Ambassador to the United States from 1962 to 1986, claimed that "from the long-term geopolitical point of view, the developments in that part of Africa were unmistakably of local importance, and the political leadership in Moscow regarded them as such."[6] Thus, if the Kremlin did not attribute any global significance to events in the Horn, it seems unlikely that American actions — or indeed inaction — there affected subsequent Soviet policy towards Afghanistan. This view was shared by Robert Gates, a member of the CIA who transferred to work as Brzezinski's executive assistant from June 1977 to early 1980, before returning to eventually become the Director of the CIA during the George H. W. Bush administration. In his autobiography, Gates contended that events in the Horn, with regards to either Soviet or American policy, "had no impact on the broader U.S.-Soviet relationship."[7]

There is ample reason, therefore, for questioning Brzezinski's contention that détente was buried in the sands of the Ogaden; as we have seen, the evidence presented here suggests that the opposite assertion is more accurate. As well as the crisis in Iran, it was the collapse of détente, triggered by Soviet intervention in Afghanistan, which was principally responsible for the reorientation of the Carter administration's policy not only towards the Ogaden but also to the whole of the Horn of Africa. Linkage, rather than influencing Soviet policy, retained its traditional place in American politics and the customary fear that the Democrats would be charged with being "soft on communism" remained relevant, even in 1980. Indeed, American public opinion was crucial to both the demise of détente and the legacy of the Carter administration, as will be argued shortly.

Jimmy Carter, Cold Warrior

Having considered the role of Carter's policy towards Ethiopia and Somalia at a critical moment of the Cold War, let us now appraise Carter's policy towards the Cold War in general, and examine the premise, put forward in this book, that Carter, like presidents that came before and after him, was also a Cold Warrior.

For nearly fifty years, the Cold War dominated American foreign policy. For almost thirty of those years the United States based its policy on central doctrines: containment of the communist threat and the need to "hold the line" against communist expansion; national and international security provided by the nuclear umbrella and the concept of "mutually assured destruction;" and an acceptance of a bipolar world with control over one's sphere of influence only. But, by the mid 1970s, many of these basic premises had been severely challenged, if not abandoned. No longer was communism seen as a monolithic threat, and the Vietnam War had demonstrated to the United States some of the pitfalls of the theory of containment. It had also combined with the Watergate scandals to damage, perhaps irrevocably, the credibility and trustworthiness of the federal government in the eyes of the American people. In 1976, as the United States celebrated its bicentennial, the pride that was on display masked a deeper sense of malaise, insecurity and anxiety.

Jimmy Carter came to the presidency in the shadow of Vietnam and Watergate, well aware of the difficulties of the task before him. He had to restore American pride and faith at home, and the prestige of the United States abroad. He also had to wage the Cold War in the era of the Vietnam syndrome, at a time when traditional methods were either suspect or inappropriate. Carter rose to the challenges facing him and called for a new approach in foreign policy, which was designed to overcome the stigmas of Vietnam and Watergate, while also successfully waging the Cold War. The new president clearly understood the importance of demonstrating American power and influence and, as he wrote in his memoirs, he acknowledged that the United States possessed "weapons" other than those commanded by the military:

> I was familiar with the widely accepted argument that we had to choose between idealism and realism, or between morality and the exertion of power; but I rejected those claims. To me, the demonstration of American idealism was a practical and realistic approach to foreign affairs, and moral principles were the best foundation for the exertion of American power and influence.[8]

Hence the cornerstone of Carter's reorientation of American foreign policy was the prioritization of, and emphasis upon, human rights. This would fight the Cold War on moral, rather than military, grounds, win the "hearts and minds" of the people of the developing world by offering economic and military aid regardless of the political orientation of the ruling regime, increase the standing of the United States in the eyes of the rest of the world by using American power for good rather than the corruption that had been perceived in Vietnam, and satisfy Carter's personal agenda as a Christian and moralist.

In addition to emphasizing human rights, Carter sought to move to a regionalist, instead of a globalist, approach when formulating foreign policy. The move reflected practical necessity in the era of the Vietnam syndrome by attempting to avoid some of the assumptions that had led to American involvement in Indochina. Developing countries would be considered in a regionalist context, and policy based towards them on their own merits, rather than the perceived implications of that country's importance, or otherwise, to East-West conflict and competition. Like the emphasis on human rights, this aspect of the reorientation of American foreign policy was multi-purpose. Such an approach would portray the United States as still active and powerful in the international environment at the same time that it removed a possible cause for involvement in future wars similar to Vietnam; it was also designed to increase the respect with which developing countries viewed the United States.

Linked to Carter's emphasis on regionalism was his belief that the world order should be built upon community, not competition. In addition to maintaining ties with nations with whom the United States already had a relationship, the Carter administration aimed to develop links with all nations around the world, and involve them, as much as possible, in shaping and governing the international community. The idea of a community of nations was not new to American diplomatic history, and Carter shared the hope of some of his predecessors in the Oval Office, including Woodrow Wilson, that such a world order would lead to a more peaceful and secure world. However, Carter also recognized the pragmatic benefits of international partnerships; indeed, the experience of Vietnam had reiterated the importance of multilateralism in foreign engagements undertaken by the United States.

The election of Jimmy Carter in 1976, as well as his reorientation of foreign policy, led commentators at the time to remark that the new president had engendered a new feeling of hope in the nation. But any hopes of a new beginning seemed to have disappeared by the end of 1979. By that time various international events, most notably the Soviet invasion of Afghanistan and the revolution and subsequent hostage crisis in Iran, brought about a second reorientation in the foreign policy of the Carter administration. Although Carter did not abandon his commitment to human rights, the issue was accorded a much lower priority in policy formulation, and a globalist perspective on the international environment replaced the administration's regionalist outlook, together with an increased emphasis on the importance of the Soviet Union and East-West issues.

As has been demonstrated here, an analysis of the foreign policy applied to Ethiopia and Somalia by Jimmy Carter reflected clearly the reorientation in the administration's stance between 1977 and 1981. Initially, policy towards both Ethiopia and Somalia was based upon human rights issues, resulting in the end of the special relationship enjoyed by Ethiopia and the United States since 1953. As Ethiopia moved closer to the Soviet Union, to the extent that communist bloc support enabled Ethiopia to triumph over Somalia in the Ogaden war fought from 1977 to 1978, so the Somali leader, Siad Barré, sought to improve relations between his country and the United States. The Carter administration, adhering to doctrines such as regionalism and human rights, resisted such efforts until international developments in late 1979 led to a reorientation of its foreign policy approach. Thereafter, more traditional Cold War tactics were applied, with priority given to containing the Soviet threat through the use of American military power. This led to an agreement under which the United States furnished Somalia with military and economic aid in return for access to military facilities, despite the continuing evident human rights problems. By 1980, therefore, the Horn of Africa had become a classic microcosm of the Cold War, with the Soviets and Cubans in Ethiopia and the Americans supporting Somalia. It appeared that national security concerns had taken precedence over issues of human rights and that global-ism had triumphed over regionalism, with the problems of the Horn of Africa seen through the Cold War prism.

Some historians cite Carter's reorientation of foreign policy, as demon-strated by this analysis of his policy towards the Horn of Africa, as evidence of Carter's lack of leadership abilities and weakness as president.[9] However, as argued here, the changes of 1980 were brought about because they were seen as the best option for addressing the contemporary circumstances, not through any thoughtless or easy abandonment of dearly held principles. The context had changed and therefore Carter's policy options changed, but his basic premise, that the United States needed to project a strong and power-ful image in the Cold War, remained constant. Rather than criticizing the president for a failure of leadership or lack of vision, it can be argued that Carter should be praised for his recognition that his early attempts to imple-ment a new system needed to be modified, and a more practical and prag-matic foreign policy approach introduced.

The Carter Presidency

Having discussed the lessons that can be learned about the Cold War through our study of the Carter administration and the Horn of Africa, let us now turn to a consideration of some aspects of the style of the Carter pres-idency.

One of the most noticeable things revealed by a study of policy towards the Horn of Africa is the interpersonal conflict apparent both between individual members of the administration, and between departments. There were clear differences between Zbigniew Brzezinski and Cyrus Vance, especially with regard to policy towards the Soviet Union. Although the media attention devoted to this internal conflict often exaggerated its extent, there was a degree of truth in the reports. Carter consistently claimed that he welcomed such differences and that he encouraged all sides of an issue to be presented to him, to facilitate his final decision. While there is some sense to this approach, it could also be argued that Carter failed to present or explain his style of government adequately to the American public or the media. Hence, there was never a clear understanding as to why the president allowed internal disputes to develop, leading to criticism from both elements of society.

The emphasis placed by the media on the conflict between Brzezinski and Vance meant that other aspects of inter-departmental discord were frequently overlooked. We have seen, particularly, many examples of differences between Paul Henze of the National Security Council and members of the Department of State. Interestingly, these differences did not exactly mirror those between Brzezinski and Vance, since Henze's perspective, too, reflected regional rather than global concerns — in his case, a clear sympathy for Ethiopia, as against Somalia. This first in-depth analysis of the policy of the Carter administration towards the Horn of Africa has provided evidence of the tension that existed at the lower levels of the administration, and has therefore demonstrated that policymaking in the Executive branch was much more complex and intricate than often is accredited.

New levels of complexity have also been provided for the argument that Carter deserves the disapproval leveled at him for his desire to micromanage all aspects of his presidency when there was simply too much for him to do. We have seen that, once Carter set the basic outlines of policy, much of the subsequent discussion and implementation of policy towards the Horn of Africa was taken at levels below that of president, not least during the final year of the administration. Thus, in this area, as with the issue of inter-departmental differences, this investigation of policy towards Ethiopia and Somalia has brought to light complexities neglected by previous evaluations of the Carter administration.

The History of the Carter Administration and the Horn of Africa Does Matter

Paul Henze, a member of staff of the National Security Council with responsibility for the Horn of Africa, asked and answered his own question, in the frontispiece of his book, *The Horn of Africa: From War to Peace*: "Does history matter? The answer in the Horn of Africa must be a resounding yes.[10]

Although he was referring to the importance of history in gaining an understanding of the region, his claim can also be applied to the importance of the Horn of Africa in allowing us to gain an understanding of the foreign policy of Jimmy Carter.

Détente, as claimed previously, may not have been "buried in the sands of the Ogaden," but the importance of Carter's policy towards the Horn of Africa should not be underestimated. The Ogaden War represented the first foreign policy crisis for the Carter administration and it was here that the president's new approach to the Cold War was put to the test. Carter de-emphasized American military power and strove for a peaceful resolution of the conflict — but failed. He invoked the principle of regionalism by insisting that African problems should have African solutions and attempted to remove all outside influence from the conflict — but failed. Nevertheless, one still might argue that Carter had been right, and that the commitment of American military power would have been even worse, both for the situation in the Horn of Africa and for American-Soviet relations.

Carter's ultimate failure, then, lay in his inability to convince the American public that his policy choices in the Horn of Africa were appropriate. He failed to "sell" his "soft power" approach of 1977, with its emphasis on human rights and regionalism; nor did he convincingly explain his policy reorientation of 1980. Brzezinski claimed that, because of the Ogaden War, "the momentum of SALT was lost" and he is correct, but it was not the Soviet momentum that was most important in 1978; it was American public opinion. Perhaps the Soviets had been emboldened by Carter's handling of the Ogaden War but ultimately it was the willingness of the American people to support SALT, not the support of the Soviet Union, that was undermined by Carter's policy choices in the Horn of Africa. The Ogaden War raised doubts among the American people, which were exacerbated by international events throughout Carter's administration, and consolidated by the Soviet invasion of Afghanistan. Subsequently, Carter withdrew SALT from consideration by the Senate, and the era of the Second Cold War began.

Carter's inability to enlist public support has been attributed by different historians to various reasons. For Gaddis Smith, although Carter's vision of foreign policy was "morally responsible and far-sighted" he failed to communicate this effectively to the American public because of his inability to successfully lead his administration or manage Soviet adventurism.[11] David Skidmore likewise praises Carter's vision for foreign policy, considering it a pragmatic response to the relative decline of American power, and makes a powerful, theoretical argument that the structure of American politics, with its crucial element of public opinion, led to Carter's failure to "sell" his initial foreign policy and ultimately to "reverse course."[12] However, this analysis of Carter's policy towards the Horn of Africa strongly supports the view of those analysts, including Jerel Rosati, who, while also crediting Carter with a coherent worldview, argues that the president's failure to gain public support lay with the rising tide of conservatism in the United States.[13] Indeed, it could be argued that public sentiment in the mid–1970s, which enabled Carter's election and facilitated his initial foreign policy approach, was a temporary aberration, an immediate reaction to Vietnam and Watergate, but one that quickly passed. The conservative right in the United States demands a tough foreign policy, but Carter was perceived as a stereotypical Democrat president; one who was "soft on communism" and his policy towards the Ogaden War was but one element, albeit an important element, in creating this perception.

Ultimately Carter failed in convincing the American people to support his vision because he, like many Democrats subsequently, was unable to combat the trend towards Republicanism in American politics; a trend that arguably began with the election of Richard Nixon in 1968, spawned the 1994 Republican Revolution, and still continues, with major impact on both the United States and the rest of the world, today.

Thus the story of the Carter administration and the Horn of Africa seems to reach a somewhat ignoble end. The legacy of the Carter administration, though, suggests that such a conclusion is undeserved. Carter's acceptance of global interdependence and complexity, and his emphasis on developing nations in their own right, are themes that have endured and been factored into the policy formulation of subsequent American presidents. Perhaps most significant, however, was Carter's emphasis on human rights. The attempt to base policy toward Ethiopia and Somalia upon human rights considerations, and related humanitarian concerns, and the publicity given to these issues, ensured that these were not forgotten, even after the administration had been forced to a different practical approach by developments in 1979 and 1980. Furthermore, it arguably made a major contribution to the resolve of both contemporary and successive agencies and governments, in the United States and around the world, to ensure that matters of human rights could never be ignored in international politics. In his farewell address to the nation, the president declared:

> The struggle for human rights overrides all differences of color, nation or language. Those who hunger for freedom, who thirst for human dignity, and who suffer for the sake of justice — they are the patriots of this cause. I believe with all my heart that America must always stand for these basic human rights — at home and abroad. This is both our history and our destiny... . The battle for human rights — at home and abroad — is far from over. We should never be surprised nor discouraged because the impact of our efforts has had, and will always have, varied

results. Rather, we should take pride that the ideals which gave birth to our nation still inspire the hopes of oppressed people around the world. We have no cause for self-righteousness or complacency. But we have every reason to persevere, both within our own country and beyond our borders.[14]

Despite its failures and shortcomings, of which there were many, the emphasis on human rights remains an enduring legacy of the Carter administration, and one of which Jimmy Carter should justifiably be proud.

Epilogue: Jimmy Carter versus President Carter

Jimmy Carter was a man raised to do his duty, whether that duty was to his family, his church, the U.S. Navy, or, while president, to the nation. One might also argue that, after leaving the White House, Carter perceived that his duty was to the world.

The issue of human rights remained dear to Jimmy Carter's heart after he left the White House in 1981; his post-presidential work with the Carter Center in Atlanta is based largely upon the concept that the human condition could and should be improved. At the farewell dinner for the Carter administration at the Metropolitan Club, in the presence of the president, first lady, White House staff and cabinet members, Vice President Mondale rose and proposed a toast: "To President and Mrs. Carter — you kept the peace, you obeyed the law, you told the truth, you did your best for the American people."[15] As a eulogy for the defeated president it was both laudatory and appropriate, suggesting that Carter had fulfilled his pledge of January 1977 to do his best. But Jimmy Carter was not finished, and in the years since he left the White House, he has become almost universally recognized as one of the best ex-presidents that the United States has produced.[16]

One of the first acts of Jimmy and Rosalynn Carter after they left the White House was the foundation of the Carter Center, an organization dedicated to the belief that "that every human being has the right to be free from preventable disease and free to live in freedom and peace."[17] Since its inception in 1982, it has helped people in more than sixty-five nations through the promotion of democracy through fair elections, peaceful resolution of conflict, the reduction of hunger by improved crop yields, the prevention or eradication of crippling diseases, and educational programs to battle the stigma of mental illness.[18] In addition to establishing an organization to further these projects, Carter remains personally involved. The former president has built houses with his own hands in low income neighborhoods for the non-profit volunteer group Habitat for Humanity.[19] Furthermore, as Hendrik Hertzberg pointed out, "when he denounced the rigging of a Panamanian election by the Manuel Noriega regime, he did so not from the safety of Washington or Atlanta, but from a sidewalk in Panama City, under the eyes — and the guns — of Noriega's armed secret police."[20]

Nor, in the post-presidential years, did Carter forget Africa, and many programs of the Carter Center are dedicated to the problems of that continent. The Carter Center Human Rights Program has attempted to ensure that constitutions and legislation are compatible with international human rights standards in many countries around the world, including Liberia, Chad and Ethiopia, while the African Governance Center works to promote democracy in the countries of sub–Saharan Africa.[21] During 2005, the Carter Center was active in ensuring that the national elections in Ethiopia were fair and democratic. In March, six observers were sent by the Center to Ethiopia to observe the pre-election preparations, and a team of 50 observers, led by Carter, observed the national elections held on May 15. A team from the Carter Center also monitored the subsequent electoral complaints investigation process and the re-elections held in 31 constituencies in August. At a meeting with the media after the electoral process had finished, Carter acknowledged that there had been some problems but that the "potential for multiparty democracy to take hold here is great. These elections could prove to be a major step forward on Ethiopia's democratic path."[22]

"Wars," asserts the website of the Carter Center, "are responsible for the greatest violations of basic human rights, causing death, destruction, and human suffering... . Ending suffering and building sustainable peace are key goals of the Carter Center's Conflict Resolution Program."[23] Currently the Center is working to ease the problems in Sudan, but one of the Center's innovations, the International Negotiation Network (INN) was to prove crucial to developments in the Horn of Africa. The INN was established by Carter to work for the peaceful resolution of conflicts, especially in the case of intranational conflicts where international organizations such as the United Nations do not have jurisdiction, or are forbidden to act by the terms of the charter. Pledged to "address the most intractable kinds of conflict" and "not look for easy victories that might be tracked on a score card, but to focus on the most horrendous conflicts in terms of human suffering or lives lost," the first project of the INN was an attempt to address the Eritrean secessionist crisis.[24] Beginning in the spring of 1989 the INN mediation team met with, and hosted talks between, representatives of the secessionist movements in Eritrea and with members of Mengistu's government. Despite the sterling work of the INN, and the apparent willingness of the parties involved to negotiate, conflict in Ethiopia continued, and the future of Eritrea was settled by military means. In May 1991 opposition movements in Addis Ababa forced Mengistu's resignation, and the EPLF seized the Eritrean capital, Asmara, leading to the formal declaration of Eritrean independence following a referendum in April 1993.[25] Nonetheless, the work and intentions of the INN should not be disparaged.

Carter also worked with the Clinton administration during 1993 to assist the new president with developments in Somalia. In that year Clinton moved from a humanitarian peacekeeping role in Somalia, and pledged to capture one of the most aggressive clan leaders, Mohamed Farah Aidid. Clinton, however, met with little success, until Aidid contacted Jimmy Carter and offered to begin negotiations. Following talks in Ethiopia, American troops were withdrawn from Somalia in 1994, and UN peacekeepers the following year. Carter's involvement not only eased the crisis but also enabled the Clinton administration to disengage from military involvement in a region where the United States had met with disaster.[26]

In addition to promoting peace and democracy, the Carter Center runs many programs aimed at alleviating health problems. In September 2005 Carter visited communities in Ethiopia, Mali and Nigeria on a tour designed to bring attention to the need for more government and international action on health issues in the developing world. Carter proclaimed that "we believe good health is a basic human right, especially among poor people afflicted with disease who are isolated, forgotten, ignored and often without hope."[27] As well as programs designed to tackle river blindness, trachoma and lymphatic filariasis, a major project of the Carter Center has been the eradication of Guinea worm disease, a chronic and painful infection caused by drinking contaminated water. Working in partnership with organizations such as the World Health Organization, UNICEF and the Centers for Disease Control and Prevention, the Carter Center has achieved great success. In 2006, the Center announced that the numbers of guinea worm disease had been reduced worldwide by more than 99.5%, "from an estimated 3.5 million cases in 1986 to 10,674 reported cases in 2005."[28] In Nigeria, only 5 cases were reported between July 2005 and January 2006 (traditionally the period when the highest number of cases are reported), compared with 148 reported cases the previous year. Dr. Donald Hopkins, associate executive director of health programs at the Carter Center, commented that "as the most populated country in Africa, Nigeria's amazing progress in the fight against Guinea worm disease sets a fast pace for the remaining endemic countries to end this painful chapter in human history."[29] A New York Times editorial of March 26, 2006, commented that "thanks to a relentless 20-year campaign led by former President Jimmy Carter, Guinea worm is poised to become the first disease since smallpox to be pushed into oblivion."[30]

When questioned by the New York Times as to his motivations for his busy post-presidential career, Carter replied:

I have one life and one chance to make it count for something. I'm free to choose what the something is and the something is my faith... . My faith demands — this is not optional — my faith *demands* that I do whatever I can, whenever I can, for as long as I can, with whatever I have, to try to make a difference.[31]

While president, Jimmy Carter had attempted to make a difference, with varying degrees of success. Freed from the constraints under which government officials are forced to operate — for example, the UN Charter forbade involvement in the conflict between Ethiopia and Eritrea, while diplomatic considerations arguably limited Clinton's ability to negotiate effectively over the American role in Somalia — Carter continues to make a difference. Again, he and his organization are meeting with varying degrees of success, but evidence suggests that this will not inhibit their attempts, and Carter, as he pledged to the American people during the presidential campaign in 1976, "will never be satisfied with less than the best."[32]

Chapter Notes

Introduction

1. Paul B. Henze, *The Horn of Africa: From War to Peace* (London: Macmillan Press, 1991).

2. Zbigniew Brzezinski, *Power and Principle: Memoirs of the National Security Adviser, 1977–1981* (London: Weidenfeld & Nicolson, 1983), p. 189.

3. Jimmy Carter, Inaugural Address, January 20, 1977.

4. Jerel Rosati, *The Carter Administration's Quest for Global Community: Beliefs & Their Impact on Behavior* (Columbia: University of South Carolina Press, 1987), p. 7.

5. It should be noted that many of the works discussed here analyze Carter's administration as a whole. In this review, I will, for the most part, focus on the sections that discuss foreign policy.

6. Lawrence Shoup, *The Carter Presidency and Beyond: Power and Politics in the 1980s* (Palo Alto, Ramparts Press, 1980).

7. Shoup, *Carter Presidency*, p. 14.

8. Shoup, *Carter Presidency*, p. 51.

9. Shoup, *Carter Presidency*, p. 117.

10. Richard Thornton, *The Carter Years: Toward a Global World Order* (Washington, D.C.: Washington Institute Press, 1991), p. 8.

11. Thornton, *Carter Years*, p. 7.

12. Thornton, *Carter Years*, p. 542.

13. Burton Kaufman, *The Presidency of James Earl Carter, Jr.* (Lawrence: University Press of Kansas, 1993), p. 3.

14. Kaufman, *Presidency*, p. 131.

15. Gaddis Smith, *Morality, Reason and Power: American Diplomacy in the Carter Years* (New York: Hill & Wang, 1986), p. 247.

16. M. Glenn Abernathy, Dilys M. Hill, and Phil Williams, eds., *The Carter Years: The President and Policy Making* (London: Francis Pinter Publishers, 1984), p. 75.

17. Abernathy, *Carter Years*, p. 75.

18. Erwin C. Hargrove, *Jimmy Carter as President: Leadership and the Politics of the Public Good* (Baton Rouge: Louisiana State University Press, 1988), p. 13.

19. Hargrove, *Carter*, p. 190.

20. John Dumbrell, *The Carter Presidency: A Re-Evaluation* (Manchester and New York: Manchester University Press, 1995), p. 214.

21. Abernathy, *Carter Years*, p. 75.

22. Joshua Muravchik, *The Uncertain Crusade: Jimmy Carter & the Dilemmas of Human Rights* (Lanham: Hamilton Press, 1986), p. 217.

23. Muravchik, *Uncertain Crusade*, p. xix.

24. Muravchik, *Uncertain Crusade*, p. 217.

25. A. Glenn Mower, *Human Rights and American Foreign Policy: The Carter and Reagan Experiences* (New York: Greenwood Press, 1987), p. 4.

26. Donald S. Spencer, *The Carter Implosion: Jimmy Carter and the Amateur Style of Diplomacy* (New York: Praeger, 1988), p. 103.

27. Spencer, *Carter Implosion*, p. 103.

28. Smith, *Morality*, p. 247.

29. Smith, *Morality*, p. 14.

30. Dumbrell, *Carter Presidency*, p. 214.

31. Mower, *Human Rights*, p. 74.

32. Spencer, *Carter Implosion*, p. 150.

33. Smith, *Morality*, p. 247.

34. Abernathy *Carter Years*, p. 75.

35. Kaufman, *Presidency*, pp. 128–130.

36. Spencer, *Carter Implosion*, p. 150.

37. David Skidmore, *Reversing Course: Carter's Foreign Policy, Domestic Politics and the Failure of Reform* (Nashville and London: Vanderbilt University Press, 1996), p. 102.

38. Garland Haas, *Jimmy Carter and the Politics of Frustration* (Jefferson, North Carolina: McFarland, 1992), p. 2.

39. Haas, *Carter*, p. 2.

40. See, for example, Robert Wilson (ed.), *Character Above All: Ten Presidents From FDR to George Bush* (New York: Simon & Schuster, 1995), p. 173.

41. Emphasis in original. Douglas Brinkley, "The Rising Stock of Jimmy Carter: The 'Hands-On' Legacy of Our Thirty-Ninth President," *Diplomatic History*, Volume 20, Fall 1996, p. 528.

42. Brinkley, "Rising Stock," p. 529.

43. Fred Halliday, *The Making of the Second Cold War* (London: Verso, 1986).

44. Raymond Garthoff, *Détente and Confrontation: American-Soviet Relations From Nixon to Reagan* (Washington: Brookings Institution, 1985), p. 1068.

45. See Garthoff; Jussi Hanhimaki, "Ironies and Turning Points: Détente in Perspective" in Odd Arne Westad, ed., *Reviewing the Cold War: Approaches, Interpretations, Theory* (London: Frank Cass, 2000); Odd Arne Westad, ed., *The Fall of Détente: Soviet-American Relations During the Carter Years* (Oslo: Scandinavian University Press, 1997).

46. For example, Zbigniew Brzezinski, 1978, in Fred Halliday, *Soviet Policy in the Arc of Crisis* (Washington: Institute for Policy Studies, 1981), p. 19.

47. Brzezinski, *Power*, p. 189.

Chapter I

1. *Time*, January 24, 1977.

2. *Time*, January 3, 1977.

3. Jimmy Carter, *Why Not the Best?: Jimmy Carter, the First Fifty Years* (Fayetteville: University of Arkansas Press, 1975), pp. 57–58.

4. Jimmy Carter, Gubernatorial Inaugural Address, Atlanta, Georgia, January 12, 1971, *A Government as Good as Its People* (Fayetteville: University of Arkansas Press, 1996), p. 6.

5. Reply to Governor Brown, Rockville, Maryland, May 1976, Carter, *Government*, p. 66.

6. *Time*, January 3, 1977.

7. The 95th Congress, in session from January 1977 to December 1978, was composed of 61 Democratic Senators, 38 Republican and one Independent, while the House had 292 Democrats to 143 Republicans; in the 96th Congress, in session from January 1979 to December 1980, 58 Democrats, 41 Republicans and one Independent were seated in the Senate, with 276 Democrats and 159 Republicans in the House. Source: *Members of Congress Since 1789, 3rd Edition*, Congressional Quarterly Inc, Washington, D.C., 1985.

8. Carter, University of Notre Dame: Address at Commencement Exercises at the University, May 22, 1977, in *Public Papers of the Presidents of the United States: Jimmy Carter 1977, Vol 1* (Washington, D.C.: United States Government Printing Office, 1977), p. 956.

9. Speech, Carter to Democratic Reception, Dallas, Texas, September 24, 1976, Carter, *Government*, pp. 162–163.

10. Jimmy Carter, *Keeping Faith: Memoirs of a President* (New York: Bantam Books, 1982), p. 27.

11. Carter, *Faith*, p. 27.

12. Laurie Johnstone, *New York Times,* May 19, 1975.

13. Two occasions were at a luncheon speech, Baltimore, Maryland, April 2, 1975, and Florida State University, Tallahassee, Florida, September 28, 1975, in Carter, *Government*, pp. 41–42 and pp. 48–49.

14. The Second Ford-Carter Debate, San Francisco, California, October 6, 1976, in Carter, *Government*, p. 181.

15. Address to the Chicago Council on Foreign Relations, March 15, 1976, in *The Presidential Campaign: 1976* (Washington: U.S. Government Printing Office, 1978), p. 112.

16. Carter, Inaugural Address, January 20, 1977 in *Public Papers 1977, Vol 1*, p. 2.

17. Carter speech, February 2, 1977 in *Public Papers, Carter 1977 Vol I*, p. 75.

18. Presidential Directive/NSC-30, "Human Rights", February 17, 1978 — No 1521, Items 1515–1521, Fiche 344, National Security Archive, Washington, D.C.

19. John Dumbrell, *The Carter Presidency: A Re-Evaluation* (Manchester: Manchester University Press, 1993), p. 192.

20. A. Glenn Mower, *Human Rights and American Foreign Policy: The Carter and Reagan Experiences* (New York: Greenwood, 1987), p. 3.

21. Carter, *Faith*, p. 143.

22. Universal Declaration of Human Rights, 1948.

23. Joshua Muravchik, *The Uncertain Crusade: Jimmy Carter & the Dilemmas of Human Rights* (Lanham: Hamilton Press, 1986), p. 75.

24. The Helsinki Accords, 1975.

25. "Remarks and a Question-and-Answer Session With a Group of Editors and News Directors" July 15, 1977, *Public Papers 1977 Vol 2*, p. 1274.

26. 1974 Foreign Assistance Act (section 502B); See also Dumbrell, p. 118.

27. International Security Assistance and Arms Export Control Act of 1976, Section 502(B).

28. Carter, *Faith*, p. 143.

29. The Bible which Carter used and annotated can be see on display in the museum at the Carter Center and Presidential Library in Atlanta, Georgia.

30. "Man of the Year," *Time*, January 3, 1977.

31. Interview with Bill Moyers, May 6, 1976, from Carter, *Government*, p. 75

32. David Kucharsky, *The Man From Plains: A Portrait of Jimmy Carter* (London: Collins, 1977), p. 42.

33. Memo, Brzezinski to Carter, January 12, 1978 — "Weekly Reports, 42–52 [1/78 — 3/78]" Folder, Box 41, Zbigniew Brzezinski Donated Historical Material, Carter Presidential Library.

34. See, for example, Richard Crockatt, *The Fifty Years War: The United States and the Soviet Union in World Politics, 1941-1991* (London: Routledge, 1995), Walter LaFeber, *America, Russia and the Cold War, 1945-1992* (New York: McGraw-Hill, 1993), Stephen Ambrose, *Rise to Globalism: American Foreign Policy Since 1938* (New York and London: Penguin, 1993).

35. Memo, Warnke to Carter/Mondale Policy Planning Group, October 24, 1976, "Cy Vance Papers" (Yale) Folder, Carter-Brezhnev Florida Conference Documents (1), National Security Archive, Washington, D.C.

36. Memo, Vance to Carter, October 10, 1976 — "Carter Presidential Campaign: Foreign Policy Issues and Positions 1976, Mid" Folder, Box 9, Carter Presidential Administration Group No. 1664 Series No. II, Cyrus R. Vance and Grace Sloan Papers, Yale University Library Manuscripts Collection.

37. Speech, Carter, Remarks at the 31st Annual Meeting of the Southern Legislative Conference, July 21, 1977, Charleston, South Carolina, *Public Papers 1977 Vol II*, p. 1310.

38. Speech, Vance to the Plenary Session of the National Association for the Advancement of Colored People, July 1, 1977 — " Speeches, Articles and Interviews by Cyrus R. Vance [while Secretary of State] 1977 — 1979" Folder, Box 39, Professional and Personal Activities, Group No 1664, Series No III, Cyrus R. Vance and Grace Sloane Papers, Yale University Library Manuscripts Collection.

39. Cyrus Vance, *Hard Choices: Critical Years in America's Foreign Policy* (New York: Simon & Schuster, 1983), p. 87.

40. Memo, Brzezinski to Carter, January 12,1978, "Weekly Reports, 42–52 [1/78 — 3/78]" Folder, Box 41, Zbigniew Brzezinski Donated Historical Material, Carter Presidential Library.

41. Address to the 32nd UN General Assembly, October 4, 1977, *Department of State Bulletin*, Volume LXVII, No 2000, October 24, 1977, Library of Congress, Washington, D.C.

42. Interview with General William Odom, Military Adviser to the National Security Council in the Carter administration, July 14, 2000, Hudson Institute, Washington, D.C.

43. "President Carter: Special Report" *Congressional Quarterly Inc*, April 1977, ed. Margaret Thompson, p. 1.

44. Carter, *Faith*, p. 46.

45. Carter, *Faith*, p. 51.

46. Exit interview, Brzezinski, February 20, 1981- Carter Presidential Library.

47. All biographical information on Brzezinski from "President Carter: Special Report" *Congressional Quarterly Inc*, April 1977, ed. Margaret Thompson, p. 37.

48. Information on the Trilateral Commission from Dumbrell, *Carter Presidency*, p. 111.

49. Jerel A Rosati, *The Carter Administration's Quest for Global Community: Beliefs and Their Impact on Behavior* (Columbia: University of South Carolina Press, 1987), p. 104.

50. Carter, *Faith*, p. 54.

51. Biographical information on Cyrus Vance from "President Carter: Special Report" *Congressional Quarterly Inc*, April 1977, ed. Margaret Thompson, pp. 26–27; David McClellan, *Cyrus Vance* (Totowa NJ: Rowland & Allenheld, 1985), pp. 7–9; Obituary, *New York Times*, January 13, 2002.

52. "President Carter: Special Report" *Congressional Quarterly Inc*, April 1977, ed. Margaret Thompson, pp. 26–27.

53. Carter, *Faith*, p. 35.

54. Biographical information on Mondale from "President Carter: Special Report" *Con-*

gressional Quarterly, Inc. April 1977, ed. Margaret Thompson, p. 14.

55. Speech, Carter, Service to America Summit 2000, Washington, D.C., June 12, 2000.

56. Conversation with author, The Carter Center, Atlanta, Georgia, March 25, 2000.

57. *Washington Post,* April 25, 1977.

58. See, for example, interview with Bill Moyers, PBS, May 6, 1976, in Carter, *Government,* p. 73.

59. Report, Brzezinski to Carter, undated, "NSC, 1/77–10/80" Folder, Box 24, Zbigniew Brzezinski Donated Historical Material, Carter Presidential Library.

60. Report, Brzezinski to Carter, undated.

61. Report, Brzezinski to Carter, undated.

62. Press Release, January 22, 1977, in *Public Papers 1977 Vol I,* p. 8.

63. Carter, Remarks at the Ceremony, "Swearing In Ceremony for Members of the Cabinet," January 23, 1977, *Public Papers 1977 Vol I,* p. 15.

64. Paul B. Henze, conversation with author, April 1999.

Chapter II

1. William Odom, *On Internal War: American and Soviet Approaches to Third World Approaches to Third World Clients and Insurgents* (Durham: Duke University Press, 1992), p. 158. See also, Haggai Erlich, *The Struggle over Eritrea, 1962–1978* (Stanford: Hoover Institute, 1983), p. 55.

2. Paul B. Henze, *The Horn of Africa: From War to Peace* (London: Macmillan Press, 1991), p. 188–189.

3. Henze, *Horn of Africa,* p. 162.

4. Henze, *Horn of Africa,* p. 163.

5. "Basic Data on Sub-Saharan Africa," *Department of State Bulletin,* Vol. 80, No 2036, March 1980, Library of Congress, Washington, D.C.

6. Samuel M. Makinda, *Superpower Diplomacy in the Horn of Africa* (New York: St Martin's, 1987), p. 58.

7. See for example statement by William E Schaufele, Jr., Assistant Secretary of State for African Affairs, to Senate Subcommittee on African Affairs, August 6, 1976, *Ethiopia and the Horn of Africa,* August 4–6, 1977, S381–13, 95th Congress, 1st Session, Library of Congress, Washington, D.C.

8. Statement, Schaufele to Senate Subcommittee on African Affairs, August 6, 1976.

9. Statement, Schaufele to Senate Subcommittee on African Affairs, August 6, 1976.

NB: U.S. aid for Somalia was terminated in 1970 because of a Congressional provision in the Foreign Assistance Act forbidding aid to countries whose flag was flown on ships trading with North Vietnam.

10. Note, Henze to Brzezinski, March 10, 1978, "3/78" Folder, Box Horn/Special: 2, NSA Staff Material, Carter Presidential Library.

11. Presidential Review Memorandum NSC/21, "The Horn of Africa," April 1, 1977, No 1558, Items 1552 (cont)—1558, Fiche 352, National Security Archive, Washington, D.C.

12. Interview with Paul Henze, *Cold War Television Series* — National Security Archive, Washington, D.C.

13. Peter J. Schraeder, *United States Foreign Policy Toward Africa: Incrementalism, Crisis and Change* (Cambridge: Cambridge University Press, 1994), p. 114. See also, Paul B. Henze, *Layers of Time: A History of Ethiopia* (London: Hurst & Company, 2000), pp. 83–86.

14. In *Arms for the Horn: U.S. Security Policy in Ethiopia and Somalia, 1953–1991* (Pittsburgh: University of Pittsburgh Press, 1991), p. 4. J. A. Lefebvre claims that one of the reasons that the Horn of Africa provides such an interesting area for study is that the Cold War led to two of the world's poorest countries, namely Ethiopia and Somalia, becoming the most heavily armed states in the African continent, as the United States and the Soviet Union provided their respective clients with military aid.

15. I. M. Lewis, ed., *Nationalism and Self-Determination in the Horn of Africa* (London: Ithaca Press, 1983), p. 74.

16. "Basic Data on Sub-Saharan Africa," *Department of State Bulletin,* Vol. 80, No 2036, March 1980, Library of Congress, Washington, D.C.

17. Testimony, Tom Farer to House Subcommittee on Africa, March 28, 1977, *Foreign Assistance Legislation for FY78 Part 3: Economic and Military Assistance Programs in Africa,* March 17, 18, 23, 28, 29, April 28, 1977, H461–37, 95th Congress, 1st Session, Library of Congress, Washington, D.C.

18. Bereket H. Selassie, "The American Dilemma in the Horn," in Gerald Bender, James S. Coleman and Richard L. Sklar (eds.), *African Crisis Areas and United States Foreign*

Policy (Berkeley and Los Angeles: University of California Press, 1985), p. 173.

19. Report, *The Horn of Africa*, House Committee on International Relations, November 11, 1976, H462–62, 95th Congress, 1st Session, Library of Congress, Washington, D.C.

20. Henze, *Horn of Africa*, p. 131.

21. Testimony, Talcott Seelye to House Subcommittee on Africa, March 29, 1977, *Foreign Assistance Legislation for FY78 Part 3: Economic and Military Assistance Programs in Africa*, March 17, 18, 23, 28, 29, April 28, 1977, H461–37, 95th Congress, 1st Session, Library of Congress, Washington, D.C. See also *Newsweek*, May 9, 1977.

22. David Korn, *Ethiopia, the United States and the Soviet Union* (London: Croom Helm, 1986), p. 112.

23. Korn, *Ethiopia*, p. 109.

24. Telegram, Mengistu to State Department, January 22, 1977, "Ethiopia, CO49 1/20/77–1/20/78" Folder, Box CO-25, WHCF, Countries (CO), Carter Presidential Library.

25. Biographical information from interview with Henze, July 19, 2000, Bethesda, Maryland.

26. Transcript of Proceedings, Conference on Global Competition and the Deterioration of U.S.-Soviet Relations, 1977–1980, February 23–26, 1995, "USSR-U.S. Conference 3/95, Transcript (1)" Folder, Box USSR/U.S. Conference 5/6–9/94 (2) through USSR-Vienna Summit, Vertical File, Carter Presidential Library.

27. Interview, Henze for *Cold War* Television Series, National Security Archive, Washington, D.C.

28. Speech, Vance to the Plenary Session of the National Association for the Advancement of Colored People, July 1, 1977, "Speeches, Articles and Interviews by Cyrus R. Vance [while Secretary of State] 1977 —1979" Folder, Box 39, Professional and Personal Activities, Group No 1664, Series No III, Cyrus R. Vance and Grace Sloane Papers, Yale University Library Manuscripts Collection.

29. Report, *An Overview of U.S. Policy Toward Africa*, December 14, 1977, "Foreign Affairs (General) [CF, O/A 47] [1]" Folder, Box 208, Stuart Eizenstat Collection, Carter Presidential Library.

30. The term "special relationship" was often used to describe the association between the United States and Ethiopia. See, for example, *New York Times*, April 25, 1977.

31. *New York Times*, February 4, 1977.

32. *Los Angeles Times*, March 9, 1977.

33. Minutes, Policy Review Committee Meeting, April 11, 1977, "Meetings PRC-10 4/11/77" Folder, Box 24, Zbigniew Brzezinski Donated Historical Material, Carter Presidential Library.

34. Memo, Henze to Brzezinski, March 16, 1977, "Evening Reports File: 2–6/77" Folder, Box Horn/Special: 5, NSA Staff Material, Carter Presidential Library.

35. Memo, Henze to Brzezinski, March 17, 1977, "Evening Reports File: 2–6/77" Folder, Box Horn/Special: 5, NSA Staff Material, Carter Presidential Library.

36. *Los Angeles Times*, March 9, 1977.

37. *New York Times*, July 18, 1977.

38. *Los Angeles Times*, June 22, 1977.

39. Testimony, Dr. Arnt K. Meyer-Lie, Amnesty International, to House Subcommittee on Africa, March 28, 1977, *Foreign Assistance Legislation for FY78 Part 3: Economic and Military Assistance Programs in Africa*, March 17, 18, 23, 28, 29, April 28, 1977, H461–37, 95th Congress, 1st Session, Library of Congress, Washington, D.C.

40. Statement, William E. Schaufele Jr., Assistant Secretary of State for African Affairs, to Senate Subcommittee on African Affairs, August 6, 1976, *Ethiopia and the Horn of Africa*, August 4–6, 1977, S381–13, 95th Congress, 1st Session, Library of Congress, Washington, D.C.

41. Speech, Representative Derwinski to House of Representatives, June 6, 1977, *Congressional Record*, 95th Congress, 1st Session, pp. 17668–17669.

42. *New York Times*, February 1, 1977.

43. *Time*, February 14, 1977.

44. *Washington Post*, February 11, 1977.

45. *U.S. News and World Report*, August 29, 1977.

46. *Time*, May 9, 1977.

47. *New York Times*, May 20, 1977.

48. *New York Times*, March 1, 1977.

49. *Time*, February 14, 1977.

50. Testimony, Tom Farer to House Subcommittee on Africa, March 28, 1977, *Foreign Assistance Legislation for FY78 Part 3: Economic and Military Assistance Programs in Africa*, March 17, 18, 23, 28, 29, April 28, 1977, H461–37, 95th Congress, 1st Session, Library of Congress, Washington, D.C.

51. Memo, Henze to Brzezinski, March 17, 1977, "Evening Reports File: 206/77" Folder, Box Horn/Special: 5, NSA Staff Material, Carter Presidential Library.

52. Interview with Henze, July 19, 2000, Bethesda, Maryland.

53. Memo, Brown to Brzezinski, March 21, 1977, "3/77" Folder, Box Horn/Special: 1, NSA Staff Material, Carter Presidential Library.

54. Memo, Brown to Brzezinski, March 21, 1977.

55. Memo, Henze to Brzezinski, March 31, 1977, "3/77" Folder, Box Horn/Special: 1, NSA Staff Material, Carter Presidential Library.

56. Memo, Brzezinski to Brown, undated, "3/77" Folder, Box Horn/Special: 1, NSA Staff Material, Carter Presidential Library.

57. *New York Times*, April 27, 1977.

58. Carter, News Conference, November 15, 1976, "President Carter Special Report" *Congressional Quarterly Inc*, April 1977, ed. Margaret Thompson. See also, A. Glenn Mower, *Human Rights and American Foreign Policy: The Carter and Reagan Experiences* (New York: Greenwood, 1987), p. 100.

59. *New York Times*, February 25, 1977. It should be noted that Ethiopia was not singled out for exclusion from military aid. For example, aid was also terminated to Argentina and Uruguay, and restrictions were made on aid to Zimbabwe and Zaire.

60. Testimony, Talcott Seelye to House Subcommittee on Africa, March 29, 1977, *Foreign Assistance Legislation for FY78 Part 3: Economic and Military Assistance Programs in Africa*, March 17, 18, 23, 28, 29, April 28, 1977, H461-37, 95th Congress, 1st Session, Library of Congress, Washington, D.C. See also, Lefebvre, *Arms for the Horn*, p. 153.

61. Minutes, Policy Review Committee April 11, 1977, "PRC-10 4/11/77" Folder, Box 24, Zbigniew Brzezinski Donated Historical Material, Carter Presidential Library.

62. Letter, Representative Pease to Carter, March 28, 1977, "HU [3/1/77–3/31/77]" Folder, Box HU-1, Human Rights Collection, Carter Presidential Library.

63. Transcript, *Recommendations of the Subcommittee on Africa, Committee Markup Session, House Committee on International Relations*, April 20, 21, 25, 27, 28, May 2–4, 1977, p. 229, H461-37, 95th Congress, 1st Session, Library of Congress, Washington, D.C.

64. Report, *International Security Assistance and Arms Export Control Act of 1977*, Committee on Foreign Relations, May 16, 1977 — S383-15, 95th Congress, 1st Session, Library of Congress, Washington, D.C.

65. Memo, Brzezinski to Carter, June 15, 1977, "6–7/77" Folder, Box Horn/Special: 1, NSA Staff Material, Carter Presidential Library.

66. Note, Henze to Brzezinski, April 21, 1977, "4–5/77" Folder, Box Horn/Special: 1, NSA Staff Material, Carter Presidential Library. See also, *New York Times*, April 28, 1977.

67. *Washington Post*, February 25, 1977.

68. Carter's Presentation to the Platform Committee, June 12, 1976, "President Carter Special Report" *Congressional Quarterly Inc*, April 1977, ed. Margaret Thompson.

69. Speech, Vance to the Plenary Session of the National Association for the Advancement of Colored People, July 1, 1977, "Speeches, Articles and Interviews by Cyrus R Vance [while Secretary of State] 1977 —1979" Folder, Box 39, Professional and Personal Activities, Group No 1664, Series No III, Cyrus R. Vance and Grace Sloane Papers, Yale University Library Manuscripts Collection.

70. *New York Times*, January 8, 1977, January 9, 1977.

71. Statement, Philip Habib, April 4, 1977, *Department of State Bulletin*, Volume LXXVI, Number 1971, p. 319.

72. News Conference, Cyrus Vance, January 31, 1977, *Department of State Bulletin*, Volume LXXVI, Number 1965, p. 143.

73. News Conference, Cyrus Vance, March 4, 1977, *Department of State Bulletin*, Volume LXXVI, Number 1970, p. 283.

74. Speech, Vance to the Plenary Session of the National Association for the Advancement of Colored People, July 1, 1977, "Speeches, Articles and Interviews by Cyrus R. Vance [while Secretary of State] 1977 —1979" Folder, Box 39, Professional and Personal Activities, Group No 1664, Series No III, Cyrus R. Vance and Grace Sloane Papers, Yale University Library Manuscripts Collection.

75. Memo, Vance to Carter/Mondale Policy Planning Group, October 24, 1976, "Carter Presidential Campaign: Foreign Policy Issues and Positions 1976, Mid" Folder, Box 9, Group No 1664, Series No II, Cyrus R. Vance and Grace Sloane Papers, Yale University Library Manuscripts Collection.

76. Testimony, Talcott Seelye to House Subcommittee on Africa, March 29, 1977, *Foreign Assistance Legislation for FY78 Part 3: Economic and Military Assistance Programs in Africa*, March 17, 18, 23, 28, 29, April 28, 1977, H461-37, 95th Congress, 1st Session, Library of Congress, Washington, D.C. See also, *Newsweek*, May 9, 1977.

77. *Washington Post*, May 4, 1977 and May 7, 1977, *New York Times*, May 6, 1977.

78. Interview, Paul Henze, *Cold War* Television Series, National Security Archive, Washington, D.C.

79. *Washington Post*, March 15, 1977.

80. Memo, Henze to Brzezinski, March 16, 1977, "Evening Reports File: 2–6/77" Folder, Box Horn/Special: 5, NSA Staff Material, Carter Presidential Library.

81. Minutes, Meeting between Erich Honecker and Fidel Castro, March 3, 1977, "Carter-Brezhnev Translations" Folder, Carter-Brezhnev Florida Conference Documents, National Security Archive, Washington, D.C.

82. *New York Times*, March 26, 1977.

83. *Washington Post* April 18, 1977.

84. *New York Times*, March 26, 1977.

85. *Washington Post*, March 25, 1977.

86. Memo, Henze to Brzezinski, March 31, 1977, "3/77" Folder, Box Horn/Special: 1, NSA Staff Material, Carter Presidential Library. See also, Robert G. Patman, *The Soviet Union in the Horn of Africa* (Cambridge: Cambridge University Press, 1990), p. 151.

87. Presidential Review Memorandum/NSC-21, *The Horn of Africa*, April 1, 1977, No 1558, Items 1552 (cont)— 1558, Fiche 352, National Security Archive, Washington, D.C.

88. *Time*, May 9, 1977.

89. Presidential Review Memorandum/NSC-21, *The Horn of Africa*, April 1, 1977.

90. *New York Times*, May 13, 1977.

91. *Time*, May 9, 1977.

92. Print, *Report of the Delegation to the Middle East and Africa*, House Committee on Armed Services, February 6, 1978, H202–2, 95th Congress, 2nd Session, Library of Congress, Washington, D.C.

93. *Newsweek*, August 29, 1977.

94. Testimony, Talcott Seelye to House Subcommittee on Africa, March 29, 1977, *Foreign Assistance Legislation for FY78 Part 3: Economic and Military Assistance Programs in Africa*, March 17, 18, 23, 28, 29, April 28, 1977, H461–37, 95th Congress, 1st Session, Library of Congress, Washington, D.C.

95. Presidential Review Memorandum/NSC-21, *The Horn of Africa*, April 1, 1977, No 1558, Items 1552 (cont)— 1558, Fiche 352, National Security Archive, Washington, D.C.

96. Minutes, Policy Review Committee Meeting, April 11, 1977, "Meetings PRC-10 4/11/77" Folder, Box 24, Zbigniew Brzezinski Donated Historical Material, Carter Presidential Library.

97. Minutes, PRC, April 11, 1977.

98. Minutes, PRC, April 11, 1977.

99. *New York Times*, April 26, 1977 and *Time*, May 9, 1977.

100. *Washington Post*, April 26, 1977 and *New York Times*, April 26, 1977.

101. Report, Vance to the Cabinet, Minutes of the Cabinet Meeting, April 25, 1977, "Cabinet Minutes, 1–5/77" Folder, Cabinet Minutes 1–5/77 through Cabinet Minutes 1980, Plains Subject File, Carter Presidential Library.

102. Interview, Henze for *Cold War* Television Series, National Security Archive, Washington, D.C.

103. Memo, Henze to Brzezinski, April 25, 1977, "4–5/77" Folder, Box Horn/Special: 1, NSA Staff Material, Carter Presidential Library.

104. *Time*, May 9, 1977.

105. *Los Angeles Times*, January 9, 1977; *New York Times* January 8, 1977, January 9, 1977; Memo, Lake to Vance, January 16, 1978, "HU [1/20/77 –1/20/81]" Folder, Box HU-1, Human Rights Collection, Carter Presidential Library.

106. Henze, *Horn of Africa,* p. 146.

107. Memo, Brzezinski to Vance, May 2, 1977, "4–5/77" Folder, Box Horn/Special: 1, NSA Staff Material, Carter Presidential Library.

108. Minutes, Meeting Between Siad Barré and G. V. Samsonov, Soviet Ambassador to Somalia, February 23, 1977, "I-1 Angola/Shaba" Folder, Carter-Brezhnev Florida Conference Documents (1), National Security Archive, Washington, D.C.

109. *Newsweek*, June 27, 1977.

110. *Washington Post*, February 22, 1977.

111. Lewis, ed., *Nationalism*, p. 4.

112. *New York Times*, July 11, 1977.

113. *New York Times*, July 11, 1977.

114. *Washington Post*, February 3, 1977. See also, Haggai Erlich, *The Struggle over Eritrea, 1962–1978* (Stanford: Hoover Institute, 1983), pp. 77/78.

115. See, for example, David Skidmore, *Reversing Course: Carter's Foreign Policy, Domestic Politics and the Failure of Reform* (Nashville and London: Vanderbilt University Press, 1996), who contends that "Carter's approach to foreign policy rested on a belief that the world was too complicated to be reduced to a doctrine (e.g. anti-communism)," p. 87.

116. Carter, Inaugural Address, January 20, 1980, *Public Papers 1977 Vol 1*, p. 4.

117. News Conference, Cyrus Vance, May 4, 1977, *Department of State Bulletin*, Volume LXXVI, Number 1978, May 23, 1977, pp. 519–520.

118. President Carter's News Conference, March 24, 1977, *Public Papers 1977 Vol I*, p. 497. See also *Newsweek*, April 4, 1977.

119. Presidential Review Memorandum NSC-21, *The Horn of Africa*, April 1, 1977, No 1558, Items 1552 (cont)—1558, Fiche 352, National Security Archive, Washington, D.C.

120. PRM/NSC-21.

121. PRM/NSC-21.

122. PRM/NSC-21.

123. Note, Henze to Brzezinski, May 3, 1977, "4–5/77" Folder, Box Horn/Special: 1, NSA Staff Material, Carter Presidential Library.

124. PRM/NSC-21.

125. *New York Times*, April 5, 1977.

126. PRM/NSC-21.

127. Testimony, James Akins to Senate Subcommittee on Multinational Corporations, May 4, 1976, *Multinational Corporations and U.S. Foreign Policy Part 14*, February 4, 6, May 4, 1976, S381–1, 95th Congress, 1st Session, Library of Congress, Washington, D.C.

128. *Washington Post*, February 28, 1977.

129. *Newsweek*, November 28, 1977.

130. *Newsweek*, May 9, 1977.

131. *Time*, May 9, 1977.

132. *Newsweek*, November 28, 1977.

133. *Time*, May 9, 1977.

134. *Newsweek*, June 13, 1977.

135. See, for example, Jerel A. Rosati, *The Carter Administration's Quest for Global Community: Beliefs & their Impact on Behavior* (Columbia: University of South Carolina Press, 1987), p. 39.

136. *U.S. News and World Report*, May 30, 1977.

137. *U.S. News and World Report*, November 7, 1977.

138. Memo, Brzezinski to Mondale, March 24, 1977, "4/78" Folder, Box Horn/Special: 2, NSA Staff Material, Carter Presidential Library.

139. *Time*, April 18, 1977.

140. Memo, Brzezinski to Mondale, March 24, 1977.

141. Minutes, Policy Review Committee Meeting, April 11, 1977, "PRC-10 4/11/77" Folder, Box 24, Zbigniew Brzezinski Donated Historical Material, Carter Presidential Library.

142. Minutes, PRC, April 11, 1977.

143. Minutes, PRC, April 11, 1977.

144. Henze, *Horn of Africa*, p. 147

145. Memo, Tarnoff to Brzezinski, June 2, 1977, "6–7/77" Folder, Box Horn/Special: 1, NSA Staff Material, Carter Presidential Library.

146. Memo, Brzezinski to Carter, undated, "6–7/77" Folder, Box Horn/Special: 1, NSA Staff Material, Carter Presidential Library.

147. *New York Times*, January 9, 1977

148. Memo, Tarnoff to Brzezinski, June 2, 1977, "6–7/77" Folder, Box Horn/Special: 1, NSA Staff Material, Carter Presidential Library.

149. Memorandum for the Record, Meeting with Addou, Carter, Brzezinski, Henze and Seelye, June 16, 1977, "6–7/77" Folder, Box Horn/Special: 1, NSA Staff Material, Carter Presidential Library.

150. Memorandum for the Record, Meeting with Addou, June 16, 1977.

151. Testimony, Tom Farer to House Subcommittee on Africa, March 28, 1977, *Foreign Assistance Legislation for FY78 Part 3: Economic and Military Assistance Programs in Africa*, March 17, 18, 23, 28, 29, April 28, 1977, H461–37, 95th Congress, 1st Session, Library of Congress, Washington, D.C.

152. Presidential Review Memorandum NSC-21, *The Horn of Africa*, April 1, 1977, No 1558, Items 1552 (cont)—1558, Fiche 352, National Security Archive, Washington, D.C.

153. *Newsweek*, June 27, 1977.

154. *Newsweek*, August 29, 1977.

155. *New York Times*, June 21, 1977.

156. Report, *Factfinding Mission to Egypt, Sudan, Ethiopia, Somalia and Kenya* to House Committee on International Relations, February 3, 1978, H462–9, 95th Congress, 2nd Session, Library of Congress, Washington, D.C.; Memo, Mondale to Carter, May 12, 1977, "4–5/77" Folder, Box Horn Special: 1, NSA Staff Material, Carter Presidential Library.

157. *Washington Post*, July 16, 1977.

158. *Newsweek*, May 9, 1977.

159. *Newsweek*, June 27, 1977.

160. *Newsweek*, June 27, 1977.

161. Memorandum for the Record, Meeting with Addou, Carter, Brzezinski, Henze and Seelye, June 16, 1977, "6–7/77" Folder, Box Horn/Special: 1, NSA Staff Material, Carter Presidential Library.

162. Memorandum for the Record, Meeting with Addou, June 16, 1977.

163. Statement, William E. Schaufele Jr., Assistant Secretary of State for African Affairs, to Senate Subcommittee on African Affairs, August 6, 1976, *Ethiopia and the Horn of Africa*, August 4–6, 1976 — S381-13, 95th Congress, 1st Session, Library of Congress, Washington, D.C.

164. Memo, Peter Bourne to Carter, June 6, 1977, "Somalia, CO140 1/20/77 —1/20/81" Folder, Box CO-53, WHCF, Countries (CO), Carter Presidential Library.

165. *Washington Post*, July 26, 1977.

166. Memorandum for the Record, Meeting with Addou, Carter, Brzezinski, Henze and Seelye, June 16, 1977, "6–7/77" Folder, Box Horn/Special: 1, NSA Staff Material, Carter Presidential Library.

167. Memo, Tarnoff to Brzezinski, July 12, 1977, "6–7/77" Folder, Box Horn/Special: 1, NSA Staff Material, Carter Presidential Library.

168. Memo, Mondale to Carter, May 12, 1977, "4–5/77" Folder, Box Horn/Special: 1, NSA Staff Material, Carter Presidential Library.

169. Memo, Mondale, May 12, 1977.

170. Memo, Mondale, May 12, 1977.

171. Presidential Review Memorandum NSC-21, *The Horn of Africa*, April 1, 1977, No 1558, Items 1552 (cont) —1558, Fiche 352, National Security Archive, Washington, D.C.

172. Memo, Brzezinski to Carter, undated, "4–5/77" Folder, Box Horn/Special: 1, NSA Staff Material, Carter Presidential Library.

173. Presidential Review Memorandum NSC-21, *The Horn of Africa*, April 1, 1977, No 1558, Items 1552 (cont) —1558, Fiche 352, National Security Archive, Washington, D.C.

174. Memo, Henze to Brzezinski, May 14, 1977, "4–5/77" Folder, Box Horn/Special: 1, NSA Staff Material, Carter Presidential Library.

175. Memo, Brzezinski to Mondale, March 24, 1977, "3/77" Folder, Horn Special: 1, NSA Staff Material, Carter Presidential Library.

176. Memorandum for the Record, Meeting with Addou, Carter, Brzezinski, Henze and Seelye, June, 16, 1977, "6–7/77" Folder, Box Horn/Special: 1, NSA Staff Material, Carter Presidential Library.

177. Memo, Henze to Brzezinski, May 14, 1977, "4–5/77" Folder, Box Horn/Special: 1, NSA Staff Material, Carter Presidential Library.

178. Memo, Tarnoff to Brzezinski, July 12, 1977, "6–7/77" Folder, Box Horn/Special: 1, NSA Staff Material, Carter Presidential Library.

179. Memo, Brzezinski to Mondale, March 24, 1977, "3/77" Folder, Box Horn/Special: 1, NSA Staff Material, Carter Presidential Library.

180. Speech, Vance to the Plenary Session of the National Association for the Advancement of Colored People, July 1, 1977, "Speeches, Articles and Interviews by Cyrus R. Vance [while Secretary of State] 1977–1979" Folder, Box 39, Professional and Personal Activities, Group No 1664, Series No III, Cyrus R. Vance and Grace Sloane Papers, Yale University Library Manuscripts Collection.

181. Note, Henze to Brzezinski, March 10, 1978, "3/78" Folder, Horn/Special: 2, NSA Staff Material, Carter Presidential Library.

182. Memorandum for the Record, Meeting with Addou, Carter, Brzezinski, Henze and Seelye, June 16, 1977, "6–7/77" Folder, Box Horn/Special: 1, NSA Staff Material, Carter Presidential Library.

183. *Washington Post*, April 25, 1977.

184. Speech, Representative Waggonner to the House, March 22, 1977, *Congressional Record*, 95th Congress, 1st Session, p. 8455.

185. Speech, Representative Crane to the House, April 25, 1977, *Congressional Record*, 95th Congress, 1st Session, p. 12144.

186. Speech, Representative McDonald to the House, June 2, 1977, *Congressional Record*, 95th Congress, 1st Session, p. 17394. NB: Representative McDonald was killed when the Soviet Union shot down the Korean Air Lines flight 007 over the Sea of Japan on September 1, 1983 — arguably an act of Cold War sabotage.

187. Speech, Representative McDonald to the House, June 8, 1977, *Congressional Record*, 95th Congress, 1st Session, pp. 18085/18086.

188. Speech, Representative Derwinski to the House, August 6, 1977, *Congressional Record*, 95th Congress, 1st Session, pp. 17668/17669.

189. Speech, Representative Derwinski to the House, July 14, 1977, *Congressional Record*, 95th Congress, 1st Session, p. 23149.

190. *Washington Post*, February 28, 1977.

191. *U.S. News and World Report*, April 4, 1977.

192. Emphasis added. Report, "Overview of Foreign Policy Issues and Positions," Cyrus Vance, October 24, 1976, "Cy Vance Papers (Yale)" Folder, Carter-Brezhnev Florida Conference Documents 1, National Security Archive, Washington, D.C.

193. Second Election Debate, October 6, 1976, "President Carter Special Report" *Congressional Quarterly Inc*, April 1977, ed. Margaret Thompson.

194. Carter, Address to the American People, February 2, 1977, *Public Papers 1977 Vol I*, p. 75. See also *Newsweek*, April 4, 1977.

195. Presidential Directive/NSC-18, *U.S. National Strategy*, August 24, 1977, No 1509, Items 1508–1514, Fiche 343, National Security Archive, Washington, D.C.

196. Presidential Review Memorandum NSC-21, *The Horn of Africa*, April 1, 1977, No 1558, Items 1552 (cont)—1558, Fiche 352, National Security Archive, Washington, D.C.

197. Memo, Henze to Brzezinski, July 14, 1977, "6–7/77" Folder, Box Horn/Special: 1, NSA Staff Material, Carter Presidential Library.

198. Address by the Honorable Cyrus R. Vance before the Plenary Session of the National Association for the Advancement of Colored People, St Louis, Missouri, July 1, 1977, Folder: "Speeches, Articles and Interviews by Cyrus R .Vance [while Secretary of State] 1977 —1979" Folder, Box 39, Group 1664, Series III, Cyrus R Vance and Grace Sloane Papers, Professional and Personal Activities, Yale University Library Manuscripts Collection.

Chapter III

1. *New York Times*, August 7, 1977; as well as the war in the Ogaden, Buxton was referring to the Eritrean secessionist insurgency.

2. *Washington Post*, August 15, 1977.

3. *Los Angeles Times*, August 1, 1977.

4. *New York Times*, August 4, 1977.

5. *Time*, August 22, 1977.

6. *New York Times*, September 8, 1977.

7. *Time*, October 24, 1977.

8. Jimmy Carter, *Keeping Faith: Memoirs of a President* (London: Collins, 1982), p. 301.

9. Jody Powell, *The Other Side of the Story* (New York: William Morrow, 1984), p. 76.

10. Powell, *Other Side*, p. 77.

11. *New York Times*, July 27, 1977.

12. *Washington Post*, July 26, 1977.

13. *New York Times*, June 12, 1977.

14. *Los Angeles Times*, August 1, 1977.

15. *Newsweek*, September 26, 1977.

16. *Newsweek*, September 26, 1977.

17. Report, *War in the Horn of Africa: A Firsthand Report on the Challenges for United States Policy. Report of a Factfinding Mission to Egypt, Sudan, Ethiopia, Somalia and Kenya, December 12 to 22, 1977*, to the House Committee on International Relations, February 3, 1978, 95th Congress, 2nd Session, H462-9, Library of Congress, Washington, D.C.

18. Memo, Henze to Brzezinski, March 10, 1978, "3/78" Folder, Box Horn/Special: 2, NSA Staff Material, Carter Presidential Library.

19. Letter, Jimmy Carter to Siad Barré, August 18, 1977, "8–9/77" Folder, Box Horn/Special: 1, NSA Staff Material, Carter Presidential Library.

20. Draft letter, Brzezinski on behalf of Jimmy Carter to Siad Barré, August 18, 1977, "8–9/77" Folder, Box Horn/Special: 1, NSA Staff Material, Carter Presidential Library.

21. *Washington Post*, September 20, 1977.

22. *Newsweek*, September 26, 1977.

23. Letter, Henze to Dr. Albert Henn, Agency for International Development, American Embassy, Cameroon, December 30, 1977, "Somalia, CO140 1/20/77–1/20/81" Folder, Box CO-53, WHCF, Countries (CO), Carter Presidential Library.

24. *Newsweek*, September 26, 1977.

25. *U.S. News and World Report*, November 28, 1977.

26. *Los Angeles Times*, September 21, 1977.

27. Memo, Brzezinski to Carter, August 26, 1977, "Meetings: PRC 33 [8/23/77]" Folder, Box 24, Zbigniew Brzezinski Donated Historical Material, Carter Presidential Library.

28. Letter, Jimmy Carter to Siad Barré, August 18, 1977, "8–9/77" Folder, Box Horn/Special: 1, NSA Staff Material, Carter Presidential Library.

29. Summary of Conclusion, Policy Review Committee Meeting, August 25, 1977, "Meetings: PRC 33 [8/23/77]" Folder, Box 24, Zbigniew Brzezinski Donated Historical Material, Carter Presidential Library.

30. Minutes, Policy Review Committee, August 25, 1977 —"Meetings: PRC 33 [8/25/77]" Folder, Box 24, Zbigniew Brzezinski Donated Historical Material, Carter Presidential Library.

31. *New York Times*, August 5, 1977.

32. *New York Times*, August 9, 1977.

33. *Washington Post*, August 9, 1977.

34. *New York Times*, August 12, 1977.

35. *Washington Post,* September 8, 1977.
36. *Newsweek,* June 27, 1977.
37. *New York Times,* August 12, 1977.
38. *Washington Post,* August 15, 1977.
39. *Newsweek,* August 29, 1977.
40. *Newsweek,* September 26, 1977.
41. Memo, Brzezinski to Carter, August 18, 1977, "8–9/77" Folder, Box Horn/Special: 1, NSA Staff Material, Carter Presidential Library.
42. Minutes, Cabinet Meeting, September 12, 1977, "Cabinet Minutes, 6–10/77" Folder, Subject File: Cabinet Minutes 1–5/77 through Cabinet Minutes, 1980, Plains File, Carter Presidential Library.
43. *Washington Post,* August 7, 1977.
44. *Washington Post,* September 22, 1977, *New York Times,* September 24, 1977.
45. *Los Angeles Times,* August 1, 1977.
46. *New York Times,* September 6, 1977.
47. Letter, Douglas J. Bennett, Jr., Assistant Secretary for Congressional Relations, State Department, to Representative Hamilton (D-In), October 6, 1977, *Congressional Record,* October 14, 1977, p. 33825.
48. Memo, Brzezinski to Carter, August 26, 1977, "USSR-U.S. Conference, 3/95 Briefing Book (I)" Folder, Vertical File, Carter Presidential Library.
49. Summary of Conclusions, Policy Review Committee Meeting, August 25, 1977, "Meetings: PRC 33 [8/23/77]" Folder, Box 24, Zbigniew Brzezinski Donated Historical Material, Carter Presidential Library.
50. Memo, Henze to Brzezinski, August 17, 1977, "8–9/77" Folder, Box Horn/Special: 1, NSA Staff Material, Carter Presidential Library.
51. Memo, Henze to Brzezinski, August 17, 1977.
52. *New York Times,* August 15, 1977.
53. According to conversations between the author and Stansfield Turner, Zbigniew Brzezinski, David Aaron, William Odom and Paul Henze, June and July 2000.
54. *New York Times,* October 19, 1977.
55. *Washington Post,* September 17, 1977.
56. Speech, Representative Sikes (D-Fl), October 25, 1977, *Congressional Record,* p. 35101.
57. Speech, Sikes, November 29, 1977, *Congressional Record,* p. 38050.
58. Address, Anthony Lake, Director of the Policy Planning Staff, at Johns Hopkins University School of Advanced International Studies, Washington, D.C., October 27, 1977, *Department of State Bulletin,* Vol LXXVII, No

2007, December 12, 1977, Library of Congress, Washington, D.C.
59. Press Release, "Secretary Vance's Activities at the United Nations," October 8, 1977, *Department of State Bulletin,* Vol LXXVII, No 2002, November 7, 1977.
60. *New York Times,* October 7, 1977.
61. *New York Times,* October 17, 1977.
62. Press Release, "United States Contributes to Ogaden Relief Appeal," October 28, 1977, *Department of State Bulletin,* Vol LXXVII, No 2005, November 28, 1977.
63. *New York Times,* September 19, 1977.
64. *New York Times,* September 12, 1977.
65. *Washington Post,* September 13, 1977.
66. *Time,* November 28, 1977.
67. *Newsweek,* November 28, 1977, *Time,* November 28, 1977.
68. Minutes, Cabinet Meeting, November 14, 1977, "Cabinet Minutes, 11/77–3/78" Folder, Subject File: Cabinet Minutes 1–5/77 through Cabinet Minutes, 1980, Plains File, Carter Presidential Library.
69. *Newsweek,* November 28, 1977.
70. *New York Times,* September 30, 1977.
71. *Washington Post,* October 21, 1977.
72. *New York Times,* November 5, 1977.
73. *Washington Post,* November 14, 1977.
74. *Washington Post,* November 15, 1977.
75. *New York Times,* November 5, 1977.
76. Memo, Henze to Brzezinski, December 7, 1977, "12/77" Folder, Box Horn/Special: 1, NSA Staff Material, Carter Presidential Library.
77. *Washington Post,* November 15, 1977.
78. Tsongas had been a Peace Corp volunteer in Ethiopia before becoming a member of Congress.
79. *Washington Post,* December 15, 1977.
80. Report, *War in the Horn of Africa: A Firsthand Report on the Challenges for United States Policy. Report of a Factfinding Mission to Egypt, Sudan, Ethiopia, Somalia and Kenya, December 12 to 22, 1977,* to the House Committee on International Relations, February 3, 1978, 95th Congress, 2nd Session — H462-9, Library of Congress, Washington, D.C.
81. *New York Times,* December 17, 1977.
82. Cyrus Vance, *Hard Choices: Critical Years in America's Foreign Policy* (New York: Simon & Schuster, 1983), p. 103.
83. *New York Times,* November 6, 1977.
84. Telegram, Secretary of State to American Embassies, December 13, 1977, "Meetings: SCC 45 [12/12/77]" Folder, Box 27, Zbigniew Brzezinski Donated Historical Material, Carter Presidential Library.

85. Report, *War in the Horn of Africa: A Firsthand Report on the Challenges for United States Policy. Report of a Factfinding Mission to Egypt, Sudan, Ethiopia, Somalia and Kenya, December 12 to 22, 1977*, to the House Committee on International Relations, February 3, 1978, 95th Congress, 2nd Session, H462–9, Library of Congress, Washington, D.C.

86. *New York Times*, December 17, 1977.

87. NSC Weekly Report #40, December 16, 1977, "Weekly Reports, 31–41 [10/77–1/78]" Folder, Box 41, Zbigniew Brzezinski Donated Historical Material, Carter Presidential Library.

88. Minutes, Cabinet Meeting, November 14, 1977, "Cabinet Minutes, 11/77–3/78" Folder, Subject File: Cabinet Minutes 1–5/77 through Cabinet Minutes, 1980, Plains File, Carter Presidential Library.

89. Zbigniew Brzezinski, *Power and Principle: Memoirs of the National Security Adviser, 1977–1981* (London, Weidenfeld & Nicolson, 1983), p. 179.

90. Telegram, Secretary of State to American Embassies, December 13, 1977, "Meetings: SCC 45 [12/12/77]" Folder, Box 27, Zbigniew Brzezinski Donated Historical Material, Carter Presidential Library.

91. Telegram, Vance to Brzezinski, December 12, 1977, "Meetings: SCC 45 [12/12/77]" Folder, Box 27, Zbigniew Brzezinski Donated Historical Material, Carter Presidential Library.

92. *New York Times*, November 18, 1977.

93. Report, *War in the Horn of Africa: A Firsthand Report on the Challenges for United States Policy. Report of a Factfinding Mission to Egypt, Sudan, Ethiopia, Somalia and Kenya, December 12 to 22, 1977*, to the House Committee on International Relations, February 3, 1978, 95th Congress, 2nd Session, H462–9, Library of Congress, Washington, D.C.

94. Report, *War in the Horn of Africa*, February 3, 1978.

95. NSC Weekly Report #37, November 18, 1977, "Weekly Reports, 31–41 [10/77–1/78]" Folder, Box 41, Zbigniew Brzezinski Donated Historical Material, Carter Presidential Library.

96. Memo, Henze to Brzezinski, December 7, 1977, "12/77" Folder, Box Horn/Special: 1, NSA Staff Material, Carter Presidential Library.

97. *New York Times*, December 10, 1977.

98. *Washington Post*, December 29, 1977.

99. Memo, Henze to Brzezinski, December 7, 1977.

100. *New York Times*, February 1, 1978.

101. See Chapter II, page 41.

102. *New York Times*, December 17, 1977.

103. *Washington Post*, January 27, 1978.

104. Summary of Conclusions, Policy Review Committee Meeting, August 25, 1977, "Meetings: PRC 33 [8/23/77]" Folder, Box 24, Zbigniew Brzezinski Donated Historical Material, Carter Presidential Library.

105. *Washington Post*, December 23, 1977.

106. *Washington Post*, January 18, 1978.

107. Briefing Prepared for Carter's Meeting with Black Leaders' Forum, December 14, 1977, "Foreign Affairs (General) [CF, O/A 47] [1]" Folder, Box 208, Stuart Eizenstat's Files, Carter Presidential Library.

108. President's News Conference, January 12, 1978, *Public Papers of the Presidents of the United States: Jimmy Carter 1978 Volume I* (Washington, D.C.: United States Government Printing Office, 1978), p. 57.

109. *Washington Post*, January 18, 1978.

110. *Washington Post*, January 19, 1978.

111. *New York Times*, January 30, 1978.

112. Memo, Henze to Brzezinski, January 12, 1978, "1/78" Folder, Box Horn/Special: 1, NSA Staff Material, Carter Presidential Library.

113. Summary of Conclusions, SCC Meeting, February 21, 1978, "Meetings: SCC 59 [2/21/78]" Folder, Box 28, Zbigniew Brzezinski Donated Historical Material, Carter Presidential Library.

114. Minutes, SCC Meeting, February 22, 1978, "Meetings: SCC 59 [2/21/78]" Folder, Box 28, Zbigniew Brzezinski Donated Historical Material, Carter Presidential Library.

115. *New York Times*, January 21, 1978.

116. *Washington Post*, January 22, 1978.

117. *New York Times*, January 22, 1978.

118. Minutes, Five Power Meeting on the Horn of Africa, January 24, 1978, "1/78" Folder, Box Horn/Special: 1, NSA Staff Material, Carter Presidential Library.

119. Minutes, Five Power Meeting on the Horn of Africa, January 24, 1978.

120. *New York Times*, January 23, 1978.

121. *Washington Post*, January 23, 1978.

122. Toasts of the President and the Shah at a State Dinner, December 31, 1977, Tehran, Iran, *Public Papers 1977 Vol II*, p. 2221.

123. Letter, Jimmy Carter to Marshal Tito of Yugoslavia, January 30, 1978, "Meetings: SCC 56 [2/10/78]" Folder, Box 28, Zbigniew Brzezinski Donated Historical Material, Carter Presidential Library.

124. *New York Times*, January 19, 1978.

125. Interview with Zbigniew Brzezinski, National Security Adviser to the Carter Administration, July 6, 2000, Center for Strategic and International Studies, Washington, D.C.

126. Memo, Henze to Brzezinski, January 23, 1978, "1/78" Folder, Box Horn/Special: 1, NSA Staff Material, Carter Presidential Library.

127. Minutes, NSC Meeting, February 23, 1978, "Ethiopia-Somalia [4/77–2/22/78]" Folder, Box 11, Zbigniew Brzezinski Donated Historical Material, Carter Presidential Library.

128. *Los Angeles Times*, March 3, 1978.

129. *New York Times*, February 25, 1978.

130. Letter, Brzezinski to Representative Richmond (D-NY), January 11, 1978, "Africa, CO 1–1 [1/20/77–9/1/78]" Folder, Box CO-4, WHCF Countries (CO) Collection, Carter Presidential Library.

131. Remarks and a question-and-answer session with a group of editors and news directors, November 11, 1977, *Public Papers 1977 Vol II*, p. 2010; The President's News Conference of January 12, 1978, *Public Papers of the Presidents of the United States: Jimmy Carter 1978 Volume I* (Washington, D.C.: United States Government Printing Office, 1978), pp. 56–57; State of the Union Message (text delivered to Congress), January 19, 1978, *Public Papers 1978 Vol I*, p. 121.

132. The President's News Conference, January 12, 1978, *Public Papers: Carter 1978 Vol I*, p. 57.

133. Letter, Carter to President Valery Giscard d'Estaing of France, January 27, 1978, "Meetings: SCC 56, [2/10/78]" Folder, Box 28, Zbigniew Brzezinski Donated Historical Material, Carter Presidential Library.

134. Letter, Carter to Prime Minister Morarji Desai of India, January 30, 1978, "Meetings: SCC 56 [2/10/78]" Folder, Zbigniew Brzezinski Donated Historical Material, Carter Presidential Library.

135. Letter, Carter to President Carlos Andres Perez of Venezuela, January 19, 1978, "Meetings: SCC 56 [2/10/78]" Folder, Zbigniew Brzezinski Donated Historical Material, Carter Presidential Library.

136. Letter, Carter to Perez, January 19, 1978.

137. Letter, Carter to President Jose Lopez Portillo of Mexico, February 13, 1978, "Ethiopia, CO49 1/20/77–1/20/81" Folder, Box CO-25, WHCF Countries (CO), Carter Presidential Library.

138. Letter, Carter to Brezhnev, January 25, 1978, "B-C Correspondence 1978" Folder, Subject File: Accomplishments: White House and Miscellaneous [2] 12/80 through B-C correspondence 1980, Plains File, Carter Presidential Library.

139. Telegram, State Department to American Embassy, Havana, February 10, 1978, "2/78" Folder, Box Horn/Special: 2, NSA Staff Material, Carter Presidential Library.

140. Summary of Conclusions, SCC Meeting, February 21, 1978, "Meetings: SCC 59 [2/21/78]" Folder, Box 28, Zbigniew Brzezinski Donated Historical Material, Carter Presidential Library.

141. *New York Times*, February 7, 1978.

142. *Washington Post*, February 7, 1978.

143. *New York Times*, February 8, 1978, *Washington Post*, February 8, 1978.

144. Memo, Henze to Brzezinski, January 12, 1978, "1/78" Folder, Box Horn/Special: 1, NSA Staff Material, Carter Presidential Library.

145. Memo, Henze to Brzezinski, January 12, 1978.

146. Briefing for Vice President Mondale, January 19, 1978, "1/78" Folder, Box Horn Special: 1, NSA Staff Material, Carter Presidential Library.

147. Telegram, American Embassy, Moscow, to Secretary of State, February 4, 1978, "2/78" Folder, Box Horn/Special: 2, NSA Staff Material, Carter Presidential Library.

148. Speech, Representative Sikes (D-Fl), January 19, 1978, *Congressional Record*, pp. 146/7.

149. Speech, Senator Eagleton (D-Mo), February 8, 1978, *Congressional Record*, p. 2664.

150. Memo, Henze to Brzezinski, January 21, 1978, "1/78" Folder, Box Horn/Special: 1, NSA Staff Material, Carter Presidential Library.

151. Speech, Senator McGovern, March 16, 1978, *Congressional Record*, p. 7262.

152. Memo, Tarnoff to Brzezinski, February 24, 1978, "Africa, CO 1–1 [1/20/77–9/1/78]" Folder, Box CO-4, WHCF, Countries (CO), Carter Presidential Library.

153. Memo, Henze to Brzezinski, January 16, 1978, "1/78" Folder, Box Horn/Special: 1, NSA Staff Material, Carter Presidential Library.

154. Memo, Henze to Brzezinski, January 16, 1978.

155. Memo, Henze to Brzezinski, January 16, 1978.

156. Oral message, Carter to Mengistu, January 19, 1978, "1/78" Folder, Box Horn/Special: 1, NSA Staff Material, Carter Presidential Library.

157. Memo, Henze to Brzezinski, January 12, 1978, "1/78" Folder, Box Horn/Special: 1, NSA Staff Material, Carter Presidential Library.

158. Note, Henze to Brzezinski, January 16, 1978, "1/78" Folder, Box Horn/Special: 1, NSA Staff Material, Carter Presidential Library.

159. Summary of Conclusions, SCC Meeting, January 26, 1978, "USSR-U.S. Conference, 3/95 Briefing Book (I)" Folder, Vertical File, Carter Presidential Library.

160. Letter, Mengistu to Carter, February 3, 1978, "2/78" Folder, Box Horn/Special: 2, NSA Staff Material, Carter Presidential Library.

161. Summary of conclusions, SCC Meeting, January 26, 1978, "USSR-U.S. Conference, 3/95 Briefing Book (I)" Folder, Vertical File, Carter Presidential Library.

162. Minutes, SCC Meeting, February 10, 1978, "U.S.-Horn 1978 Chronological" File, Carter Administration NSC Documents Collection, National Security Archives, Washington, D.C.

163. Interview with David Aaron, Deputy Director of the National Security Council in the Carter Administration, July 24, 2000, Washington, D.C.

164. Interview with Aaron, July 24, 2000.

165. Interview with Aaron, July 24, 2000.

166. NSC Weekly Report #47, February 17, 1978, "Weekly Reports, 42–52 [1/78–3/78]" Folder, Box 41, Zbigniew Brzezinski Donated Historical Material, Carter Presidential Library.

167. NSC Weekly Report #47, February 17, 1978, "Weekly Reports, 42–52 [1/78–3/78]" Folder, Box 41, Zbigniew Brzezinski Donated Historical Material, Carter Presidential Library.

168. *Washington Post*, February 22, 1978.

169. Memo, Henze to Brzezinski, January 21, 1978, "1/78" Folder, Box Horn/Special: 1, NSA Staff Material, Carter Presidential Library.

170. *Washington Post*, January 18, 1978.

171. Secretary of State's News Conference, February 10, 1978, *Department of State Bulletin*, Vol 78, No 2012, March 1978, Library of Congress, Washington, D.C.

172. Remarks and a question-and-answer session with representatives of black media

associations, February 16, 1978, *Public Papers 1978 Vol I*, p. 325.

173. Memo, Brzezinski to Vance, March 1978, "3/78" Folder, Box Horn/Special: 2, NSA Staff Material, Carter Presidential Library.

174. *Newsweek*, February 13, 1978.

175. *Newsweek*, February 13, 1978.

176. Vance, *Hard Choices*, p. 87.

177. Memo, Henze to Brzezinski, January 12, 1978, "1/78" Folder, Box Horn/Special: 1, NSA Staff Material, Carter Presidential Library.

178. Minutes, NSC Meeting, February 23, 1978, "Ethiopia-Somali [2/23/78–3/78]" Folder, Box 11, Zbigniew Brzezinski Donated Historical Material, Carter Presidential Library.

179. *Los Angeles Times*, February 8, 1978.

180. *New York Times*, February 5, 1978.

181. *Washington Post*, February 12, 1978.

182. *New York Times*, February 12, 1978.

183. Memo, Tarnoff to Brzezinski, February 24, 1978, "Africa, CO 1–1 [1/20/77–9/1/78]" Folder, Box CO-4, WHCF Countries (CO), Carter Presidential Library.

184. Brzezinski, *Power*, p. 184.

185. Minutes, NSC Meeting, February 23, 1978, "Ethiopia-Somali [2/23/78–3/78]" Folder, Box 11, Zbigniew Brzezinski Donated Historical Material, Carter Presidential Library.

186. *Washington Post*, January 19, 1978.

187. Memo, Vance to Carter, February 22, 1978, "USSR-U.S. Conference, 3/95: Briefing Book (I)" Folder, Vertical File, Carter Presidential Library.

188. NSC Weekly Report #47, February 17, 1978, "Weekly Reports, 42–52 [1/78–3/78]" Folder, Box 41, Zbigniew Brzezinski Donated Historical Material, Carter Presidential Library.

189. Telegram, Vance to Brzezinski, December 12, 1977, "Meetings: SCC 45 [12/12/77]" Folder, Box 27, Zbigniew Brzezinski Donated Historical Material, Carter Presidential Library; The President's News Conference, March 2, 1978, *Public Papers 1978 Vol I*, p. 442.

190. Dobrynin served as Soviet Ambassador to the United States from 1962 to 1986, thus making him the longest serving Soviet Ambassador in one post. Source: Anatoly Dobrynin, *In Confidence: Moscow's Ambassador to America's Six Cold War Presidents (1962–1986)* (New York: Random House 1995), p. 3.

191. Minutes of Conversation, Depart-

ment of State, February 14, 1978, "USSR-U.S. Conference, 3/95: Briefing Book (I)" Folder, Vertical File, Carter Presidential Library; Brzezinski, *Power*, p. 179.

192. Minutes, Cabinet Meeting, March 6, 1978, "Cabinet Minutes, 11/77–3/78" Folder, Subject File: Cabinet Minutes 1–5/77 through Cabinet Minutes, 1980, Plains File, Carter Presidential Library.

193. Interview with Paul Henze, National Security Council Staffer responsible for the Horn of Africa in the Carter Administration, July 19, 2000, Bethesda, Maryland.

194. Interview with Zbigniew Brzezinski, National Security Adviser to the Carter Administration, July 6, 2000, Center for Strategic and International Studies, Washington, D.C.

195. Minutes, SCC Meeting, March 2, 1978, "Meetings: SCC 61 [3/2/78]" Folder, Box 28, Zbigniew Brzezinski Donated Historical Material, Carter Presidential Library.

196. Brzezinski, *Power*, p. 178.

197. NSC Weekly Report #46, February 9, 1978, "Weekly Reports, 42–52 [1/78–3/78]" Folder, Box 41, Zbigniew Brzezinski Donated Historical Material, Carter Presidential Library.

198. NSC Weekly Report #48, February 24, 1978, "Weekly Reports, 42–52 [1/78–3/78]" Folder, Box 41, Zbigniew Brzezinski Donated Historical Material, Carter Presidential Library.

199. Memo, Brzezinski to Carter, March 3, 1978, "Meetings: SCC 61 [3/2/78]" Folder, Box 28, Zbigniew Brzezinski Donated Historical Material, Carter Presidential Library.

200. Brzezinski, *Power*, p. 179.

201. Minutes, SCC Meeting, March 2, 1978, "Meetings: SCC 61 [3/2/78]" Folder, Box 28, Zbigniew Brzezinski Donated Historical Material, Carter Presidential Library.

202. Minutes, SCC Meeting, March 2, 1978.

203. Interview with Zbigniew Brzezinski, National Security Adviser to the Carter Administration, July 6, 2000, Center for Strategic and International Studies, Washington, D.C.

204. Minutes, SCC Meeting, February 21, 1978, "U.S. Duplicates 1977–78" Folder, Carter-Brezhnev Florida Conference Documents (1), National Security Archives, Washington, D.C.

205. Minutes, SCC Meeting, March 2, 1978, "Meetings: SCC 61 [3/2/78]" Folder, Box 28, Zbigniew Brzezinski Donated Historical Material, Carter Presidential Library.

206. Minutes, SCC Meeting, March 2, 1978.

207. *Washington Post*, March 2, 1978.

208. The President's News Conference, March 2, 1978, *Public Papers 1978 Vol I*, p. 442.

209. Memo of Conversation, State Department, February 7, 1978, "USSR-U.S. Conference, 5/94: Briefing Book (II)" Folder, Vertical File, Carter Presidential Library.

210. Secretary of State's News Conference, February 10, 1978, *Department of State Bulletin*, Vol 78, No 2012, March 1978, Library of Congress, Washington, D.C.

211. Minutes, SCC Meeting, March 2, 1978, "Meetings: SCC 61 [3/2/78]" Folder, Box 28, Zbigniew Brzezinski Donated Historical Material, Carter Presidential Library.

212. *Washington Post*, March 2, 1978.

213. *Washington Post*, March 2, 1978.

214. Letter, Carter to Brezhnev, January 25, 1978, "B-C Correspondence 1978" Folder, Subject File: Accomplishments: White House and Miscellaneous [2] 12/80 through B-C Correspondence 1980, Plains File, Carter Presidential Library.

215. Presidential Message to Heads of State of Sudan, Saudi Arabia, Iran and Egypt, January 1978, "1/78" Folder, Box Horn/Special: 1, NSA Staff Material, Carter Presidential Library.

216. Summary of Conclusions, SCC Meeting, February 21, 1978, "Meetings: SCC 59 [2/21/78]" Folder, Box 28, Zbigniew Brzezinski Donated Historical Material, Carter Presidential Library.

217. Summary of Conclusions, SCC Meeting, February 21, 1978.

218. Vance, *Hard Choices*, p. 87.

219. Brzezinski, *Power*, p. 182.

220. Minutes, SCC Meeting, March 2, 1978, "Meetings: SCC 61 [3/2/78]" Folder, Box 28, Zbigniew Brzezinski Donated Historical Material, Carter Presidential Library.

221. President's News Conference, March 9, 1978, *Public Papers 1978 Vol I*, p. 490.

222. *Los Angeles Times*, March 12, 1978.

223. President's News Conference, March 9, 1978, *Public Papers Carter 1978 Vol I*, p. 490.

224. Summary of Conclusions, SCC meeting, March 10, 1978, "U.S.-Horn 1978 Chronological" Folder, Carter Administration NSC Documents Collection, National Security Archive, Washington, D.C.

225. President's News Conference, March 9, 1978, *Public Papers Carter 1978 Vol I*, p. 490.

226. *Washington Post*, March 11, 1978.

227. *Los Angeles Times*, March 12, 1978.

Chapter IV

1. See, for example, John Dumbrell, *The Carter Presidency: A Re-Evaluation* (Manchester: Manchester University Press, 1993), p. 110; Jerel A. Rosati, *The Carter Administration's Quest for Global Community: Beliefs & Their Impact on Behavior.* (Columbia: University of South Carolina Press, 1987), p. 69; Odd Arne Westad, ed., *The Fall of Detente: Soviet-American Relations During the Carter Years*, (Oslo & Oxford: Scandinavian University Press, 1997), p. 21.

2. Interview with Henze, July 19, 2000, Bethesda, Maryland.

3. Handwritten note, Cyrus Vance, 1976, "Carter Presidency Transition: Notes, Background and Proposals 1976" Folder, Box 8, Series II, Group 1664, Cyrus R. Vance and Grace Sloane Papers, Carter Presidential Administration, Yale University Library Manuscripts Collection.

4. Cyrus Vance, *Hard Choices: Critical Years in America's Foreign Policy* (New York: Simon & Schuster, 1983), p. 35.

5. All quotes from Vance, *Hard Choices*, pp. 91–92.

6. Zbigniew Brzezinski, *Power and Principle: Memoirs of the National Security Adviser, 1977–1981* (London: Weidenfeld & Nicolson, 1983), p. 186.

7. Kim Willenson with Lloyd Norman, Eleanor Clift and Elaine Shannon in Washington, and James Pringle in Addis Ababa, *Newsweek*, February 27, 1978.

8. Bernard Gwertzman, Washington, *New York Times*, March 3, 1978.

9. David Ottaway, Lusaka, Zambia, *Washington Post*, February 14, 1978.

10. State of the Union Address, Carter to Congress, January 19, 1978, *Public Papers of the Presidents of the United States: Jimmy Carter 1978 Volume I* (Washington, D.C.: United States Government Printing Office, 1978), p. 95.

11. For example, *U.S. News & World Report*, March 14, 1977.

12. The difficulties encountered by the administration are discussed at length in various secondary sources on Carter's presidency, including M. Glenn Abernathy, Dilys M. Hill and Phil Williams (eds.), *The Carter Years: The President and Policy Making* (London: Francis Pinter, 1984), Dumbrell, *Carter Presidency*, David Forsythe, "American Foreign Policy and Human Rights: Rhetoric and Reality" in *Human Rights Quarterly*, July — September

1980, Volume 2, Natalie Kaufman Hevener, ed., *The Dynamics of Human Rights in U.S. Foreign Policy* (New Brunswick: Transaction Books, 1981), A. Glenn Mower, *Human Rights and American Foreign Policy: The Carter and Reagan Experiences* (New York: Greenwood, 1987) and Sandy Vogelgesang, *American Dream, Global Nightmare: The Dilemma of United States Human Rights Policy* (New York: WW Norton & Co., 1980).

13. Mower, *Human Rights*, p. 38.

14. *Washington Post*, February 9, 1978.

15. *New York Times*, February 9, 1978.

16. Briefing for Mondale, January 19, 1978, "1/78" Folder, Horn/Special: 1, NSA Staff Material, Carter Presidential Library.

17. Memo, Henze to Brzezinski, January 12, 1978, "1/78" Folder, Horn/Special: 1, NSA Staff Material, Carter Presidential Library.

18. Memo, Henze to Brzezinski, February 6, 1978, "2/78" Folder, Box Horn/Special: 2, NSA Staff Material, Carter Presidential Library.

19. Emphasis in original. Memo, Henze to Brzezinski, March 27, 1978, "4/78" Folder, Box Horn/Special: 2, NSA Staff Material, Carter Presidential Library.

20. Memo, Henze to Brzezinski, March 10, 1978, "3/78" Folder, Box Horn/Special: 2, NSA Staff Material, Carter Presidential Library.

21. Minutes, SCC Meeting, March 16, 1978, "U.S.-Horn 1978 Chronological" Folder, Carter Administration NSC Documents Collection, National Security Archive, Washington, D.C.

22. Memo, Wauchope to Moose, March 7, 1978, "3/78" Folder, Box Horn/Special: 2, NSA Staff Material, Carter Presidential Library.

23. Memo, Carter to Vance, March 23, 1978, *Public Papers 1978 Vol I*, p. 959.

24. As well as offering access to the sea, Eritrea had provided the staging point for foreign forces on the two occasions that Ethiopia had suffered invasion, in 1896 and 1935. Haile Selassie therefore claimed that control over Eritrea was vital for Ethiopian national security. See J. A. Lefebvre, *Arms for the Horn: U.S. Security Policy in Ethiopia and Somalia, 1953–1991* (Pittsburgh: University of Pittsburgh Press, 1991), p. 59.

25. Memo, Wauchope to Moose, March 7, 1978.

26. Summary of Conclusions, SCC Meeting, March 10, 1978, "Carter Administration NSC documents collection" Folder, Box:

U.S.-Horn 1978 Chronological, National Security Archive, Washington, D.C.

27. Discussion Paper, SCC Meeting, March 27, 1978, "Meetings: SCC 68, 3/27/78" Folder, Box 28, Zbigniew Brzezinski Donated Historical Material, Carter Presidential Library.

28. Discussion Paper, SCC Meeting, March 27, 1978.

29. Memo, Wauchope to Moose, March 7, 1978, "3/78" Folder, Box Horn/Special: 2, NSA Staff Material, Carter Presidential Library.

30. Discussion Paper, SCC Meeting, March 27, 1978.

31. Discussion Paper, SCC Meeting, March 27, 1978.

32. Memo, Wauchope to Moose, March 7, 1978.

33. Memo, Henze to Brzezinski, March 11, 1978, "3/78" Folder, Box Horn/Special: 2, NSA Staff Material, Carter Presidential Library.

34. Statement, Tom Farer to House Subcommittee on Africa, March 28, 1977, *Report and Recommendations of the House Subcommittee on Africa to the Committee on International Relations, Foreign Assistance Legislation for FY78, Part 3: Economic and Military Assistance Programs in Africa*, March 17, 18, 23, 28, 29, April 28 1977, H461-37, 95th Congress, 1st Session, Library of Congress, Washington, D.C. See also Ruth Iyob, "Regional Hegemony: Domination and Resistance in the Horn of Africa" in *Journal of Modern African Studies*, Volume 31, June 1993, and Anthony Lake, *Third World Radical Regimes: U.S. Policy Under Carter and Reagan* (New York: Foreign Policy Association, 1979), p. 80.

35. Memo, Wauchope to Moose, March 7, 1978, "3/78" Folder, Box Horn/Special: 2, NSA Staff Material, Carter Presidential Library.

36. Minutes, SCC Meeting, March 27, 1978, "Meetings: SCC 3/27/78" Folder, Box 28, Zbigniew Brzezinski Donated Historical Material, Carter Presidential Library.

37. Handwritten note by Carter on Memo, Brzezinski to Carter, March 28, 1978, "Meetings: SCC 3/27/78" Folder, Box 28, Zbigniew Brzezinski Donated Historical Material, Carter Presidential Library.

38. Memo, Wauchope to Moose, March 7, 1978, "3/78" Folder, Box Horn/Special: 2, NSA Staff Material, Carter Presidential Library.

39. Discussion Paper, SCC Meeting, March 27, 1978, "Meetings: SCC 68, 3/27/78" Folder, Box 28, Zbigniew Brzezinski Donated Historical Material, Carter Presidential Library.

40. Discussion Paper, SCC Meeting, March 27, 1978.

41. State Department Briefing Document for SCC Meeting on Horn of Africa, March 23, 1978, "USSR-U.S. Conference, 3/95: Briefing Book (I)" Folder, Vertical File, Carter Presidential Library.

42. John Bushnell, Deputy Assistant Secretary of State for Inter-American Affairs, to House Subcommittee on Inter-American Affairs, March 15, 1978, *Hearings before the Subcommittee on Inter-American Affairs, Impact of Cuban-Soviet Ties in the Western Hemisphere*, March 14, 15, April 5, 12, 1978, H461-53, 95th Congress, 2nd Session, Library of Congress, Washington, D.C.

43. Memo of Conversation, Vance and Dobrynin, March 16, 1978, "USSR-U.S. Conference, 3/95: Briefing Book (II)" Folder, Vertical File, Carter Presidential Library.

44. Memo, Henze to Brzezinski, March 16, 1978, "Meetings: SCC 65 [3/16/78]" Folder, Box 28, Zbigniew Brzezinski Donated Historical Material, Carter Presidential Library. Negative opinions of Siad were expressed in interviews by David Aaron, Deputy Director of the National Security Council in the Carter Administration, July 24, 2000, Washington, D.C.; Admiral Stansfield Turner, Director of the CIA in the Carter Administration, June 30, 2000, Watergate Complex, Washington, D.C.

45. Memo, Henze to Brzezinski, March 27, 1978, "3/78" Folder, Horn/Special: 2, NSA Staff Material, Carter Presidential Library.

46. Discussed in detail in Chapter I.

47. Memo, Henze to Brzezinski, March 10, 1978, "3/78" Folder, Box Horn/Special: 2, NSA Staff Material, Carter Presidential Library.

48. Memo, Henze to Brzezinski, March 27, 1978, "3/78" Folder, Horn/Special: 2, NSA Staff Material, Carter Presidential Library.

49. Meeting, SCC meeting, March 16, 1978, "U.S.-Horn 1978 Chronological" Folder, Carter Administration NSC Documents Collection, National Security Archive, Washington, D.C.

50. Memo, Henze to Brzezinski, March 27, 1978, "3/78" Folder, Horn/Special: 2, NSA Staff Material, Carter Presidential Library.

51. Memo, Henze to Brzezinski, March 10, 1978, "10/78" Folder, Horn/Special: 2, NSA Staff Material, Carter Presidential Library.

52. Memo, Henze to Brzezinski, March 16, 1978, "Meetings: SCC 65 [3/16/78]" Folder, Box 28, Zbigniew Brzezinski Donated Historical Material, Carter Presidential Library.

53. Emphasis in original. Memo, Henze to Brzezinski, March 9, 197, "Meetings: SCC 64 [3/10/78]" Folder, Box 28, Zbigniew Brzezinski Donated Historical Material, Carter Presidential Library.

54. See, for example, Chapter II, page 58.

55. Memo, Henze to Brzezinski, March 16, 1978.

56. Summary of Conclusions, SCC Meeting, March 16, 1978, "Meetings: SCC 65 [3/16/78]" Folder, Box 28, Zbigniew Brzezinski Donated Historical Material, Carter Presidential Library.

57. Summary of Conclusions, SCC Meeting, March 16, 1978.

58. *Washington Post*, March 16, 1978.

59. Minutes, SCC Meeting, March 16, 1978, "U.S.-Horn 1978 Chronological" Folder, Carter Administration NSC Documents Collection, National Security Archive, Washington, D.C.

60. Minutes, SCC meeting, March 27, 1978, "Meetings: SCC 3/27/78" Folder, Box 28, Zbigniew Brzezinski Donated Historical Material, Carter Presidential Library.

61. *Washington Post*, March 16, 1978.

62. Memo, Henze to Brzezinski, March 16, 1978, "Meetings: SCC 65 [3/16/78], Box 28, Zbigniew Brzezinski Donated Historical Material, Carter Presidential Library.

63. Memo, Henze, to Brzezinski, March 16, 1978.

64. *New York Times*, March 24, 1978.

65. Minutes, SCC Meeting, March 27, 1978, "Meetings: SCC 68 [3/27/78]" Folder, Box 28, Zbigniew Brzezinski Donated Historical Material, Carter Presidential Library.

66. Memo, Henze to Brzezinski, March 27, 1978, "3/78" Folder, Horn/Special: 2, NSA Staff Material, Carter Presidential Library.

67. Minutes, SCC meeting, March 27, 1978.

68. Minutes, SCC Meeting, March 27, 1978.

69. Memo of Conversation, Vance and Dobrynin, March 16, 1978, "USSR-U.S. Conference 3/95: Briefing Book (II)" Folder, Vertical File, Carter Presidential Library.

70. Note, Henze to Brzezinski, April 18, 1978, "4/78" Folder, Horn/Special: 2, NSA Staff Material, Carter Presidential Library.

71. Note, Henze to Brzezinski, April 18, 1978.

72. Emphasis in original. Memo, Henze to Brzezinski, March 27, 1978, "3/78" Folder, Horn/Special: 2, NSA Staff Material, Carter Presidential Library.

73. Minutes, SCC Meeting, April 7, 1978, "U.S.-Horn 1978 Chronological" Folder, Carter Administration NSC Documents Collection, National Security Archive, Washington, D.C.

74. Memo, Henze to Brzezinski, April 21, 1978, "Meetings: SCC 69 [4/7/78]" Folder, Box 28, Zbigniew Brzezinski Donated Historical Material, Carter Presidential Library.

75. Minutes, SCC meeting, April 7, 1978.

76. Speech, Vance at the CENTO Opening Session, London, April 19, 1978, *Department of State Bulletin*, Vol. 78, No 2015, June 1978, Library of Congress, Washington, D.C.

77. Speech, Vance at the CENTO Opening Session, London, April 19, 1978.

78. *Washington Post*, April 1, 1978.

79. Memo, Henze to Brzezinski, April 21, 1978, "Meetings: SCC 69 [4/7/78]" Folder, Box 28, Zbigniew Brzezinski Donated Historical Material, Carter Presidential Library.

80. *Washington Post*, April 1, 1978.

81. Interview, Vance with *Time* correspondents Strobe Talbott and Christopher Ogden, *Time*, April 24, 1978.

82. *Washington Post*, April 17, 1978.

83. Speech, Senator Dole (R-Kan) to Senate, April 20, 1978, *Congressional Record*, pp. 10964–10965.

84. Speech, Representative Goldwater (R-Az), May 23, 1978, *Congressional Record*, p. 15122.

85. Speech, Representative Sikes (D-Fl) to House, May 31, 1978, *Congressional Record*, p. H4661.

86. Republican Statement, May 3, 1978, *Congressional Quarterly*, May 13, 1978, p. 1160.

87. *Washington Post*, August 20, 1978.

88. *New York Times*, April 10, 1978.

89. CIA Intelligence Memorandum, May 8, 1978, "4/78" Folder, Horn/Special: 2, NSA Staff Material, Carter Presidential Library.

90. Memo, Denend to Brzezinski, May 5, 1978, "Meetings: SCC 77 [5/15/78]" Folder, Box 28, Zbigniew Brzezinski Donated Historical Material, Carter Presidential Library.

91. Minutes, SCC Meeting, May 15, 1978, "Meetings SCC 77 [5/15/78]" Folder, Box 28, Zbigniew Brzezinski Donated Historical Material, Carter Presidential Library.

92. Memo, Denend to Brzezinski, May 5, 1978.

93. Hearing, Vance to Senate Subcommit-

tee on African Affairs, May 12, 1978, *U.S. Policy Toward Africa*, May 12, 1978, S381–31, 95th Congress, 2nd Session Library of Congress, Washington, D.C.

94. Minutes, SCC meeting, May 15, 1978.

95. CIA Intelligence Memorandum, May 9, 1978, "5/78" Folder, Horn/Special: 2, NSA Staff Material, Carter Presidential Library.

96. Memo, Henze to Brzezinski, May 26, 1978, "5/78" Folder, Horn/Special: 2, NSA Staff Material, Carter Presidential Library.

97. Remarks and a Question-and-Answer Session with a Group of Editors and News Directors, May 19, 1978, *Public Papers 1978 Vol I*, p. 941.

98. Memo of Conversation, Carter and Gromyko, May 27, 1978, "USSR-U.S. Conference 5/94: Briefing Book (III)" Folder, Vertical File, Carter Presidential Library.

99. Interview, Brzezinski on "Meet the Press," May 28, 1978, *Department of State Bulletin*, Vol. 78, Number 2016, July 1978, Library of Congress, Washington, D.C.

100. Testimony, Vance to House Subcommittee on African Affairs, May 12, 1978, *U.S. Policy Toward Africa*, May 12, 1978, S381–31, 95th Congress, 2nd Session Library of Congress, Washington, D.C.

101. *Washington Post,* May 17, 1978.

102. *Washington Post,* May 17, 1978.

103. Minutes, SCC meeting, May 15, 1978, "Meetings: SCC 5/15/78" Folder, Box 28, Zbigniew Brzezinski Donated Historical Material, Carter Presidential Library.

104. Memo of Conversation, Carter and Gromyko, May 27, 1978, "USSR-U.S. Conference, 5/94: Briefing Book (III)" Folder, Vertical File, Carter Presidential Library.

105. *Washington Post,* May 25, 1978.

106. *Washington Post,* May 30, 1978.

107. Joseph Fromm, "Tug of War Over Foreign Policy," deputy editor, *U.S. News & World Report,* June 19, 1978.

108. Fromm, *U.S. News & World Report,* June 19, 1978.

109. Don Oberdorfer, staff writer, *Washington Post,* June 20, 1978.

110. Martin Schram, *Washington Post,* August 6, 1978.

111. Interviews with Admiral Stansfield Turner, Director of the CIA in the Carter Administration, June 30, 2000, Watergate Complex, Washington, D.C., Paul Henze, National Security Council Staffer responsible for the Horn of Africa in the Carter Administration, July 19, 2000, Bethesda, Maryland, and Zbigniew Brzezinski, National Security Adviser to the Carter Administration, July 6, 2000, Center for Strategic and International Studies, Washington, D.C.

112. Letter, Ambassador Mohammed Warsama, United Nations, to *New York Times,* June 20, 1978.

113. Memo, Henze to Brzezinski, June 8, 1978, "Meetings: SCC 6/8/78" Folder, Box 28, Zbigniew Brzezinski Donated Historical Material, Carter Presidential Library.

114. David Lamb, Mogadishu, *Los Angeles Times,* June 7, 1978.

115. Michael Kaufman, Nairobi, *New York Times,* June 7, 1978.

116. Memo, Henze to Brzezinski, June 8, 1978, "Meetings: SCC 6/8/78" Folder, Box 28, Zbigniew Brzezinski Donated Historical Material, Carter Presidential Library.

117. Telegram, Secretary of State to USDEL Secretary NIACT, copy to American Embassy, Mogadishu, June 3, 1978, "Evening Reports File 6–8/78" Folder, Horn/Special: 6, NSA Staff Material, Carter Presidential Library.

118. *New York Times,* June 8, 1978.

119. *New York Times,* June 2, 1978.

120. *Washington Post,* June 2, 1978.

121. Memo, Henze to Brzezinski, July 27, 1978, "7/78" Folder, Box Horn/Special: 2, NSA Staff Material, Carter Presidential Library.

122. Memo, Henze to Brzezinski, July 27, 1978.

123. Nomination of Frederic L. Chapin, May 31, 1978, *Public Papers 1978 Vol I*, p. 1023.

124. Memo, Henze to Brzezinski, June 21, 1978, "6/78" Folder, Box Horn/Special: 2, NSA Staff Material, Carter Presidential Library.

125. Letter, Henze to Professor Ullendorff, Oxford University, Great Britain, June 26, 1978, "6/78" Folder, Box Horn/Special: 2, NSA Staff Material, Carter Presidential Library.

126. Memo, Henze to Brzezinski, June 8, 1978, "Meetings: SCC 77 [5/15/78]" Folder, Box 28, Zbigniew Brzezinski Donated Historical Material, Carter Presidential Library.

127. Memo, Henze to Brzezinski, June 8, 1978.

128. Memo, Henze to Brzezinski, June 8, 1978.

129. Memo, Henze to Brzezinski, June 8, 1978.

130. Memo, Henze to Brzezinski, June 2, 1978, "6/78" Folder, Box Horn/Special: 2, NSA Staff Material, Carter Presidential Library.

131. Agenda and Papers, Policy Review Committee Meeting July 31, 1978, "U.S.-Horn 1978 Chronological" Folder, Carter Administration NSC Documents Collection, National Security Archive, Washington, D.C.

132. Memo, Henze to Brzezinski, July 27, 1978, "7/78" Folder, Horn/Special: 2, NSA Staff Material, Carter Presidential Library.

133. Agenda and Papers, Policy Review Committee Meeting July 31, 1978, "U.S.-Horn 1978 Chronological" Folder, Carter Administration NSC Documents Collection, National Security Archive, Washington, D.C.

134. Minutes, Policy Review Committee Meeting, July 31, 1978, "U.S.-Horn 1978 Chronological" Folder, Carter Administration NSC Documents Collection, National Security Archive, Washington, D.C.

135. Speech, Carter to the Graduating Class at the U.S. Naval Academy, Annapolis, June 7, 1978, *Congressional Quarterly*, June 10, 1978.

136. The President's News Conference of June 14, 1978, *Public Papers 1978 Vol. I*, p. 1095.

137. Address, Vance to the Fifty-Eighth Annual Meeting of the U.S. Jaycees in Atlantic City, June 20, 1978, *Department of State Bulletin*, Vol. 78, No. 2017, August 1978, Library of Congress, Washington, D.C.

138. *Washington Post*, June 15, 1978.

139. Karen De Young, Havana, Cuba, *Washington Post*, June 22, 1978.

140. Memo, Henze to Brzezinski, June 8, 1978, "Meetings: 6/8/78" Folder, Box 28, Zbigniew Brzezinski Donated Historical Material, Carter Presidential Library.

141. Memo, Henze to Brzezinski, July 27, 1978, "7/78" Folder, Box Horn/Special: 2, NSA Staff Material, Carter Presidential Library.

142. Letter, Henze to Professor Harold Marcus, Editor, *Ethiopianist Notes*, Michigan State University, August 9, 1978, "8/78" Folder, Box Horn/Special: 2, NSA Staff Material, Carter Presidential Library.

143. *Washington Post*, June 4, 1978.

144. Memo, Henze to Brzezinski, June 8, 1978, "Meetings: SCC 77 [5/15/78]" Folder, Box 28, Zbigniew Brzezinski Donated Historical Material, Carter Presidential Library.

145. Address, Vance to the Fifty-Eighth Annual Meeting of the U.S. Jaycees in Atlantic City, June 20, 1978, *Department of State Bulletin*, Vol. 78, No. 2017, August 1978, Library of Congress, Washington, D.C.

146. Memo, Henze to Brzezinski, June 8, 1978, "Meetings: SCC 77 [5/15/78]" Folder,

Box 28, Zbigniew Brzezinski Donated Historical Material, Carter Presidential Library.

147. See the Hickenlooper Amendment to the Foreign Assistance Act of 1961 and the Gonzalez Amendment of March 10, 1972 to the Inter-American Development Bank Act.

148. Memo, Henze to Brzezinski, June 8, 1978.

149. Memo, Henze to Brzezinski, July 27, 1978, "7/78" Folder, Box Horn/Special: 2, NSA Staff Material, Carter Presidential Library.

150. Minutes, Policy Review Committee Meeting, July 31, 1978, "U.S.-Horn 1978 Chronological" Folder, Carter Administration NSC Documents Collection, National Security Archive, Washington, D.C.

151. Minutes, Policy Review Committee Meeting, July 31, 1978.

152. Memo, Henze to Brzezinski, July 27, 1978, "7/78" Folder, Horn/Special: 2, NSA Staff Material, Carter Presidential Library.

153. Agenda and Papers for Policy Review Meeting, July 31, 1978, "U.S.-Horn 1978 Chronological" Folder, Carter Administration NSC Documents Collection, National Security Archive, Washington, D.C.

154. David Ottaway, Khartoum, *Washington Post*, July 23, 1978.

155. Agenda and Papers, Policy Review Committee Meeting July 31, 1978, "U.S.-Horn 1978 Chronological" Folder, Carter Administration NSC Documents Collection, National Security Archive, Washington, D.C.

156. *New York Times*, July 3, 1978.

157. Memo, Henze, to Brzezinski, June 2, 1978, "6/78" Folder, Horn/Special: 2, NSA Staff Material, Carter Presidential Library.

158. Nomination of Donald K Petterson, September 21, 1978, *Public Papers 1978 Vol. II*, p. 1562.

159. Memo, Henze to Rick Inderfurth, August 8, 1978, "8/78" Folder, Box Horn/Special: 2, NSA Staff Material, Carter Presidential Library.

160. Memo, Tarnoff to Brzezinski, October 25, 1978, "10/78" Folder, Horn/Special: 2, NSA Staff Material, Carter Presidential Library.

161. Memo, McGiffert to Aaron, October 4, 1978, "10/78" Folder, Horn/Special: 2, NSA Staff Material, Carter Presidential Library.

162. Memo, Henze to Aaron, November 28, 1978, "11/78" Folder, Horn/Special: 2, NSA Staff Material, Carter Presidential Library.

163. *New York Times*, November 21, 1978.

164. *Washington Post,* November 22, 1978.

165. Memo, Henze to Brzezinski, December 8, 1978, "12/78" Folder, Box Horn/Special: 3, NSA Staff Material, Carter Presidential Library.

166. Memo, Henze to Brzezinski, December 8, 1978.

167. *Washington Post,* November 30, 1978.

168. Memo, Henze to Brzezinski, December 8, 1978.

169. *New York Times,* December 1, 1978.

170. *Washington Post,* November 30, 1978.

171. Memo, Brzezinski to Mondale, December 1978, "12/78" Folder, Horn/Special: 3, NSA Staff Material, Carter Presidential Library.

172. John Darnton, Mogadishu, *New York Times,* December 27, 1978.

173. Memo, Brzezinski to Mondale, December 1978, "12/78" Folder, Horn/Special: 3, NSA Staff Material, Carter Presidential Library.

174. *Washington Post,* November 16, 1978.

175. Telegram, Department of State to American Embassy, Addis Ababa, December 16, 1978, "12/78" Folder, Box Horn/Special: 3, NSA Staff Material, Carter Presidential Library.

176. Republican Statement in Response to President Carter's State of the Union Message, January 24, 1979, *U.S. News & World Report,* February 5, 1979.

177. Statement of Richard Moose, Assistant Secretary of State for African Affairs, to Subcommittee on African Affairs, February 4, 1979, *Foreign Assistance Legislation for FY80-FY81, Part 6: Economic and Military Assistance Programs in Africa,* February 13, 14, 21, 22, 27, 28, March 5–7, 12, 1979, H381-13, 96th Congress, 1st Session, Library of Congress, Washington, D.C.

178. Statement, Moose to Subcommittee on African Affairs, February 4, 1979.

179. Statement, Moose to Subcommittee on African Affairs, February 4, 1979.

180. *Washington Post,* February 3, 1979.

181. William Campbell, Sasabeneh, Ethiopia *Los Angeles Times,* March 7, 1979.

182. Memo, Henze to Brzezinski, February 8, 1979, "2/79" Folder, Horn/Special: 3, NSA Staff Material, Carter Presidential Library.

183. Memo, Henze to Brzezinski, March 16, 1979, "3/79" Folder, Horn/Special: 3, NSA Staff Material, Carter Presidential Library.

184. Memo, Brzezinski to Carter, March 27, 1979, "3/79" Folder, Box Horn/Special: 3, NSA Staff Material, Carter Presidential Library.

185. Memo of Conversation, Carter and Brezhnev, June 17, 1979, "C-B: Shulman Docs from DOS on Afghanistan (originals) (3/9/95)" Folder, Box: Carter-Brezhnev Collection 1 Florida Conference Documents, National Security Archive, Washington, D.C.

186. Memo of Conversation, Carter and Brezhnev, June 17, 1979.

187. Memo, Henze to Brzezinski, May 2, 1979, "5/79" Folder, Horn/Special: 3, NSA Staff Material, Carter Presidential Library.

188. Memo, Henze to Brzezinski, May 8, 1979, "5/79" Folder, Horn/Special: 3, NSA Staff Material, Carter Presidential Library. Note: PNG stands for *persona non grata* and is a term used in diplomatic circles, and elsewhere, to request the departure of an official. The "Newsom" referred to by Henze was the Under Secretary of State for Political Affairs, David Newsom.

189. Memo, Henze to Brzezinski, July 6, 1979, "6–7/79" Folder, Box Horn/Special: 3, NSA Staff Material, Carter Presidential Library.

190. Paul B Henze, *The Horn of Africa: From War to Peace* (London, Macmillan Press, 1991), p. 162.

191. Memo, Henze to Brzezinski, July 6, 1979, "6–7/79" Folder, Horn/Special: 3, NSA Staff Material, Carter Presidential Library.

192. Memo, Brzezinski to Tarnoff, October 2, 1979, "10/78" Folder, Horn/Special: 4, NSA Staff Material, Carter Presidential Library.

193. Statement of David Newsom, Under Secretary of State for Political Affairs, to House Subcommittee on Africa, October 18, 1979, *U.S. Interests in Africa,* October 16, 18, 19, 22, 24, 25, 29, November 13, 14, 1979, H381-37, 96th Congress, 1st Session, Library of Congress, Washington, D.C.

194. *New York Times,* November 13, 1979.

195. Memo, Henze to Brzezinski, October 24, 1979, "9–10/79" Folder, Horn/Special: 4, NSA Staff Material, Carter Presidential Library.

196. Memo, Henze to Brzezinski, December 10, 1980, "10–12/80" Folder, Horn/Special: 5, NSA Staff Material, Carter Presidential Library.

197. Nicholas Proffitt, Ethiopia, *Newsweek,* December 10, 1979.

198. Memo, Henze to Brzezinski, December 10, 1980.

199. Gregory Jaynes, Mogadishu, *New York Times,* October 29, 1979.

200. Gregory Jaynes, Somalia, *New York Times,* November 19, 1979.

201. NSC Weekly Report #109, September 13, 1979, "Weekly Reports (to the President), 102–120 [7/79–12/79]" Folder, Box 42, Zbigniew Brzezinski Donated Historical Material, Carter Presidential Library.

Chapter V

1. Although 90 hostages were originally taken, some, mostly women and African Americans, were subsequently released. The remaining 52 hostages were held for 444 days.

2. Interview, Carter for *Cold War* Television Series, National Security Archive, Washington, D.C.

3. See, for example, Zbigniew Brzezinski *Power and Principle: Memoirs of the National Security Adviser, 1977–1981* (London: Weidenfeld & Nicolson, 1983), p. 432.

4. Paul B Henze, *The Horn of Africa: From War to Peace* (London: Macmillan Press, 1991), p. 3.

5. Henze, *Horn of Africa*, p. 189.

6. Henze, *Horn of Africa*, p. 155. See also, Gaddis Smith, *Morality, Reason and Power: American Diplomacy in the Carter Years* (New York: Hill & Wang, 1986), p. 10; J. A. Lefebvre, *Arms for the Horn: U.S. Security Policy in Ethiopia and Somalia, 1953–1991* (Pittsburgh: University of Pittsburgh Press, 1991), p. 199.

7. Jimmy Carter, *Keeping Faith: Memoirs of a President* (London: Collins, 1982), p. 459.

8. Interview with Admiral Stansfield Turner, Director of the CIA in the Carter Administration, June 30, 2000, Watergate Complex, Washington, D.C.

9. Interview with David Aaron, Deputy Director of the National Security Council in the Carter Administration, July 24, 2000, Washington, D.C.

10. Interview with Paul Henze, National Security Council Staffer responsible for the Horn of Africa in the Carter Administration, July 19, 2000, Bethesda, Maryland.

11. Although Carter made the speech on January 23, the text had been delivered on January 21, and it is this date that is often quoted with reference to the Carter Doctrine.

12. Jimmy Carter, "The State of the Union," Address Delivered Before a Joint Session of the Congress, January 23, 1980, *Public Papers of the Presidents of the United States: Jimmy Carter 1980 Volume I* (Washington, D.C.: United States Government Printing Office, 1980), p. 197.

13. John Dumbrell, *Was There a Clinton Doctrine? President Clinton's Foreign Policy Reconsidered*, Paper presented to American Politics Group Conference, University of Lancaster, January 3, 2001.

14. Pat Towell, "Carter's response to Soviets Will Mean Abandoning Early Foreign Policy Goals" *Congressional Quarterly*, January 12, 1980.

15. Don Oberdorfer, *Washington Post*, January 24, 1980.

16. "America's Lonely Role," *U.S. News & World Report*, January 28, 1980.

17. Don Oberdorfer, *Washington Post*, January 24, 1980.

18. Brzezinski, *Power*, p. 446.

19. Lefebvre, *Arms for the Horn*, p. 200.

20. Richard Halloran, Washington, D.C., *New York Times*, December 23, 1979.

21. Interview with Admiral Stansfield Turner, Director of the CIA in the Carter Administration, June 30, 2000, Watergate Complex, Washington, D.C.

22. Don Oberdorfer, *Washington Post*, January 24, 1980.

23. Richard Halloran, Washington, D.C., *New York Times*, December 23, 1979.

24. Excerpts from question-and-answer session with John Chancellor of NBC News, January 7, 1980, *Public Papers 1980 Vol. I*, p. 35.

25. Robert Toth, Washington, D.C., *Los Angeles Times*, January 4, 1980.

26. *New York Times*, January 11, 1980.

27. *New York Times*, January 10, 1980.

28. Memo, Henze to Ermath, January 16, 1980, "1/80" Folder, Box Horn/Special: 4, NSA Staff Material, Carter Presidential Library.

29. Memo, Henze to Ermath, January 22, 1980, "1/80" Folder, Box Horn/Special: 4, NSA Staff Material, Carter Presidential Library.

30. Interview with Paul Henze, National Security Council Staffer responsible for the Horn of Africa in the Carter Administration, July 19, 2000, Bethesda, Maryland.

31. Interview with General William Odom, Military Adviser to the National Security Council in the Carter Administration, July 14, 2000, Hudson Institute, Washington, D.C.

32. Graham Hovey, Washington, D.C., *New York Times*, February 10, 1980.

33. Drew Middleton, *New York Times*, January 11, 1980.

34. Telegram, American Embassy Moga-

dishu to Secretary of State, January 21, 1980, "1/80" Folder, Box Horn/Special: 4, NSA Staff Material, Carter Presidential Library.

35. David Lamb, Mogadishu, *Los Angeles Times*, February 3, 1980.

36. Richard Burt, Washington, D.C., *New York Times*, February 12, 1980.

37. Burt, *New York Times*, February 12, 1980.

38. Annual Report, State Department to Congress, *Country Reports on Human Rights Practices for 1979*, February 4, 1980, H382–4, Library of Congress, Washington, D.C.

39. Statement, William C Harrop, Deputy Assistant Secretary of State for African Affairs, to House Subcommittee on Africa, February 25, 1980, *Foreign Assistance Legislation for FY81. Part 7: Economic and Security Assistance Programs in Africa*, February 7, 12, 13, 20, 25–28, March 5, 6, 1980, H381–67, Library of Congress, Washington, D.C.

40. Statement, Harrop, February 25, 1980.

41. Statement, Harrop, February 25, 1980.

42. Memo, Vance to Carter, February 25, 1980, "National Security Affairs" Folder, Brzezinski Material Subject File, Presidential Determinations 8/79–5/80 Collection, Carter Presidential Library.

43. Memo, Madeleine Albright to Brzezinski, February 29, 1980, "National Security Affairs" Folder, Brzezinski Material Subject File, Presidential Determinations 8/79–5/80 Collection, Carter Presidential Library.

44. Statement, Franklin D. Kramer, Principal Deputy Assistance Secretary of Defense for International Security Affairs, to House Subcommittee on Africa, February 25, 1980, *Foreign Assistance Legislation for FY81. Part 7: Economic and Security Assistance Programs in Africa*, February 7, 12, 13, 20, 25–28, March 5, 6, 1980, H381–67, Library of Congress, Washington, D.C.

45. Hearing, Solarz to House Subcommittee on Africa, February 25, 1980, *Foreign Assistance Legislation for FY81. Part 7: Economic and Security Assistance Programs in Africa*, February 7, 12, 13, 20, 25–28, March 5, 6, 1980, H381–67, Library of Congress, Washington, D.C.

46. Statement, William C. Harrop, Deputy Assistant Secretary of State for African Affairs, to House Subcommittee on Africa, February 25, 1980, *Foreign Assistance Legislation for FY81. Part 7: Economic and Security Assistance Programs in Africa*, February 7, 12, 13, 20, 25–28, March 5, 6, 1980, H381–67, Library of Congress, Washington, D.C.

47. Statement, Franklin D. Kramer, Principal Deputy Assistant Secretary of Defense for International Security Affairs, to House Subcommittee on Africa, February 25, 1980, *Foreign Assistance Legislation for FY81. Part 7: Economic and Security Assistance Programs in Africa*, February 7, 12, 13, 20, 25–28, March 5, 6, 1980, H381–67, Library of Congress, Washington, D.C.

48. Discussion and Questions, Hearings before the House Subcommittee on Africa, February 25, 1980, *Foreign Assistance Legislation for FY81. Part 7: Economic and Security Assistance Programs in Africa*, February 7, 12, 13, 20, 25–28, March 5, 6, 1980, H381–67, Library of Congress, Washington, D.C.

49. Discussion and Questions, Hearings before the Subcommittee on Africa, February 25, 1980.

50. *New York Times*, February 25, 1980.

51. Graham Hovey, Washington, D.C., *New York Times*, February 10, 1980.

52. *New York Times*, February 25, 1980.

53. *New York Times*, February 25, 1980.

54. Emphasis in original. Memo, Henze to Brzezinski, February 28, 1980, "2–3/80" Folder, Horn/Special: 4, NSA Staff Material, Carter Presidential Library.

55. Memo, Vance to Carter, February 25, 1980, "National Security Affairs" Folder, Brzezinski Material Subject File, Presidential Determinations 8/79–5/80 Collection, Carter Presidential Library.

56. Dennis Mullin, Mogadishu, *U.S. News & World Report*, March 3, 1980.

57. Memo, Vance to Carter, February 25, 1980, "National Security Affairs" Folder, Brzezinski Material Subject File, Presidential Determinations 8/79–5/80 Collection, Carter Presidential Library.

58. Memo, Vance to Carter, February 25, 1980.

59. Justification for President Determination No. 80–12 on the Eligibility of Somalia to Purchase Defense Articles and Defense Services Under the Arms Export Control Act, March 3, 1980, "National Security Affairs" Folder, Brzezinski Material Subject File, Presidential Determinations 8/79–5/80 Collection, Carter Presidential Library.

60. Interview with Paul Henze, National Security Council Staffer responsible for the Horn of Africa in the Carter Administration, July 19, 2000, Bethesda, Maryland.

61. Interview with David Aaron, Deputy Director of the National Security Council in

the Carter Administration, July 24, 2000, Washington, D.C.

62. Note, Henze to Pat Malone, March 13, 1980, "2–3/80" Folder, Box Horn/Special: 4, NSA Staff Material, Carter Presidential Library.

63. Richard Halloran, Washington, D.C., *New York Times*, March 30, 1980.

64. Richard Burt, Washington, D.C., *New York Times*, April 22, 1980.

65. Memo, Henze to Classified Recipient, April 17, 1980, "4/80" Folder, Box: Horn/Special: 4, NSA Staff Material, Carter Presidential Library.

66. Memo, Henze to Brzezinski, April 3, 1980, "4/80" Folder, Horn/Special: 4, NSA Staff Material, Carter Presidential Library.

67. Memo, Henze to Brzezinski, April 3, 1980.

68. An interesting point to note is that Masire Island, newly acquired as part of the arms-for-bases deals, was important in staging the rescue attempt, thereby offering evidence in support of those who argued for the strategic importance of the United States having access to military facilities in the Indian Ocean region. Source: Interview with General William Odom, Military Adviser to the National Security Council in the Carter Administration, July 14, 2000, Hudson Institute, Washington, D.C.

69. Obituaries for Cyrus Vance, *International Herald Tribune*, January 14, 2002 and *New York Times*, January 13, 2002.

70. *Time*, May 12, 1980.

71. *Newsweek*, May 12, 1980.

72. Biographical information on Muskie from *Time*, May 12, 1980.

73. *Time*, May 12, 1980.

74. Information from biographical notes compiled by Christopher Beam, director, Edmund S. Muskie Archives, Bates College, Maine.

75. *U.S. News & World Report*, May 12, 1980.

76. *Time*, May 12, 1980.

77. *Time*, May 12, 1980.

78. *U.S. News & World Report*, May 12, 1980.

79. *Time*, May 12, 1980.

80. *U.S. News & World Report*, May 12, 1980.

81. See Chapter IV, page 103.

82. Emphasis in original. Memo, Billings to Muskie, June 4, 1980, "State Department Correspondence Chron June 1–15 1980 [Folder 3 of 5]" Folder, Box 14, Series: Secretary of State, Muskie Archives, Bates College, Maine.

83. Press Briefing by Muskie, Memphis Tennessee, October 6, 1980, "Public Statements May 1980—January 1981 [Folder 2 of 4]" Folder, Box 16, Series: Secretary of State, Muskie Archives, Bates College, Maine.

84. Memo, Henze to Brzezinski, June 3, 1980, "6–7/80" Folder, Box Horn/Special: 5, NSA Staff Material, Carter Presidential Library.

85. Bernard Gwertzman, Ankara, *New York Times*, June 25, 1980.

86. Memo, Henze to Brzezinski, June 3, 1980, "6–7/80" Folder, Box Horn/Special: 5, NSA Staff Material, Carter Presidential Library.

87. Gwertzman, *New York Times*, June 25, 1980; Interview with General William Odom, Military Adviser to the National Security Council in the Carter Administration, July 14, 2000, Hudson Institute, Washington, D.C.

88. Christopher Wren, Berbera, *New York Times*, May 21, 1980.

89. Memo, Odom to Brzezinski, July 2, 1980, "Meetings: Muskie-Brzezinski-Brown [7/80–9/80]" Folder, Box 23, Zbigniew Brzezinski Donated Historical Material, Carter Presidential Library.

90. Telegram, State Dept to American Embassy, Mogadishu, July 2, 1980, "Meetings: Muskie-Brzezinski-Brown [7/80–9/80]" Folder, Box 23, Zbigniew Brzezinski Donated Historical Material, Carter Presidential Library.

91. Editorial, Representative Solarz (D-NY), Chairman of House Subcommittee on Africa, July 6, 1980, *New York Times*.

92. Letter to the Editor, Representative Stratton (D-NY), *New York Times*, July 27, 1980.

93. *Los Angeles Times*, July 30, 1980.

94. Henze, *Horn of Africa*, p. 162. See also, David A. Korn, *Ethiopia, the United States and Soviet Union* (London: Croom Helm, 1986), p. 55.

95. Interview with Admiral Stansfield Turner, Director of the CIA in the Carter Administration, June 30, 2000, Watergate Complex, Washington, D.C.

96. Interview with Zbigniew Brzezinski, National Security Adviser to the Carter Administration, July 6, 2000, Center for Strategic and International Studies, Washington, D.C.

97. NSC Weekly Report #149, Brzezinski to Carter, August 7, 1980, "Weekly Reports (to the President) 136–150 [4/80–8/80]" Folder, Box 42, Zbigniew Brzezinski Donated

Historical Material, Carter Presidential Library.

98. *New York Times,* August 12, 1980.

99. Richard Burt, Washington, D.C., *New York Times,* August 19, 1980.

100. Burt, *New York Times,* August 19, 1980.

101. State Department Announcement, August 22, 1980, *Department of State Bulletin,* Vol. 80, No. 2043, October 1980, Library of Congress, Washington, D.C.

102. Testimony, Matthew Nimetz to House Foreign Operations Subcommittee, September 17, 1980, *Congressional Quarterly,* September 20, 1980.

103. Richard Burt, Washington, D.C., *New York Times,* August 19, 1980.

104. *New York Times,* August 22, 1980.

105. Graham Hovey, Washington, D.C., *New York Times,* August 23, 1980.

106. Hovey, *New York Times,* August 23, 1980.

107. Memo, Henze to Jerry Funk, August 15, 1980, "8–9/80" Folder, Horn/Special: 5, NSA Staff Material, Carter Presidential Library.

108. Statement, Richard Moose, Assistant Secretary for African Affairs, to House Subcommittee on Africa, August 26, 1980, *Department of State Bulletin,* Vol. 80, No. 2043, October 1980.

109. Statement, Moose, August 26, 1980.

110. George Wilson, Washington, D.C., *Washington Post,* August 28, 1980.

111. Richard Whittle, *Congressional Quarterly,* August 30, 1980.

112. Graham Hovey, Washington, D.C., *New York Times,* August 23, 1980.

113. Don Oberdorfer, Washington, D.C., *Washington Post,* August 22, 1980.

114. Memo, Henze to Brzezinski, September 3, 1980, "8–9/80" Folder, Box Horn/Special: 5, NSA Staff Material, Carter Presidential Library.

115. Memo, Henze to Brzezinski, September 3, 1980.

116. *New York Times,* August 27, 1980.

117. George Wilson, Washington, D.C., *Washington Post,* August 28, 1980.

118. Memo, Henze to Brzezinski, September 3, 1980, "8–9/80" Folder, Box Horn/Special: 5, NSA Staff Material, Carter Presidential Library.

119. Juan de Onis, Washington, D.C., *New York Times,* August 29, 1980.

120. Onis, *New York Times,* August 29, 1980.

121. Hearing, Matthew Nimetz, Under Secretary of State for Security Assistance, to House Subcommittee on Foreign Operations Appropriations, September 16, 1980, *Foreign Assistance and Related Programs Appropriations for 1981, Part 6,* June 10, July 22, August 19, September 16, 1980, H181–113, Library of Congress, Washington, D.C.

122. Hearing, Nimetz, September 16, 1980.

123. Hearing, Nimetz, September 16, 1980.

124. Hearing, Representative Solarz (D-NY), Chairman, Subcommittee on African Affairs, to House Subcommittee on Foreign Operations Appropriations, September 16, 1980, *Foreign Assistance and Related Programs Appropriations for 1981, Part 6,* June 10, July 22, August 19, September 16, 1980, H181–113, Library of Congress, Washington, D.C.

125. *New York Times,* September 19, 1990.

126. John Felton, "House Panel Votes Down Aid to Somalia," *Congressional Quarterly,* September 20, 1980.

127. Pat Towell, "Senate OK's Funds for Indian Ocean Bases," *Congressional Quarterly,* September 27, 1980.

128. Juan de Onis, Washington, D.C., *New York Times,* October 1, 1980.

129. Onis, *New York Times,* October 1, 1980.

130. Letter, Mengistu to Carter, August 30, 1980, "8–9/80" Folder, Box Horn/Special: 5, NSA Staff Material, Carter Presidential Library.

131. Memo, Henze to Brzezinski, September 3, 1980, "8–9/80" Folder, Box Horn/Special: 5, NSA Staff Material, Carter Presidential Library.

132. Letter, Carter to Mengistu, September 30, 1980, "8–9/80" Folder, Box Horn/Special: 5, NSA Staff Material, Carter Presidential Library.

133. Reagan won the Electoral College by 489 votes to 49, and the popular vote by 43,899,248 to 35,481,435.

134. See, for example, M. Glenn Abernathy, Dilys M. Hill & Phil Williams (eds.), *The Carter Years: The President and Policy Making* (London: Francis Pinter, 1984); John Dumbrell, *The Carter Presidency: A Re-Evaluation* (Manchester and London: Manchester University Press, 1993); Garland A Haas, *Jimmy Carter and the Politics of Frustration* (Jefferson, N.C.: McFarland, 1992); Burton Kaufman, *The Presidency of James Earl Carter, Jr.* (Lawrence: University Press of Kansas, 1993); Gaddis Smith, *Morality, Reason and Power: American Diplomacy in*

the Carter Years (New York: Hill & Wang, 1986).

135. *Los Angeles Times,* November 19, 1980.

136. *Los Angeles Times,* November 19, 1980

137. Memo, Henze to Brzezinski, December 8, 1980, "10–12/80" Folder, Box Horn/Special: 5, NSA Staff Material, Carter Presidential Library.

138. Henze, *Horn of Africa,* p. 4.

139. Brzezinski, *Power,* p. 56.

140. Memo, Muskie to Carter, December 11, 1980—"State Department Evening Papers, 1/81" Folder, Subject File: State Department Evening Reports, 11/80 through Transition: State and Defense Option Papers [3], Plains File, Carter Presidential Library.

141. Indeed, Henze argued in an interview in 2000 that there had, in fact, been no change in policy by the Administration but an "acceptance of reality." Source: Interview with Paul Henze, National Security Council Staffer responsible for the Horn of Africa in the Carter Administration, July 19, 2000, Bethesda, Maryland.

142. Brzezinski, *Power,* p. 129.

143. Remarks at First Annual Dinner, Jimmy Carter to Asian/Pacific American Democratic Caucus, May 22, 1980, *Public Papers of the Presidents of the United States: Jimmy Carter 1980 Volume I* (Washington, D.C.: United States Government Printing Office, 1980), p. 962.

144. Speech, Senator Kennedy to Senate, January 24, 1980, *Congressional Record,* p. 709, Library of Congress, Washington, D.C.

145. Speech, Representative Petri (R-Wis), January 31, 1980, *Congressional Record,* pp. 1546–1547, Library of Congress, Washington, D.C.

146. Speech, Representative Maguire (D-NJ), May 13, 1980, *Congressional Record,* pp. 11108–11109, Library of Congress, Washington, D.C.

147. Speech, Senator Proxmire (D-Wis), April 2, 1980, *Congressional Record,* p. 7497, Library of Congress, Washington, D.C.

148. Speech, Senator McGovern (D-SD), April 23, 1980, *Congressional Record,* p. 8763, Library of Congress, Washington, D.C.

149. Edward Cody, Gobieri Outpost, Rebel-Held Ogaden, *Washington Post,* May 22, 1980.

150. Robin Knight, Mozambique, *U.S. News & World Report,* September 1, 1980.

151. Gregory Jaynes, Lugh, Somalia, *New York Times,* October 12, 1980.

152. Report, *Assessment of the Refugee Situation in Somalia,* Senate Committee on Foreign Relations, September 1980—S382–24, Library of Congress, Washington, D.C.

153. Speech, Representative Maguire (D-NJ), August 25, 1980, *Congressional Record,* p. 23084, Library of Congress, Washington, D.C.

154. Speech, Representative Dornan (R-Ca), November 12, 1980, *Congressional Record,* p. 29232, Library of Congress, Washington, D.C.

155. Speech, Dornan, November 12, 1980, *Record,* p. 29443.

Conclusion

1. For a discussion of the various historiographical viewpoints concerning the demise of détente, see page 25.

2. For example, Zbigniew Brzezinski, 1978 in Fred Halliday, *Soviet Policy in the Arc of Crisis* (Washington, D.C.: Institute for Policy Studies, 1981), p. 19.

3. Zbigniew Brzezinski, *Power and Principle: Memoirs of the National Security Adviser, 1977–1981* (London: Weidenfeld & Nicolson, 1983), p. 189.

4. Peter J. Schraeder, *United States Foreign Policy Toward Africa: Incrementalism, Crisis and Change* (Cambridge: Cambridge University Press, 1994), p. 13. See also, Brzezinski, *Power and Principle,* Cyrus Vance, *Hard Choices: Critical Years in America's Foreign Policy* (New York: Simon & Schuster, 1983) and Jimmy Carter, *Keeping Faith: Memoirs of a President* (London: Collins, 1982).

5. David McLellan, *Cyrus Vance* (Totowa, NJ: Rowman & Allanheld, 1985), p. 156.

6. Anatoly Dobrynin, *In Confidence: Moscow's Ambassador to American's Six Cold War Presidents (1962–1986)* (New York: Random House, 1995), p. 403.

7. Robert M. Gates, *From the Shadows: The Ultimate Insider's Story of Five Presidents and How They Won the Cold War* (New York: Simon & Schuster, 1996), p. 74.

8. Carter, *Faith,* p. 143.

9. For more details of the historiography on the Carter administration, see pages 12–27.

10. Henze, Paul B. *The Horn of Africa: From War to Peace* (London: Macmillan Press, 1991)

11. Gaddis Smith, *Morality, Reason and Power* (New York: Hill & Wang, 1986), p. 247.

12. David Skidmore, *Reversing Course: Carter's Foreign Policy, Domestic Politics and the Failure of Reform* (Nashville and London: Vanderbilt University Press, 1996).

13. Jerel Rosati, "The Rise and Fall of America's First Cold-War Foreign Policy" in Herbert Rosenbaum and Alexej Ugrinsky, eds., *Jimmy Carter: Foreign Policy and Post-Presidential Years* (Westport, CT: Greenwood Press, 1994).

14. Carter, "Farewell Address to the Nation," January 14, 1981, *Public Papers of the Presidents of the United States: Jimmy Carter 1980/1 Volume III* (Washington, D.C.: United States Government Printing Office, 1980), p. 2892.

15. Hamilton Jordan, *Crisis: The Last Year of the Carter Presidency* (New York: Putnam's Sons, 1982), p. 388.

16. See, for example, Robert Wilson (ed.), *Character Above All: Ten Presidents from FDR to George Bush* (New York: Simon & Schuster, 1995), p. 173.

17. Jimmy Carter, *The Carter Center at a Glance*, Information Publication from The Carter Center, Atlanta, 1997.

18. *The Carter Center at a Glance*, Information Publication from The Carter Center, Atlanta, 1997.

19. *Washington Post*, October 13, 1998.

20. Wilson, *Character*, p. 179.

21. Rod Troester, *Jimmy Carter as Peacemaker: A Post-Presidential Biography* (New York: Praeger, 1996), p. 44, 114.

22. "Elections in Ethiopia, Liberia Advance Democracy in Africa," *The Carter Center News*, Fall 2005.

23. www.cartercenter.org/peacekeeping programs, June 2006.

24. Troester, *Carter,* p. 59.

25. For a full account of the Eritrean peace talks, see Troester, *Carter*, pp. 58–66.

26. Gary M. Fink and Hugh Davis Graham (eds.), *The Carter Presidency: Policy Choices in the Post-New Deal Era* (Lawrence: University Press of Kansas, 1998), p. 271

27. "President Carter Visits Africa, Urges Leaders to Intensify Global Health Promotion," Press Release, The Carter Center, September 7, 2005.

28. "Committed to International Health Through Guinea Worm Disease Eradication," The Carter Center, April 2006, www.cartercenter.org.

29. "In Nigeria, Guinea Worm Chapter Nears End," *The Carter Center News*, Spring 2006.

30. Donald McNeil, "Dose of Tenacity Wears Down an Ancient Horror," *The New York Times*, March 26, 2006.

31. Emphasis in original. *The Guardian*, February 7, 1998.

32. Reply to Governor Brown, Rockville, Maryland, May 1976, Jimmy Carter, *A Government as Good as Its People* (Fayetteville: University of Arkansas Press, 996), p. 66.

Bibliography

Primary Sources

Archival Material

CARTER PRESIDENTIAL LIBRARY, ATLANTA, GEORGIA

Chief of Staff Files, 1977–1980 (Hamilton Jordan)
National Security Agency, Staff Material Collection
National Security Agency, Brzezinski Material
President's Files: Plains Files
President's Files: Staff Secretary's Files
Records of Louis Martin, Special Assistant to the President, 1978–1981
Records of Martha (Bunny) Mitchell, Special Assistant to the President
Records of the Office of Peter Bourne, Special Assistant to the President for Health Issues
Records of the Office of Science and Technology Policy
Records of the Office of the Assistant for Public Liaison, Margaret Costanza Files
Records of the Office of the Assistant for Public Liaison, Seymour Wishman Files
Records of the Office of the Assistant to the President for Communications (Gerald Rafshoon)
Records of the Office of the Staff Secretary
Records of the Speechwriter's Office
Records of the White House Office of Counsel to the President, Margaret A. McKenna Files
Records of the White House Office of Counsel to the President, Robert J. Lipshutz Files
Records of the White House Press Office (Anne Edwards)
Records of the White House Press Office (Jody Powell)
Records of Tim Kraft, Special Assistant to the President
Roddey E. Mims Collection, 1976–1982
Stuart Eizenstat Collection
Vertical File
White House Central Files: Country Collection
White House Central Files: Human Rights Collection
White House Central Files: International Organisations
Zbigniew Brzezinski Collection

215

THE EDMUND S. MUSKIE COLLECTION: BATES COLLEGE, MAINE

Secretary of State Series
Appointment Books and Guest Registers, 1955–1980 Series

THE CYRUS R. VANCE AND GRACE SLOAN PAPERS: YALE UNITED STATES
LIBRARY MANUSCRIPTS COLLECTION

NATIONAL SECURITY ARCHIVES, WASHINGTON, D.C.

Carter-Brezhnev Collection
Carter Administration NSC Documents Collection

Official Publications

Congressional Record, 1977–1981
Department of State Bulletin, 1977–1981
US Congress Committee Reports, 1977–1981
Public Papers of the Presidents of the United States: Jimmy Carter (Washington, D.C.,: United
States Government Printing Office, 1977–1981)
The Presidential Campaign: 1976 (Washington, D.C., U.S. Government Printing Office, 1978)

Newspapers and Periodicals

The New York Times, 1977–1981
The Washington Post, 1977–1981
The Los Angeles Times, 1977–1981
Time, 1977–1981
Newsweek, 1977–1981
U.S. News and World Report, 1977–1981

Oral Interviews

David Aaron, Deputy Director of the National Security Council in the Carter Adminis-
tration, July 24, 2000, Washington, D.C.
Zbigniew Brzezinski, National Security Adviser to the Carter Administration, July 6, 2000,
Center for Strategic and International Studies, Washington, D.C.
Paul Henze, National Security Council Staffer responsible for the Horn of Africa in the
Carter Administration, July 19, 2000, Bethesda, Maryland
Willard Hoing, Director of the Peace Corps in Ethiopia, July 6, 2000, College Park, Mary-
land.
General William Odom, Military Adviser to the National Security Council in the Carter
Administration, 14/7/2000, Hudson Institute, Washington, D.C.
Wardell Townsend, Campaign Worker and Personal Friend of the Carter Family, July 5,
2000, Silver Spring, Maryland.
Admiral Stansfield Turner, Director of the CIA in the Carter Administration, June 30,
2000, Watergate Complex, Washington, D.C.

Memoirs and Autobiographies

Brzezinski, Zbigniew. *Power and Principle: Memoirs of the National Security Adviser,
1977–1981* (London: Weidenfeld & Nicolson, 1983).
Carter, Jimmy. *Why Not the Best?: Jimmy Carter, The First Fifty Years* (Fayetteville: University of Arkansas Press, 1975).

Carter, Jimmy. *A Government as Good as Its People* (Fayetteville: University of Arkansas Press, 1996).

Carter, Jimmy. *Keeping Faith: Memoirs of a President* (London: Collins, 1982).

Carter, Jimmy. *Negotiation: The Alternative to Hostility* (Macon: Mercer University Press, 1984).

Dobrynin, Anatoly. *In Confidence: Moscow's Ambassador to American's Six Cold War Presidents (1962–1986)* (New York: Random House, 1995).

Henze, Paul B. *The Horn of Africa: From War to Peace* (London: Macmillan Press, 1991).

Gates, Robert M. *From the Shadows: The Ultimate Insider's Story of Five Presidents and How They Won the Cold War* (New York, Simon & Schuster, 1996).

Jordan, Hamilton. *Crisis: The Last Year of the Carter Presidency* (New York: Putnam's Sons, 1982).

Powell, Jody. *The Other Side of the Story* (New York: William Morrow and Company, Inc., 1984).

Vance, Cyrus. *Hard Choices: Critical Years in America's Foreign Policy* (New York: Simon & Schuster, 1983).

Young, Andrew. 'The United States and Africa: Victory for Détente," *Foreign Affairs: America and the World 1980*, Volume 59, 1980–1981.

Secondary Sources

Articles

Aluko, Olajide. "African Response to External Intervention in Africa Since Angola," *African Affairs*, Volume 80, April 1981.

Araya, Mesfin. "The Eritrean Question: An Alternative Explanatio," *Journal of Modern African Studies*, Volume 28, March 1990.

Birnbaum, Karl E. "Human Rights and East-West Relations," *Foreign Affairs*, Volume 55, July 1977.

Brinkley, Douglas. "The Rising Stock of Jimmy Carter: The Hands-On Legacy of Our Thirty-Ninth President," *Diplomatic History*, Volume 20, Fall 1996.

Burt, Richard. "The Scope and Limits of SALT," *Foreign Affairs*, Volume 56, July 1978.

Carleton, David, and Michael Stohl. "The Foreign Policy of Human Rights: Rhetoric and Reality from Jimmy Carter to Ronald Reagan," *Human Rights Quarterly*, Volume 7, May 1985.

Cohen, S B. "Conditioning US Security Assistance on Human Rights Practices," *The American Journal of International Law*, Vol. 76, April 1982.

Derian, Patricia. "Human Rights and American Foreign Policy," *Human Rights Quarterly*, Volume 1, January-March 1979.

Donnelly, Jack. "Human Rights as Natural Rights," *Human Rights Quarterly*, Volume 4, Summer 1982.

Falk, Pamela S. "Cuba in Africa," *Foreign Affairs*, Volume 65, Summer 1987.

Forsythe, David P. "American Foreign Policy and Human Rights: Rhetoric and Reality," *Human Rights Quarterly*, Volume 2, July — September 1980.

Garthoff, Raymond. "The Crumbling Triangle: Detente and Confrontation," *Economist*, December 9, 1978.

Iyob, Ruth. "Regional Hegemony: Domination and Resistance in the Horn of Africa," *Journal of Modern African Studies*, Volume 31, June 1993.

Kaufman, Victor. "The Bureau of Human Rights during the Carter Administration," *The Historian*, Fall 1998.

LaFeber, Walter. "From Confusion to Cold War: The Memoirs of the Carter Administration," *Diplomatic History*, Volume 8, Winter 1984.

Laitin, David. "The War in the Ogaden: Implications for Siyaad's Role in Somali History," *Journal of Modern African Studies*, Volume 17, March 1979.

Leffler, Melvyn. "From the Truman Doctrine to the Carter Doctrine: Lessons and Dilemmas of the Cold War" *Diplomatic History*, Volume 7, Fall 1983.

Legum, Colin. "The African Crisis," *Foreign Affairs: America and the World 1978*, Volume 57, 1978–79.

Legum, Colin, and Bill Lee. "Crisis in the Horn: International Dimensions of the Somali-Ethiopian Conflict," *Africa Contemporary Record: Annual Survey and Documents*, 1977–78.

Legvold, Robert. "The Super Rivals: Conflict in the Third World," *Foreign Affairs*, Volume 57, Spring 1979.

Levering, Ralph B. "Public Opinion, Foreign Policy and American Politics Since the 1960s," *Diplomatic History*, Volume 13, Summer 1989.

Lewis, I M. "The Ogaden and the Fragility of Somali Segmentary Nationalism," *African Affairs*, Volume 88, October 1989

Maynard, E S. "The Bureaucracy and Implementation of US Human Rights Policy," *Human Rights Quarterly*, Vol. 11, May 1989.

Morison, David. "Soviet and Chinese Policies in Africa in 1978," *Africa Contemporary Record*, 1978–79.

Ogunbadejo, Oye. "Soviet Policies in Africa," *African Affairs*, Volume 79, July 1980.

Oudes, Bruce, with Michael Clough. "The United States' Year in Africa: From Confidence to Caution," *Africa Contemporary Record*, 1978–1979.

Oudes, Bruce. "From Caution to the Carter Doctrine," *Africa Contemporary Record*, 1979–80.

Petterson, Donald. "Ethiopia Abandoned? An American Perspective," *International Affairs (London)*, Volume 62, number 4, Autumn 1986.

Schneider, M. "Human Rights Policy under the Carter Administratio," *Law and Contemporary Problems*, 1979.

Schwab, Peter. "Cold War on the Horn of Africa," *African Affairs*, Volume 77, January 1978.

Selassie, Bereket Habte. "The American Dilemma on the Horn," *Journal of Modern African Studies*, Volume 22, June 1984.

Schlesinger, Arthur M., Jr. "Human Rights and the American Tradition," *Foreign Affairs: America and the World 1978*, Volume 57, 1978–1979.

Schlesinger, Arthur M., Jr. "Foreign Policy and the American Character," *Foreign Affairs*, Volume 62, Fall 1983.

Skidmore, David. "Carter & the Failure of Foreign Policy Reform," *Political Science Quarterly*, Volume 108, Winter 1993–1994.

Tower, John G. "Congress Versus the President: The Formulation and Implementation of American Foreign Policy," *Foreign Affairs*, Volume 60, Winter 1981–1982.

Yankelovich, Daniel. "Farewell to "President Knows Best"" *Foreign Affairs: America and the World 1978*, Volume 57, 1978–1979

Zagoria, Donald. "Into the Breach: New Soviet Alliances in the Third World" *Foreign Affairs*, Volume 57, Spring 1979.

Books

Abernathy, M. Glenn, Dilys M. Hill, & Phil Williams (eds.). *The Carter Years: The President and Policy Making* (London: Francis Pinter, 1984).

Baker, James T. *A Southern Baptist in the White House* (Philadelphia: Westminster Press, 1977).

Bender, Gerald, James S. Coleman, and Richard L. Sklar, (eds.). *African Crisis Areas and United States Foreign Policy* (Berkeley and Los Angeles: University of California Press, 1985).

Bourne, Peter G. *Jimmy Carter: A Comprehensive Biography from Plains to Postpresidency* (New York: Scribner, 1997).

Brinkley, Douglas. *The Unfinished Presidency* (New York: Viking, 1998).

Dougherty, James. *The Horn of Africa: A Map of Political-Strategic Conflict* (Cambridge, MA: Institute for Foreign Policy Analysis, 1982).

Dumbrell, John. *The Carter Presidency: A Re-Evaluation* (Manchester: Manchester University Press, 1993).

Erlich, Haggai. *The Struggle over Eritrea, 1962–1978* (Stanford: Hoover Institute, 1983).

Farer, Tom J. *War Clouds on the Horn of Africa: the Widening Storm* (New York: Carnegie Endowment for International Peace, 1979).

Fink, Gary M. and Hugh Davis Graham, (eds.). *The Carter Presidency: Policy Choices in the Post–New Deal Era* (Lawrence: University Press of Kansas, 1998).

Garthoff, Raymond. *Detente and Confrontation: American-Soviet Relations from Nixon to Reagan* (Washington, D.C.: Brookings Institution, 1994).

Gaver, Jessyca R. *The Faith of Jimmy Carter* (New York: Manor Books, 1977).

Glad, Betty. *Jimmy Carter: In Search of the Great White House* (New York: Norton, 1980).

Gorman, Robert F. *Political Conflict on the Horn of Africa* (New York: Praeger, 1981).

Grover, William F. *The President as Prisoner: A Structural Critique of the Carter and Reagan Years* (Albany: State University of New York Press, 1989).

Haas, Garland A. *Jimmy Carter and the Politics of Frustration* (Jefferson, North Carolina: McFarland, 1992).

Hargrove, E C. *Jimmy Carter as President: Leadership and the Politics of the Public Good* (Baton Rouge: Louisiana State University Press, 1988).

Henze, Paul B. *Layers of Time: A History of Ethiopia* (London: Hurst & Company, 2000).

Henze, Paul B. *Rebels and Separatists in Ethiopia: Regional Resistance to a Marxist Regime* (Washington, D.C.: The Rand Corporation, 1985).

Hevener, Natalie Kaufman (ed.). *The Dynamics of Human Rights in U.S. Foreign Policy* (New Brunswick: Transaction Books, 1981).

Jones, Charles O. *The Trusteeship Presidency: Jimmy Carter and the United States Congress* (Baton Rouge: Louisiana State University Press, 1988).

Kaufman, Burton. *The Presidency of James Earl Carter, Jr.* (Lawrence: University Press of Kansas, 1993).

Klunk, Brian. *Consensus and the American Mission* (Lanham: University Press of America, 1986).

Korn, David A. *Ethiopia, the United States and Soviet Union* (London: Croom Helm, 1986).

Kucharsky, David. *The Man From Plains: A Portrait of Jimmy Carter* (London: Collins, 1977).

Lake, Anthony. *Third World Radical Regimes: US Policy Under Carter and Reagan* (New York: Foreign Policy Association, 1979).

Lasky, Victor. *Jimmy Carter: The Man and the Myth* (New York: Richard Marek Publishers, 1979).

Lefebvre, J A. *Arms for the Horn: U.S. Security Policy in Ethiopia and Somalia, 1953–1991* (Pittsburgh: University of Pittsburgh Press, 1991).

Lewis, I. M. (ed.). *Nationalism and Self-Determination in the Horn of Africa* (London: Ithaca Press, 1983).

Little, Richard and Steve Smith (eds.). *Belief Systems and International Relations* (Oxford:Blackwell, 1988).

Maddox, Robert L. *Preacher at the White House* (Nashville: Broadman Press, 1984).

Makinda, Samuel M. *Superpower Diplomacy in the Horn of Africa* (New York: St. Martin's, 1987).

Mazlish, Bruce, and Edwin Diamond. *Jimmy Carter: A Character Portrait* (New York: Simon & Schuster, 1979).

McLellan, David S. *Cyrus Vance* (Totowa, NJ: Rowman & Allanheld, 1985).

Melanson, R. A. *Reconstructing Consensus: American Foreign Policy Since the Vietnam War* (New York: St Martin's Press, 1991).

Miller, William L. *Yankee from Georgia: The Emergence of Jimmy Carter* (New York: Times Books, 1978).

Moens, Alexander. *Foreign Policy Under Carter* (Boulder, CO: Westview Press, 1990).

Mollenhoff, C. R. *The President Who Failed: Carter Out of Control* (New York: Macmillan, 1980).

Mower, A. Glenn. *Human Rights and American Foreign Policy: The Carter and Reagan Experiences* (New York: Greenwood, 1987).

Muravchik, J. *The Uncertain Crusade: Jimmy Carter & the Dilemmas of Human Rights* (Lanham: Hamilton Press, 1986).

Newsum, H. E. and Olayiwola Abergunrin. *United States Foreign Policy Towards Southern Africa: Andrew Young and Beyond* (London: Macmillan Press, 1987).

Niebuhr, Reinhold. *The Irony of American History* (New York: Charles Scribner's Sons, 1952).

Nielsen, N.C. *The Religion of President Carter* (London: Mowbrays, 1977).

Odom, William E. *On Internal War: American and Soviet Approaches to Third World Clients and Insurgents* (Durham: Duke University Press, 1992).

Ottaway, Marina. *Soviet and American Influence in the Horn of Africa* (New York: Praeger, 1982).

Patman, Robert G. *The Soviet Union in the Horn of Africa* (Cambridge: Cambridge University Press, 1990).

Richardson, Don (ed.). *Conversations with Carter* (Boulder: Lynne Rienner Publishers, Inc., 1998).

Rosati, Jerel A. *The Carter Administration's Quest for Global Community: Beliefs & Their Impact on Behaviour* (Columbia: University of South Carolina Press, 1987)

Rosenbaum, Herbert D & Ugrinsky, Alexej (eds). *Jimmy Carter: Foreign Policy and Post-Presidential Years* (New York, Greenwood Press, 1994).

Rozell, Mark J. *The Press and the Carter Presidency* (Boulder and London: Westview, 1989).

Schraeder, Peter J. *United States Foreign Policy Toward Africa: Incrementalism, Crisis and Change* (Cambridge: Cambridge University Press, 1994).

Selassie, Bereket Habte. *Conflict and Intervention in the Horn of Africa* (New York: Monthly Review Press, 1980).

Shoup, Lawrence. *The Carter Presidency and Beyond: Power and Politics in the 1980s* (Palo Alto: Ramparts Press, 1980).

Skidmore, David. *Reversing Course: Carter's Foreign Policy, Domestic Politics and the Failure of Reform* (Nashville and London: Vanderbilt University Press, 1996).

Smith, Gaddis. *Morality, Reason and Power: American Diplomacy in the Carter Years* (New York: Hill & Wang, 1986).

Spencer, Donald S. *The Carter Implosion: Jimmy Carter and the Amateur Style of Diplomacy* (New York: Praeger, 1988).

Steele, Jonathan. *The Limits of Soviet Power: The Kremlin's Foreign Policy, Brezhnev to Chernenko* (New York: Simon & Schuster, 1984).

Strong, Robert A. *Working in the World: Jimmy Carter and the Making of American Foreign Policy* (Baton Rouge: Louisiana State University Press, 2000).

Thornton, Richard. *The Carter Years: Toward a Global World Order* (Washington, D.C.: Washington Institute Press, 1991).

Troester, Rod. *Jimmy Carter as Peacemaker: A Post-Presidential Biography* (New York: Praeger, 1996).

Vogelgesang, Sandy. *American Dream, Global Nightmare: The Dilemma of United States Human Rights Policy* (New York: WW Norton and Co., 1980).

Westad, Odd Arne (ed.). *The Fall of Detente: Soviet-American Relations During the Carter Years*, (Oslo and Oxford: Scandinavian University Press, 1997).

Wilson, Robert (ed.). *Character Above All: Ten Presidents from FDR to George Bush* (New York: Simon & Schuster, 1995).

Zartman, I. William. *Ripe for Resolution: Conflict and Intervention in Africa* (New York and Oxford: Oxford University Press, 1985).

Index